Gift of the

John D. Walthour

Trust

Silent Revolution

Silent Revolution

HOW THE LEFT ROSE TO POLITICAL POWER AND CULTURAL DOMINANCE

Barry Rubin

BROADSIDE BOOKS
An Imprint of HarperCollins*Publishers*
www.broadsidebooks.net

HarperCollins books may be purchased for educational, business, or sales promotional use.
For information, please e-mail the Special Markets Department at
SPsales@harpercollins.com.

Broadside Books™ and the Broadside logo are registered
trademarks of HarperCollins Publishers.

FIRST EDITION

Designed by Michael Correy

Library of Congress Cataloging-in-Publication Data has been applied for.

ISBN 978-0-06-223176-5

14 15 16 17 18   OV/RRD   10 9 8 7 6 5 4 3 2 1

FOR JUDY, GABRIELLA, AND DANIEL

ACKNOWLEDGMENTS

Thanks to Yeru Chernilovsky and Jonathan Spyer.

7

CONTENTS

Silent Revolution

INTRODUCTION

This is a contrarian book. A political and social movement has transformed the United States. That movement and President Barack Obama, who was, we should remember, only a small part of it, is praised, exalted, and celebrated by many millions of people who call themselves "liberals." Meanwhile, they are condemned, derided, and ridiculed by many "conservatives."

And yet that is a strange deviation from all of American history. In fact, it is a break from, a break with, the entire history of liberalism as well. Indeed, it is an ideological defacing of liberalism. But that is because it is to camouflage the real identity of this doctrine, which seeks to impersonate liberalism: radicalism. There is a big difference.

It is that impersonation that has brought this movement the success it has enjoyed. Without this disguise, it would appeal to few people. Words like *radicalism, extremism, Socialism, Communism, Marxism, anti-patriotism* sound less attractive than *multiculturalism*. One reason, of course, is that these ideologies are well-known failures, even disasters that bear little in common with what has made America a brilliant success, ever expanding its liberties and prosperity.

Yet that is the key to an explanation of what happened in America in the early twenty-first century. Put very simply there was a four-stage process.

Step One: Radicalism took over liberalism.

Step Two: The new "liberalism" portrayed its only opponent as a reactionary, right-wing conservatism.

Step Three: The radicalism (liberalism) represents all that is good in America and a correction to all (a lot of it) that was evil.

Step Four: The new radicalism (liberalism) has a monopoly on truth and a right to fundamentally transform America.

All that is good in American history—racial equality, worker's rights, environmentalism, women's rights, the very acts of intellectualism or cultural creativity themselves—are awarded to "liberalism," yet nothing is acceded to conservatism or traditional liberalism.

But if there was a "one percent" in American history, those were the radicals. The liberal-conservative spectrum was the "ninety-nine percent."

This requires a considerable contradiction. On the one hand, the radicals ("liberals") want to claim everything good about America's greatness and achievements. On the other hand, they claim that America has mostly been evil.

As for traditional liberalism, it has become extinct. A doctrine that enjoyed at least 25 percent support among the population and periodically won a majority of votes is simply gone.

Was the fruit of radicalism in U.S. history so splendid that they can claim credit for substantial achievement? Of course not. Has conservatism not meant the real ballast of American society, contributing the moral, religious stabilizing factors? Of course.

Then there is the balance of the degree of free enterprise in the economy, the balance between freedom and responsibility, and other social factors. The liberal–conservative spectrum has been the basis of America's success and freedom. Wrecking it would destroy them. This new situation is a terrible threat to everything that has gone right in America for two centuries.

CHAPTER 1

America's Fundamental Transformation Has Already Happened

On January 20, 2013, President Barack Obama used his second inaugural address to express his views on American history, political philosophy, and strategy.

Although his phrases rang with continuity with his predecessors, they showed how unprecedented Obama's views and measures were. This combination of "fundamentally transforming" America—a phrase Obama used just before his first inauguration[1]—and concealment of the drastic change happening was a hallmark of contemporary American politics.

> What makes us exceptional—what makes us American—is our allegiance to an idea, articulated in a declaration made more than two centuries ago: "We hold these truths to be self-evident, that all men are created equal, that they are endowed by their Creator with certain unalienable rights, that among these are Life, Liberty, and the pursuit of Happiness."[2]

Here was an appeal to patriotism and the basis of American democracy—the Constitution, American exceptionalism, and Declaration of Independence—which Obama had not used during his first term. On the contrary, according to him, the Constitution provided only "negative liberties" and there was no such thing as American exceptionalism. On several occasions he had even misquoted the very words he used from the Declaration of Independence.

Obama was merely adjusting to criticisms that he did not accept the American political structure as previously accepted, that he was off the liberal-conservative spectrum. Indeed, Obama continually proved that point, albeit in the guise that his reinterpretation was merely modernization needed "to bridge the meaning of those words with the realities of our time."

In fact, though, he was indeed forging a new and very different path toward "fundamentally transforming" the American system, to use his words. The altered approach was one of an unprecedented degree of statism, an imperial presidency that went far beyond Richard Nixon's dreams: record high levels of government regulation, taxation, and debt.

These policies were accompanied by social developments in American institutions, imposing a "politically correct" and "multicultural" ideology; an extreme lack of diversity in universities and the mass media; and political indoctrination in schools that narrowed permissible debate.

What was being created, then, was a different system from the one through which America achieved success and prosperity. Yet the fact that such changes were occurring was everywhere denied even as it was happening.

That factor, a new political philosophy when taken as a whole, was embodied in Obama's speech and in literally thousands of media articles and broadcasts, lectures in college courses, grade and high school curricula, activities of nongovernmental organizations, regulations written by government agencies, and in every other aspect of American life. All pushed in the same direction and used the same fundamental arguments.

For example, Obama's inaugural speech was filled with loaded phrases not balanced by other, contrary ideas about independent actions by citizens or other institutions.

Rights may be "self-evident, they've never been self-executing."[3] The guarantor of rights was the federal government.

America could only succeed if there was a national infrastructure and only the government could produce or build "[r]ailroads and highways to speed travel and commerce; schools and colleges to train our workers."

"A free market only thrives when there are rules to ensure competition and fair play." But it had always thrived under fewer rules than Obama wanted, while it had plummeted with the level of rules and definition of fair play Obama had imposed during his first term.

Obama did add that there has been skepticism of central authority, and he acknowledged that government can't do everything, so for Americans, "celebration of initiative and enterprise, our insistence on hard work and personal responsibility, are constants in our character."

But that last concept was only raised to be dismissed by a very big "but."

Times have changed, continued Obama, and "so must we; that fidelity to our founding principles requires new responses to new challenges; that preserving our individual freedoms ultimately requires collective action." The collective, as he made clear repeatedly, is embodied in the national government, and that response requires a bigger government, more taxes, more spending, and more regulation.

Consider this passage in Obama's inaugural speech:

No single person can train all the math and science teachers we'll need to equip our children for the future, or build the roads and networks and research labs that will bring new jobs and businesses to our shores. Now, more than ever, we must do these things together, as one nation, and one people.

And how does that follow? Of course, no one is suggesting or has ever suggested that a single person could do all those things. But that doesn't mean Obama's proposed methods for achieving these goals are the only alternative.

Up to now, with some exceptions, like veterans' benefits and some research subsidies, all that stuff had been pretty much done by private enterprise and individual initiative. People *decided* to be teachers and went to universities established by the states and private institutions. It was taken for granted that the national government played virtually no role in education.

Equally, the creation of "new jobs and businesses" was done in the same nongovernmental way. Companies created labs and networks needed to create jobs. As for roads, most were built and maintained by states. The American view was that government interference should be limited, must be limited, for the system to work. Top-down systems had failed in many countries. And while liberals and conservatives disagreed as to exactly where the line should be drawn, they both agreed on a line of far more limited government control than in other countries.

Why does all this now have to be done collectively? In the guise of continuity, Obama simply slipped through an unprecedented centralizing of America.

"My fellow Americans," Obama continues, "we are made for this moment, and we will seize it—so long as we seize it together." That sentence might have been spoken by previous American presidents. Yet there is a profound difference. When they said "we," they meant "we the people." Obama meant "we" as the institution that he thinks best represents all, that is, the federal government.

In addition, he said that everything must be changed to meet the gigantic crisis America faced. But he did not say what that crisis was. Indeed, he claimed the economy was recovering—so *that* was not the crisis. What was it, then, that required fundamental transformation?

The answer was the way that the American system had always existed, since it innately generated inequality, injustice, prejudice, and overall failure:

> We understand that outworn programs are inadequate to the needs of our time. We must harness new ideas and technology to remake our government, revamp our tax code, reform our schools, and empower our citizens with the skills they need to work harder, learn more, and reach higher.

Yet Obama explained that all this change didn't really *change* anything, because:

> While the means will change, our purpose endures: a nation that rewards the effort and determination of every single American. That is what this moment requires. That is what will give real meaning to our creed.[4]

Yet had not America basically achieved that goal by its traditional definition, and perhaps as much as any society made up of human beings could do so? Wasn't Obama's own career proof of that? But wait—there was a land mine in that phrase. Let's reexamine it:

> While the means will change, our purpose endures: a nation that rewards the effort and determination of every single American.

This puts us in the sphere of the participation trophy, or the carny games that you know are going to cheat you but proclaim: "Everyone a winner!" How can the nation—that is, the country collectively through the government—reward everyone who, in effect, shows up?

And how hard do you have to try? How much do you have to do to merit that reward?

A society that rewards everyone will soon run out of money. A society that decouples reward from achievement will face the same fate.

Things get even more revisionist to normative American political philosophy:

> We must make the hard choices to reduce the cost of health care and the size of our deficit. But we reject the belief that America must choose between caring for the generation that built this country and investing in the generation that will build its future. . . . The commitments we make to each other—through Medicare, and Medicaid, and Social Security—these things do not sap our initiative; they strengthen us. They do not make us a nation of takers; they free us to take the risks that make this country great.

Again, on the surface this seems to make sense. Yet the implications are enormous and enormously dangerous:

- We have money for everything.
- The U.S. government must spend more to invest in the next generation. But why is that so, especially since it is plunging that same generation into hopeless debt? How come previous generations were able to handle this situation?

- More entitlements equal greater prosperity. By removing risks, they free us to take risks? How about: I'll risk not buying health insurance because I know the federal government will give it to me free (which is to say, at the expense of other people).
- The same basic approach is applied to climate change, environmentalism, and energy. There is an emergency, we must spend a lot of money, we must act as fast as possible so we cannot really have a debate or think these things through, and we must have the federal government take the lead so we don't fall behind others.
- On foreign policy—which gets only a brief mention—the two main themes are 1) America will remain the anchor of strong alliances in every corner of the globe. That is, we will lead from behind. And 2) "we will support democracy" everywhere even as those "democracies" turn into repressive Islamist dictatorships whose regimes hate America.

The closest that Obama came to defining the emergency was to say that people were treated unequally due to their gender, race, or sexual preferences. He chose as illustrations the 1848 women's suffrage convention at Seneca Falls, New York (women got the vote *nearly a century ago*, in 1920); the 1965 civil rights marches from Selma to Montgomery, Alabama (the civil rights bill passed a *half century ago*), and the 1969 series of gay demonstrations at the Stonewall Inn in Greenwich Village (almost *forty-five years* earlier).

Discrimination along these lines was already completely illegal, universally denounced, and rare by 2013. Indeed, reverse discrimination in the form of quotas, preferential hiring, and "affirmative action" was far more common. So why did America need to be turned upside down to cope with a problem that had been largely solved?

A single sentence best illustrated the Obama method:

For our journey is not complete until our wives, our mothers, and daughters can earn a living equal to their efforts.

It was a matter of publicly documented fact that in the Obama White House, women were paid disproportionately less. And it was a matter of fact that for any nongovernment enterprise to behave that way was *already illegal* under laws passed before Obama even entered politics.

Thus, what was really going on was a left-wing redefinition of America along the following strategic lines:

Portray America as a disaster zone where inequality and unfairness run rampant, even though that was demonstrably untrue. Therefore, the United States must be fundamentally transformed.

Portray those who don't support you as engaged in evil, racist, etc., practices. Thus, those who criticize you are illegitimate and don't deserve a fair hearing, much less compromise.

Get away with breaking those principles yourself.

Mobilize support by ever-larger payouts and by intensifying conflicts along the lines of racial, religious, ethnic, and sexual preferences.

Any other president would have feared putting such themes in speeches lest the mass media would produce highly critical stories, but Obama could depend on the mass media to conceal and even echo such themes.

There was not a single sentence of the speech where he referred specifically to anything he did in his first term. Far from acknowledging its failures, to help the economy, for instance, he advocated more of the same, as the crisis was so humongous and there was no time to waste, so his plans must be immediately implemented without much scrutiny: "For now decisions are upon us, and we cannot afford delay."

Indeed, Obama even admitted that this rush would be unnecessarily messy: "We must act, knowing that our work will be imperfect."

Obama's second inaugural speech was thus a shocking statement, a revolutionary one in the context of U.S. history. Yet what Obama was trying to do to America would have had no chance of success, and he would not have any chance of election, if far more was not going on, if a far larger movement was not making dramatic gains in a transformational process.

Consequently, this is not a book about Barack Obama but rather about why such dramatic changes in policy, ideology, and the way American society and history are viewed have gone mostly unnoticed. It is a book explaining the movement, worldview, and changing situation that created Obama and made both possible and relatively popular the transformation he was undertaking.

True, it is necessary to deal with him at some length, both because he wielded so much power and came to symbolize the silent revolution America has undergone. But despite his early life's unusual features, his vast popularity, and his political success, Obama was merely just another product of the ideology and indoctrination that grown-up 1960s radicals had systematically spread to his generation and its successors.

Even if no one had ever heard of Obama, the radical capture of so much social, cultural, and intellectual power was what really laid the foundation for America's fundamental transformation. And these radical forces and ideas will continue to hold the commanding heights of intellect and culture even after he moves out of the White House.

Thus, this is the story of that movement, whose ideas and policies manifested themselves in the Obama administration but went far beyond that incidental success or the politics and character of the forty-fourth president of the United States.

In January 2008, Obama announced that he would soon enter office and embark on the fundamental transformation of America. The results of the November 2012 elections extended his endeavor for four more years, making its impact and scope even greater, perhaps irreversible. How could ideas and actions that seemed bizarre to so many Americans—and even more so to their ancestors—suddenly sweep the nation and alter its most fundamental assumptions?

The answer is that America's fundamental transformation already happened to a large extent before Obama ever declared his candidacy. Indeed, if those changes had not occurred he would never have been a serious candidate, much less the victor in the 2008 election and, despite a terrible economy and widespread passionate discontent, the 2012 election as well.

This book argues that the ideas and events that took place in the United States from the twentieth century through today can be fully understood only if the hegemonic radicalism of today is critiqued from the standpoint of traditional liberal thinking. Only then can the essential break with all past American thinking and practice be fully revealed. In effect, "liberalism" in America was redefined from a mild reformist impulse to improve the existing system into a radical, anticapitalist ideology seeking to overturn the country's most fundamental premises.

As a result, real liberals faced precisely the same task as did ancestors who battled reactionary movements, Communism, and the New Left. How can individual freedom be balanced against powerful institutions like government and corporations, between a just society and a materially successful society? And how can those who believe they hold all the answers to how people should live and behave be stopped from imposing their will on everyone else?

In the current situation, this struggle has not even begun, and in fact it may never begin at all. For if the moderate liberalism that has been the principal force shaping America over the last century becomes extinct, the sole choices left are to support either a leftism that is basically destructive to America's freedom and success, or a conservatism that is by far the lesser of the two evils.

Otherwise, a radical movement that has no name will set the agenda and ideas in American society. Since it was supposed to, and did, imitate and then supplant liberalism, this new radical ideology had to be so invisible as not even to have a name or organizational identity of its own. This group's greatest power was to change the thinking of those who denied its existence altogether. Invisibility and deniability were its main assets. Many people merely see this sharp swing to the left as a mere continuation of historic liberalism. In fact, the situation was no matter of business as usual but the most effective attack of far-left thinking in American history, one that pushed historic liberal ideas and forces to the edge of extinction.

Having spent my career studying Middle Eastern and Third World radicalism, especially how such doctrines both continued and sharply revised Marxist ideology, I could see clearly how such analysis now applies to what is happening in America.

This movement, which I will call the Third Left, grew from the failure of the two previous lefts—the Communist Party of the 1920s–1950s and the New Left of the 1960s and 1970s. The Communist Party was built on a basis of Marxism-Leninism but failed to seize power in the West due to the relative indifference of the proletariat there, the ultimate success of capitalist economies, the appeals of democratic culture, and the disastrous example of Communist states.

The New Left understood generally these four points of failure but was not quite sure how to change its appeal. As a result, it also failed quickly, but not before developing some new ideas and approaches that would live on until a third kind of left, the Third Left of the twenty-first century, figured out how to achieve its goal of fundamentally transforming American society.

Out of these movements' ruins came a large group of activists who learned from their previous mistakes. Adjusting their ideas to twenty-first-century realities, they gained cultural, intellectual, and even a measure of political hegemony, winning millions of adherents who had no idea what they were actually accepting, even gaining the presidency as a result of an unforeseen, wildly unlikely opportunity.

Realizing that the clichés of Marxism-Leninism—much less the idea of armed revolution or mass uprising—were ridiculous notions for America, the New Left's survivors had changed course and used modern tools corresponding far better to a vulnerable republic's weaknesses than did dogmatic Marxism. Through this strategy, the far left converted to its views tens of millions of people, most of them unaware of how outlandish these ideas were and how fundamentally they undermined the basis of America's success.

For this movement, in contrast to all of its predecessors on the radical left, politics was the end, not the beginning, of the process. Power was to grow out of a base secured by control over such key institutions as entertainment, mass media, and the educational system. Extremist ideas were made to seem normal; liberal, and pragmatic, and scholarly values were trampled. Yet how many would notice all this if there were no one with intellectual authority to point this out?

With these ideas accepted, large numbers of politicians and voters were ready to utter positions that many of them would have scoffed at a decade earlier. Professors bragged of indoctrinating students and produced unashamedly polemical work; journalists boasted of twisting or concealing vital stories for the alleged good of their readers. The mass media systematically concealed key facts and stories, having been transformed into a cheerleading section for the Third Left and "Progressive" liberalism, where large elements of news, entire stories, and important arguments were simply self-censored out. Instead, the media is used to intimidate, smear, and use double-standard super-criticism against dissenters.

The massive funding for left-wing front groups allowed them not only to have public influence but also to employ thousands of full-time cadre—that is, ideologically and tactically sophisticated professional political activists (in Marxist terminology, cadre are trained, dedicated activists engaged in the building of a revolutionary party). Ironically, the left has far more resources than its opponents, including tremendous power in rewarding those who supported the movement with jobs, prestige, and money and punishing those who didn't. The remarkable ability to demonize critics by slanderous charges (racism, homophobia, Islamophobia, class greed, sexism) intimidated many into remaining silent and guided many others to put their hands over their ears to ignore anything said by dissenters.

One can add to this list a turn toward anticapitalism, accepted as if that were a normal American view; systematic condemnation of American society for a wide variety of failings; transforming inequality of wealth from a fact of life into a crime against social justice; a medical plan that eschewed simple needed changes for a damaging total overhaul; unprecedented government control over key industries; the celebration of antireligious and antipatriotic ideas; the twisting of the Constitution; the division of society into competing racial and ethnic groups; the handling of a recession in ways certain to fail; the turning of universities into a means of mass-producing indoctrinated students; the redistribution of wealth; the renunciation of past American foreign policy as harmful imperialism; and the rejection of a leading role in the world; and many other such concepts.

These ideas and policies infected the Democratic Party, Congress, and even the White House when in 2008, without serious debate or realization of what was happening, America elected the most left-wing government in its history, headed by the most left-wing member of the U.S. Senate.

Suddenly, America was governed by a president disconnected from the country's most basic assumptions and principles, and most of whose life was shrouded in carefully unexplored mystery and deliberately unexamined controversy. Yet without the transformation of key institutions to promote radical ideology, push a political agenda rather than do their proper job, and make their priority protecting Obama and his policies rather than defending the country's interests, Obama would have been quickly discredited in a tidal wave of criticism, ridicule, and exposés.

How dramatically had things changed, and yet for how many was that change concealed! More regulations, high taxes, wasteful spending, and other policies strangled recovery and extended a recession. Foreign policy promoted the most hostile foreign forces, contradicting historic American practices and even fundamental principles of Western statecraft. An energy policy sabotaged greater independence, reduced supplies, and encouraged higher prices. An official policy of racialism promised to bring social peace but actually deepened conflict.

What had always before failed was now exalted; what had always succeeded was demeaned. This covert revolution did fundamentally transform America, but just how deep and irreversible those changes were will be revealed only in the future. The first task, however, was to understand that something momentous had occurred, what it meant, and how it had happened.

The historian Victor Davis Hanson put it this way: "What thirty years ago was a common-sense given is now considered a landmark breakthrough."[5]

Oh, no, came the common response, nothing unusual at all was happening. The idea that America had taken a dangerously sharp swing to the far left was merely an illusion. Academia and the mass media were functioning with their historic high quality, conscientious attempt at fairness, and reasonable balance of opinion. For his part, Obama was said to be a normal Democratic president, a typical liberal in the tradition of his predecessors or even centrist who had either done little harm or much that was good.

With the radical forces posing as liberal, it was natural that people who thought themselves liberal-minded believe they were congenial. And if the critique came only from the right, those who did not like that perspective for a variety of reasons would simply reject it.

Consequently, there was a wide gap between those who thought the republic was in danger, at least of crippling debt, and those who insisted there was no problem at all except for unreasoning resistance to obviously beneficial changes to which no rational, well-intentioned person could object. Thus a critic must be an extreme rightist, a racist, or a religious fanatic to whom the proper response was hatred, ridicule, and isolation.

Yet this supposedly liberal worldview was based on trashing an America that was largely the creation of liberalism. The United States of the early twenty-first century was a system that owed more to liberal reforms than to traditional conservatism. The system that supposedly didn't work and, in Obama's words, had never worked was not some unreconstructed, laissez-faire arrangement of the late nineteenth century but had been transformed by dozens of such changes. And these developments had included, often with Republican assent, an ever larger government and ever more extensive regulation.

The radical movement's main political victim was not conservatism, which merely made a handy scapegoat, but liberalism, which the radical forces and its satellite "Progressive" mind-set detested. After all, liberalism was the main rival of radicalism and most of the new recruits were unconsciously radical, thinking that they were still advocating normative liberalism. It was liberalism that was obliterated by the new radical version. Indeed, the decline of real liberalism reinvigorated conservatism as the only apparent alternative to radical ideas and policies.

Was its rise to power a conspiracy? No, since the movement's cadres were largely acting independently or in many small groups based on their own parallel ideas without close coordination. The movement's development was all in the open, but those who would otherwise have publicized its advance—journalists and academics—did so only favorably, since so many of them were activists themselves. Indeed, the main reason for the movement's success was that, unlike in the Communist era, there was no single party and leadership whose machinations could be exposed or which might dissolve into bickering factions.

This book's purpose is to explain the bewildering gap between the image of this new radicalism (liberalism) being consistent with democracy, capitalism, and moderation, despite ample evidence to the contrary in the bizarre statements, policies, and changes wrought by the silent revolution. It seeks to persuade the many people who believe nothing has changed for the worse in America that there is a potentially fatal problem, and to help those who already understand that reality to comprehend the nature of that danger.

While there are of course long-term trends and fundamental shifts helping along the process, the main factor is that America is in steep decline due to decisions made by Americans who have no idea that they are committing civilizational suicide.

At the very moment in human history when it became obvious that the far left's ideas had failed and that statist, big-government, ever-higher-regulation policies did not work, it became possible for the first time ever to convince Americans that these things were precisely what the country needed. And at the very time in human history when Western civilization and liberal capitalism were so obviously the most successful system in history—recognized as such in most of the Third World and most of all in formerly Communist China—a camouflaged radical movement convinced many of those benefiting from this system that their own societies were in fact evil and failed.

"It is part of the human condition," the historian Walter Laqueur has written, "not to accept unpleasant facts."[6] In this case, however, a large measure of the radicals' success was to hide what was happening in plain sight.

CHAPTER 2

The Marxist Challenge
to Western Society

There is a story that the Soviet dictator Joseph Stalin saw a photo of German workers in the 1920s standing patiently in line and declared that they would never be revolutionaries. Thirty years later, after a rebellion by German workers against the Communist regime in East Germany in 1953, the Marxist writer Bertolt Brecht wrote a poem, "The Solution," containing these lines: "Would it not be easier . . . for the government to dissolve the people and elect another?"

These were the classic problems of Marxism. Its adherents insisted that the Communist system must work, but it didn't. They were sure that capitalism would collapse and yet it did not do so. Why was that so? Perhaps the workers didn't know their own interests; perhaps they were too conditioned by religious, nationalist, and capitalist propaganda that they would forever stand patiently waiting their fair share?

Until that problem was solved, the far left learned by hard knocks over the course of the twentieth century, there would be no fundamental transformation of society into a Communist utopia.

The industrial age that revolutionized Western life in the nineteenth century brought tremendous hardships and inequities as well as times of great technological and economic progress. Yet, as the historian David Thomson noted, these problems were also fixed by the system that created them in the first place, motivated by a combination of conscience among the upper classes, struggles for reform by the lower classes, and broad support for reform on both pragmatic and moral grounds:

> Hardships begin to be talked about only when they are no longer taken for granted. . . . Sweated labor and cellar dwellings were not invented by the men who made the industrial revolution: they were discovered by them, discussed by them, and in the end partially remedied by them.[1]

As an honest historian, Thomson wrote of both good and bad, stinting neither on the horrors nor the reform struggles of liberals and conservatives alike. He quoted the reformer William Cobbett's description of the hellish conditions facing early-nineteenth-century workers at the industrial revolution's start:

> Talk of serfs! Are there any of these, or did feudal times ever see any of them, so debased, so absolutely slaves, as the poor creatures who . . . are compelled to work fourteen hours a day, in a heat of eight-four degrees, and who are liable to punishment for looking out of a window of the factory![2]

The hardships began with the removal of traditional agricultural rights through the "enclosure" of land by big landowners, thus also allowing, along with technological advances, the food surplus that would release peasants to become workers in cities. This was accompanied by the invention of new machinery that vastly improved transport and increased the production of goods. Initially through capitalism the masses of people were impoverished yet they also began a long climb into the most prosperous, free societies in human history.

It was understandable that radicals, including the political philosopher and activist Karl Marx (1818–1883), thought such a system to be unsustainable during the phase of brutal capital accumulation, at a time when society was badly out of balance. The political battles of his day were in fact attempted liberal democratic revolutions and reform movements that often failed during his lifetime.

Yet Marx and other radicals thought either that democratic revolutions or reforms within the capitalist framework could not succeed, or, alternatively, that capitalism itself would collapse. It was a time when, given a rush of scientific advances and discoveries, many believed that the laws of social development could be defined with the same precision as chemical formulae. Thus Marx concluded that the natural outcome of all human history must be a Communist state, that is, one in which everything would be held communally.

Only the proletariat, the new industrial working class, by acting in its own self-interest, Marx believed, could liberate all of society and reach this utopian destination. Thereafter, and until this day, the political left has largely been defined by Marx's thought and the belief that collective ownership would be inevitably more virtuous than private ownership and that government was the medium for the holding of wealth.

Thereafter, two systems provided alternative models for Western society. As eloquently explained by the historian R. R. Palmer:

> In one form of society the control of capital is through private ownership . . . by which capital is owned by individuals, families, or corporations that are in turn owned by share-

holders. In the other form of society productive capital in principle belongs to the public and is in effect owned and controlled by the state or its agencies; such societies generally call themselves socialist. . . . In these [socialist] societies the control of capital, or decisions on saving, investment, and production, *are also in the hands of relatively few under some form of central plan.* (emphasis added)[3]

Like Marx, however, those who saw capitalism as deterministically failing and "bourgeois" democracy as a hypocritical sham were not liberals at all. On the contrary, liberalism was in fact the principal ideology of capitalism, which is why it supported the diminished power of the neofeudal state and the aristocracy that got in the way of social mobility, open markets, and the application of the new technologies.

For liberals, capitalism was the solution, at least if it were to be reformed and somewhat restrained, the power of the big corporations to be balanced by more power for workers, small businesspeople, and others. In contrast, for the Marxists, revolution and the total and highly visible overturning of the existing system was a necessity. In Vladimir Lenin's words, "No compromise was possible with the capitalist, bourgeois democratic state. . . ."[4]

Vladimir Lenin (1870–1924) was leader of the first Marxist revolution, which happened in Russia in 1917. Marx put the emphasis on the idea that revolution was inevitable. The organized working class would clearly see that its interests lay with Communism because people inevitably understood their own interests and reality. The equally inevitable collapse of capitalism would force them to do so.

Lenin, however, had to deal with the fact that in the almost seventy years between Marx's initial *Communist Manifesto* and the Russian Revolution neither of Marx's predictions—a united, revolutionary working class or capitalism's collapse—had come about.

On the contrary, the working classes had improved their living standards, in part due to liberal reforms and also to the organization of trade unions. In addition, the working class was motivated by religion and patriotism to side with their own bourgeois and even aristocratic leaders to slaughter each other in long and bloody World War I.

Regarding the more effective promotion of revolution, Lenin developed the idea of having a disciplined party—the Communist Party—composed of professional, disciplined revolutionaries. The party had a single ideological line and, after the Communists seized power in Russia, Lenin imposed on foreign Communist parties an unswerving loyalty to the new state, the Union of Soviet Socialist Republics (USSR).

Dealing with the supposedly mysterious reluctance of workers to become revolutionaries, however, was a problem that went largely unsolved during the Communist era. Lenin posited that the workers were bought off by a prosperity gained from imperialism. But this idea only became important to the post-Communist left in the 1960s. The same point applied to the problem of countering religion and patriotism as well as the broader issue of why all the workers didn't become Communists.

To make matters worse, Lenin's successor, Joseph Stalin (1878–1953), added another reason for the skepticism of Westerners toward Communism. Stalin, the longtime ruler over both the USSR and the world Communist movement, created a dreadful dictatorship whose economic successes, to the perceptive foreign observer, were limited and excessively costly. When Communism was extended to Eastern Europe by the Red Army's World War II conquests, after 1945; to China after that country's revolution in 1949; and to Cuba after the revolution there in 1959, it was not notably more attractive to most Westerners, for the same reasons.

The type of fundamental transformation offered by Communism, then, was a disaster because it destroyed all the advantages of a democratic capitalist system, including its powerful self-correcting mechanisms. Instead, it substituted all the Communist system's deep flaws, which destroyed everything aside from an all-powerful state and thus ensured the rule of an unlimited dictatorship.

Marx was a child of the Enlightenment who considered himself to be a scientist uncovering the iron laws of politics, society, and history:

> The premises from which we begin are not arbitrary ones, not dogmas, but real premises from which abstraction can only be made in the imagination. They are the real individuals, their activity and the material conditions under which they live, both those which they find already existing and those produced by their activity. These premises can thus be verified in a purely empirical way.[5]

Marx said his movement's success depended on its accurately understanding "the real process of production . . . as the basis of all history." He didn't believe there was no such thing as truth, as do the postmodernists of twenty-first-century leftism. And he believed in technology and developmentally based progress. He was no ecologist, no Third Worldist, no sentimentalist nostalgic about the past. As he wrote in *The German Ideology*, " 'Liberation' is an historical and not a mental act, and it is brought about by historical conditions, the development of industry, commerce, agriculture, the conditions of intercourse."[6]

Marx and his followers identified the industrial working class as the force that would make the revolution. Here's how the idea appears in the 1848 *Communist Manifesto*: Society as a whole is more and more splitting up into two great hostile camps, led by two powerful classes—the bourgeoisie and proletariat—with mutually exclusive goals.

Marxists posited that the workers' condition would worsen and that no reform could improve their situation, forcing them to become revolutionaries. For it to become so bad as to force men to make a revolution, Marx wrote in *The German Ideology,*

> [the society] must necessarily have rendered the great mass of humanity "propertyless," and produced, at the same time, the contradiction of an existing world of wealth and culture, both of which conditions presuppose a great increase in productive power, a high degree of its development.[7]

In other words, the society must have become a lot more prosperous but the benefits would have to be restricted to a very small portion of the population. Thus the twenty-first-century left's effort to create the myth of the wealth being monopolized by the "one percent."

The main ally of the impoverished would be the lower middle class, wiped out by big business and new technology: "The lower strata of the middle class—the small tradespeople, shopkeepers and retired tradesmen generally, the handicraftsmen and peasants—all these sink gradually into the proletariat. . . ."[8]

One reason why Marx and Lenin had such faith in the proletariat was that these were seen as courageous, hardworking, disciplined people, far superior to the peasantry, who were seen by Communists as suspiciously conservative, pious, and shortsighted. Marx and Lenin did not sentimentalize poverty.

Indeed, like some stereotype of a capitalist, the Marxist looked down on the poorest people because they did not share in the proletariat's hard work and wealth creation. Implicitly, the Marxists sensed that there might be characteristics among them that would subvert the revolutionary idealism they wanted to instill. Thus Marx described the peasantry as living in "rural idiocy" and the nonproletarian urban poor in similarly unflattering terms in *The Communist Manifesto*:

The "dangerous class" [lumpenproletariat], the social scum, that passively rotting mass thrown off by the lowest layers of the old society, may, here and there, be swept into the movement by a proletarian revolution; its conditions of life, however, prepare it far more for the part of a bribed tool of reactionary intrigue.[9]

Ultimately, though, the biggest problem for Marx, Lenin, and their followers was their concept of the state. Without a revolution, they understandably believed, the state would always be firmly in the hands of pro-capitalist forces, whether conservative, liberal, or even social democratic. Strengthening the state in a "bourgeois capitalist" society would be insane because it would make fundamental transformation impossible.

In discussing the state, Marx had transformed himself from self-styled hardheaded realist into a starry-eyed utopian who thought revolution would suspend the equally valid "laws" of human society. After having described all of history as a struggle between classes, Marx suddenly posited that the revolution would make all those hitherto irrevocable laws of history go away. In *The Communist Manifesto*, he explained that the proletariat would seize all capital and means of production and place them "in the hands of the State," which was merely "the proletariat organized as the ruling class."[10]

Magically, the government had no independent life or identity as an institution. It was not a player with its own selfish interests in the battle for power but merely the selfless representative of the masses' true will and interest. No actual human beings would shape it with their own selfishness, greed, ambition, or personal perspective. Lenin said class struggle would continue even after the revolution in the form of traitors who must be purged and punished. This was the foundation for Stalin's reign of terror.

Leon Trotsky grasped this problem even before the revolution.

In explaining what would later happen in the USSR he explained: "The party organization substitutes itself for the party, the central committee substitutes itself for the organization, and, finally, a dictator substitutes himself for the central committee."[11]

Of course, all of this could only begin to become clear when Communists actually took power in Russia in 1917. Lenin understood that Marx's utopian views were of little use for running an actual state. Thus Communism became a full-fledged dictatorship, including the creation of an all-powerful party, a single acceptable political line, slave labor camps, the destruction of religion, and the demand that all foreign Communists worship the USSR as the "socialist motherland." These tactics often meant giving orders and imprisoning or shooting everyone who didn't obey fast enough.

Yet on a theoretical level, Lenin retained Marx's utopianism and fantasy view of the state. They believed that control over the means of production would permit "the development of a totality of capacities in the individuals themselves . . . into complete individuals and the casting-off of all natural limitations."[12]

In contrast, Lenin, like Marx, insisted that reforms could never achieve anything in capitalist states, explaining: "The bourgeoisie and the opportunists within the labor movement [social democrats] concur in this doctoring of Marxism. They omit, obscure, or distort the revolutionary side of this theory, its revolutionary soul."[13] They think that the "state is an organ for the reconciliation of classes."[14] Thus the traitors would inevitably fail, at most achieving limited reforms while leaving the overall framework in place.

Lenin rejected electoral democracy. After all, the founders of America also thought of the state as an organ for the reconciliation of classes. Consequently, Lenin viewed democracy as a fraud. The traitorous reformist socialists, wrote Lenin in *The State and Revolution*, "[s]hare, and instill in the minds of the people, the false notion that universal suffrage 'in the present-day state' is really capable of revealing the will of the majority of the working people and of securing its realization."[15] Communist parties would, of course, run in elections but justified such behavior as a way of building support for revolution by proving that the ballot box didn't work in bringing about real change. In part, that meant by showing that reforms were inevitably inadequate and that only revolution would suffice.

Stalin was the inevitable result. No wonder this system degenerated into the horror of the gulags, the shot in the head, concentration camps, slave labor, and torture. True, many foreign leftists—especially intellectuals—accepted the romantic myth of the USSR but most Westerners would never do so. The USSR's example would inhibit Communist revolutions from taking place in the West.

For Lenin and Stalin, who adopted the policy of "socialism in one country," persuading foreigners to stage revolutions in their own countries was secondary to keeping the Soviet Communist regime in power. And only a strong government under the party's total control could achieve that aim. "The proletariat," Lenin wrote in *The State and Revolution*, "would need to crush the bourgeois resistance through a mechanism, and that is the state."[16]

And so the USSR's borders were closed; the state held a monopoly on everything; every institution was used for ideological indoctrination. A regime that already controlled all of society and its institutions would shape people's consciousness in a relatively crude way, by raw propaganda and open compulsion. The twenty-first-century left would develop a far more sophisticated strategy before taking power, a far harder task in a democratic country where alternatives still existed.

This approach was no deviation or accident due to Stalin's personality but resulted from the profound flaw in Marx's original concept and Lenin's antidemocratic ruthlessness. A system in which the government held overwhelming power, ran the economy, took away all the independent rights of citizens, and even dictated the definition of truth on every issue was a blueprint for a very nasty dictatorship.

Marx, and certainly Lenin, understood little about the wisdom that went into constructing the United States, which assumed that checks, balances, and guarantees of individual liberty were the only things that could prevent tyranny. In contrast, Marx's view was utopian and Lenin's was cynically opportunistic. The results would be blood-soaked and terrifying.

In the Marxian concept, all money and power would be focused in the state, but then the state would not do anything wrong with that concentration of power. The state was innocent. There would be no cronyism, no corruption, no bureaucracy, and no concentration of stupidity so as to make mistakes much bigger. And no newspaper, trade union, writer, or academic could dare contradict this claim in a Communist state, since the government controlled his job and the state would punish him severely for doing so.

Marx also expected—quite wrongly—that the Communist system would make the economy grow more effectively than capitalism. In his words, it would "[i]ncrease the total productive forces as rapidly as possible."[17]

On one hand, this belief left out the waste, corruption, ignorance, and different priorities of that state whose rulers knew nothing about creating jobs, meeting a payroll, or producing goods. Their centralized planning system had all the advantages of a clumsy dinosaur. Workers and peasants, having no hope of advancement or real personal stake in the economy, worked as little as possible and stole as much as possible. Uncorrected by free speech or pluralism, the government made expensive wrong decisions.

On the other hand, Marx expected that people would work harder and accept a smaller reward on the basis of idealism and ideology, to which Lenin and Stalin added the incentive of dire punishment. In fact, feeling alienated and knowing that more effort would not improve their lot, the workers and peasants did less, stole more, and became increasingly indifferent.

At least, though, the Communists consciously sought to build a system that increased productivity. In the USSR, someone who refused to work would have been shot.

Finally, Marxist regimes had not put an end to "the exploitation of one individual by another," as Marx had predicted. Instead they had intensified it. These Communist governments had done precisely what they accused the bourgeoisie of doing! They reduced workers to slave soldiers without property or rights. Marx predicted Communism would end "the hostility of one nation to another." But in fact it intensified war, bloodshed, and imperialistic exploitation.

Communism only achieved a second-rate imitation of its own worst stereotype of capitalism, complete with exploitation of the proletariat, class discrimination, looting of the peasantry, and massive injustice, to the point of mass murder. Communism even had racial and ethnic discrimination against non-Russians and ran the USSR as an imperialist empire, extended into Central Europe after World War II. Foreign Communists became the Soviet party's satellites and put the USSR's interests first, which often made them most unpopular, even deemed treasonous, in their own countries.

The founders of America understood the causes of all these problems; Marx, none of them. Of course, the founders would have explained, a state whose power wasn't strictly limited would be a tyranny. For Marx, the state was not a threat because it would automatically "wither away." "When . . . all production has been concentrated in the hands of a vast association of the whole nation," Marx explained in *The Communist Manifesto*, "the public power will lose its political character. . . ."[18] With the whole proletariat as ruling class there would be no ruling class! Next stop, Joe Stalin and concentration labor camps.

As to who would write the regulations, manage the money, and make the decisions on distributing assets, Marx never conceived of a "new class" that lived as rulers from its relationship to the state and its assets. Instead, he asserted, "[t]he proletariat will use its political supremacy to wrest, by degree, all capital from the bourgeoisie, to centralize all instruments of production in the hands of the state."[19] Yet through the state, a ruling class still controlled the means of production, and did so without the competition, legal restrictions, and criticism that limited the bourgeoisie's power in Western democracy.

Abandoning his own self-image as a hardheaded scientist of human society, Marx thus expected its magical transformation into a place where everyone was unselfish, sensitive, and generous, willing to work overtime (from each according to his ability) for those less fortunate (to each according to his needs) without recompense. "In place of the old bourgeois society, with its classes and class antagonisms, we shall have an association, in which the free development of each is the condition for the free development of all."[20]

Marx's panacea was a state run by "good people" (proletarians) rather than "bad people" (the bourgeoisie), a state that would be so virtuous as to do away with itself. Lenin revised that to be a state run by good, very tough people (the party leadership) who would do away with all of their endless enemies while ruling in everyone's interest without giving anyone else a say in any decision.

Yet Marx had once answered this very question in his third "Thesis on Feuerbach," published in 1845:

The materialist doctrine concerning the changing of circumstances and upbringing forgets that circumstances are changed by men and that it is essential to educate the educator himself. This doctrine must, therefore, divide society into two parts, one of which is superior to society.[21]

In other words, he rightly ridiculed people who believed there could be a sudden leap by a "superman" group—Marx's proletariat; Lenin's party; the twenty-first-century left's smart, credentialed people who know best how everyone should live, and the revolutionary Islamists' rightly guided clerics who properly interpret Sharia—that breaks all the rules that hitherto governed human history and produces an ideal society based on unbridled state power.

So the revolutions dreamed of by the "Old Left" and Marxism either failed to materialize altogether or did take place and created nightmarish societies. Marx wrote an appropriate epitaph for his own system while critiquing competing radical ideologies: "Ultimately, when stubborn historical facts had dispersed all intoxicating effects of self-deception, this form of socialism ended in a miserable hangover."[22]

The causes of that hangover for the left were not internal failures but also dramatic changes in Western capitalist societies, and most thoroughly of all in the United States:

First, capitalism didn't decline but instead advanced, raising living standards. Rather than a generalized misery, the proportion of the poor shrank while workers and even the poor lived better lives than their counterparts throughout history.

Second, the working class preferred material betterment to making revolution.

Third, the workers were responsive, often more than the elites, to the appeals of religion, patriotism, and traditional culture.

Fourth, new technology and methods of organization created by the capitalist system as well as social reforms made possible living standards high above those in Communist states.

Fifth, as anyone who has lived under Communism or Third World statist despotism knows, people work harder when they work for themselves and take better care of it when they have their own property, or at least have a reasonable hope of advancement for themselves or their children.

Finally, minority groups, women, and homosexuals eventually improved their status with relatively little disruption to the society as a whole. One reason for this is the broad support among other groups for ending discrimination, up to the point of having equal rights with everyone else, though not always beyond that point.

The same pattern applied to the failure of other Communist methods and the rejection of leftist ideology. As the USSR became more and more visibly horrible, its twists and turns as well as its obvious control of foreign Communist parties—making them the clients of a foreign and even hostile power—helped destroy the movement's credibility.

The Communist approach highlighted an us-versus-them mentality that made far more people decide to be on the other side. Having a single leading group and single political line put all the movement's marbles in one basket. Accept everything and you were a reliable militant; reject even a single position and you were an enemy.

Above all, however, Communism declined as a political force and intellectual inspiration because the proletariat did not act as Marx and Lenin had predicted. Its members raised their living standards and deserted to consumerism. To the disgust of radical intellectuals—who already enjoyed a nicer life style—as their living standards rose workers were more interested in houses, cars, and sports than in creating utopia. By the 1950s and 1960s, the Communist movement passed into crisis in the West, finally collapsing with the fall of its Soviet bloc role model.

How was the failure of Marxism-Leninism explained in the West? There were several arguments, but ultimately the most important would be taken from Lenin's short book *Imperialism, the Highest Stage of Capitalism*. He claimed that while it was true that Western capitalism prospered, it did so only by stealing from the Third World.

A second idea was developed from Marx's early concept of alienation, a splitting of man and his surrounding world that engendered "false consciousness," which is just a fancy way of saying that people don't know what is in their true interest. Marx, Lenin, and the revolutionaries and intellectuals who followed them knew that their system represented reality and that Communism was good for the vast majority of people. If that vast majority didn't agree, they must have been duped by social institutions, including religion, being misled by a nonexistent God's supposed views; patriotic loyalty to countries; and national consciousness, loyalty to some racial or ethnic group that superseded class loyalty.

Regarding the United States, there was another, special explanation as to why Communism had limited appeal. Sometimes one could read into Marx a view—though this was in contradiction to the rest of his thinking—that America didn't need and wouldn't have a revolution at all. But this had to be quelled by Lenin in line with the absolutism of their political thinking: Things had to be; there could be no doubt and no exceptions; totalitarian belief dictated that the future is completely knowable, and everything was political and right or wrong, as seen in modern political correctness.

Marx realized that something exceptional was going on in the United States, distinct from the monarchical, often dictatorial and class-ridden European societies where change was so difficult to bring about. In a letter to Abraham Lincoln, January 28, 1865, Marx wrote:

> From the commencement of the [Civil War] the working-men of Europe felt instinctively that the Star-Spangled Banner carried the destiny of their class. . . .
>
> The workingmen of Europe feel sure that, as the American War of Independence initiated a new era of ascendancy for the middle class, so the American Antislavery War will do for the working classes. They consider it an earnest of the epoch to come that it fell to the lot of Abraham Lin-

coln, the single-minded son of the working class, to lead his country through the matchless struggle for the rescue of an enchained race and the reconstruction of a social world.[23]

These were unique words on Marx's part, breaking with the usual Marxist practice of voicing only contempt toward liberals or social democrats as bourgeois pawns who subverted the forces of progress. Lenin, echoing Marx, accepted that the United States had been exceptional compared to other countries because it was relatively classless, compared to Europe, and had so much opportunity for people to improve their status.

But, Lenin suggested in 1917, America was going to change. Large-scale industrialization had turned America from a country of the frontier, small farmers, and a weak state into a place under "the complete domination of the trusts, the omnipotence of the big banks, a grand-scale colonial policy, and so forth."

This idea that the rich and corporations dominated the country was closer to the truth in Lenin's time than it was in later decades. Yet America's continued development offered even more chances for the working class to rise in society and to enjoy a better material life. Liberal reforms reduced the power of wealthy capitalists without killing the golden-egg-laying goose. And there was never any real colonial policy.

While Marxist ideas came to America in the late nineteenth century with European immigrants, the Socialist and later—after the Russian Revolution—the Communist parties never grew very large. In the 1930s, the American Communists reached their peak, developing some power in the trade unions and in intellectual life. As would happen in the 1960s, Marxism was intellectually fashionable and affected the New Left.

But the discovery of real Communist infiltration into the government during the late 1940s, Senator Joe McCarthy's exaggeration of past Communist influence in the 1950s, and most of all the U.S.-Soviet Cold War further discouraged support for leftism. Moreover, the problem of workers' high living standards, the relative conservatism of the proletariat, and the way to organize a leftist movement in America still remained unsolved.

Only with the rise of the New Left in the 1960s was the fossilized thinking of the Communist era and a rigid Marxist-Leninism begun to be thrown off. And only the twenty-first-century third round of leftism would succeed in making a breakthrough to an entirely different, post-Leninist strategy, tactics, and rethinking of basic concepts.

CHAPTER 3

Why Marxism Failed and the West Succeeded

During the 1930s, Earl Browder and other Communist Party USA leaders used the word *progressive* as a cover for their real views, and in 1948 that was the name chosen by the Communist Party for its "moderate" front party, the Progressive Party. At the same time, the Communists pretended to be patriotic and within the American historical tradition, using the slogan "Communism is twentieth-century Americanism." Front groups proliferated in which liberals were lured in for ostensibly good causes but with the direction of the organizations in radical hands.

Yet behind this façade, Marxists knew that liberalism was their main, most dangerous enemy. Consider how the Communist Party approached the New Deal. Here's Browder in an interview from 1936: "There isn't an ounce of socialism in the Roosevelt administration. [President Franklin] Roosevelt stands for capitalism but he tries to remedy this capitalism of some of its worst abuses, hoping thereby to give it longer life."[1]

That was a good definition of Roosevelt's goal. The liberals wanted to save capitalism; the radicals wanted to fundamentally transform it. Of course, Browder understood that only by obscuring this contradiction could the far left flourish. Consequently, the Communists must always seek to subvert and change liberalism by influencing it. Roosevelt, Browder continued, was being pulled by some to the left and by others to the right. Consequently, it would be wrong for "all progressives to unite around Roosevelt as the sole means to defeat reaction." But they must do everything possible to pull the New Deal to the left. The reporter conducting the interview concluded, "It seems that personally Roosevelt and [Republican leader Alf] Landon look pretty much alike to Browder," though he had a slight preference for Roosevelt. That was the traditional radical attitude toward liberals, which the Third Left continued but simply hid.

This was one of the fundamental problems for the Marxist movement in America. In 1919, after a series of terrorist bombings, the liberal president Woodrow Wilson authorized a large series of police raids that arrested radicals and expelled some from the country. The left-wing militants who wanted to follow the example of the Russian Revolution were expelled from the reform-minded Socialist Party, with the Socialists even calling in the police to protect their convention from assault.

Under the influence of Lenin's Russian Revolution and the creation of the first Communist country, the USSR, the American Communists organized separately. From the start, the Communist Party USA was under Moscow's direction. It did not grow in the 1920s, due to the prosperity of that era and the often damaging extremism of Soviet ideological and strategic orders. The left thus turned to a strategy that would be duplicated in the twenty-first century: It camouflaged itself as the Progressive movement.

The Progressive movement originally had been a late-nineteenth-century effort to revitalize liberalism in the face of conservative domination, an economically successful but unrestrained capitalism with many abuses, and corrupt big-city political bosses.

The new big corporations were dominating government and running roughshod over small businesses. Workers had few rights; the middle class had little power.

Consequently, the Progressives wanted honest government, a reasonable degree of regulation, and the breakup of trusts so that competitive capitalism could flourish. They understood that only a stronger government and trade unions could balance the power of the monopolies. Those Progressives also saw a failure to rein in uncontrolled capitalism as the most likely road to leftist revolution. Consequently, they were strongly anti-Communist and no president was tougher, even more brutal, in combatting the radical left than Woodrow Wilson.

This original Progressive movement, however, had nothing to do with the use of its name after it went out of existence after World War I, with most of its goals met. In 1924, Wisconsin senator Bob La Follette organized a left-wing Progressive Party for his presidential campaign and came in third with 17 percent of the votes. La Follette formed that party after breaking with the Communists, but the Communists would have the last laugh.

From that time on, the label *Progressive* was used mainly by the Communist Party to mask itself. Communists called themselves Progressives to hide their real aims. Just as the term *progressive* was used as a cover by Earl Browder and other Communist Party leaders in the 1930s, Obama's mentor, Frank Marshall Davis, always called himself a Progressive to conceal his being a Communist. Most notoriously of all, the Communists masterminded the 1948 Progressive Party to run against Harry Truman, whom they hated for his refusal to surrender to Stalin's aggressiveness and hostility.

As shown in the Browder quote above, the Third Left claimed to be the Progressive wing of the New Deal, merely being more energetic in support of workers' rights, government power, and friendship with the USSR. While the Communist Party did profit from its exploitation of popular causes among liberals, the apparent failure of capitalism in the Great Depression, some leadership in organizing unions, antifascist passions, and the large U.S.-Soviet alliance in World War II, the limits to its growth were also clear.

Ultimately, the movement was more seriously damaged by the rigidity of the party line and its slavishness to the USSR. Precisely because of the connection with the Soviet Union, the 1939–41 Nazi-Soviet Pact hurt the party in liberal circles, as did the brutal purge trials of the 1930s and reports of repression and suffering in the USSR.

Added to this was the Truman Administration's post–World War II discovery of Soviet subversive infiltration of the government using American Communists, most notoriously in the theft of nuclear weapons technology. As the USSR seized control of Eastern Europe and the Cold War began—which became a shooting war in 1950 in Korea—the strong American antiradical tradition returned in full force.

The Communists were driven out of the AFL-CIO unions, many of which they had built and even led in the 1930s and 1940s. Party membership plummeted and supporters faced the loss of employment. That trend was further accelerated when the Soviet premier Nikita Khrushchev made a secret speech in 1956—obtained by Israel and quickly leaked by Western intelligence services—denouncing the Stalin era as one of a "cult of personality" and vicious repression.

The later revised history written by leftist academics claimed that the anti-Communist reaction was a purely right-wing campaign in which the demagoguery of Senator Joe McCarthy of Wisconsin was prominent, a witch hunt that falsely accused people of being Communists and demonized the Communists themselves. But this was a whitewash.

In fact, liberals, social democrats, and conservatives all participated in throwing Communists out of the government, universities, unions, the media, and nongovernmental groups for good reason. The Communists were in the pocket of a dictatorial and enemy foreign power.

Nevertheless, it is true that in the 1950s and early 1960s, the powerful wave of anti-Communism effectively branded the left as Communist and subversive. In contrast, however, in the late 1960s and afterward for a half century, McCarthyism was then used by the left to show that the Communist threat had merely been an invention and a witch hunt. At any rate, for all practical purposes the left in America was wiped out as an effective force for a decade or two.

While specific historical events played a major role in the failure of Marxism or even a strong left wing to flourish in the United States, there were deeper trends involved in this outcome. Most important, the twin Marxist predictions of capitalism's failure and collapse, on one hand, and the workers' discontent leading to revolution, on the other hand, did not happen.

The "primitive accumulation" of the late nineteenth century— the raising of capital by an enhancement of low living standards for the masses and the political domination of banks and corporations—was a transitional phase in capitalism, not a permanent state. A key factor in this development was the ability of liberals to make reforms, even against the interests of the strongest capitalists. Democracy worked and in America, at least, the wealthy and powerful accepted the rules and the changes.

Ultimately, the industrial West's slums were midwife to the comforts of suburbia. And the much-maligned Victorians were not only perpetrators of injustice but most energetic in battling to remedy it. Ultimately, the industrial revolution and continuing technological developments improved people's lives. The working class didn't become more impoverished and alienated but instead organized and strove within the system. Their success would come from improving rather than subverting the workings of capitalism.

The social order changed, too. Social mobility flourished, especially as new immigrants found their footing and in the following generation. As George Orwell pointed out, writing enviously about the freedom enjoyed in the United States, American society broke down the Old World's inflexible systems: "But at least it was not the case that a man's destiny was settled from his birth. . . . In a way it was for this that the Paris mob had stormed the Bastille. . . ."[2]

True, sometimes it took too long to implement the idea that "all men are created equal," or, perhaps it's more accurate to say that certain levels of development were needed to achieve that goal.

It's true, too, that not everyone was equal by talent or fortune but, yes, over time in America everyone had more and more of a fair chance, a real opportunity to better themselves, to get a fair share, and even, something hitherto impossible, to rise far higher. Certainly they could hold such expectations for their children.

An opportunity, however, was not a right or certainty. For to claim to ensure exact equality, to force the faster runners to wear weights, would have ensured stagnation. Skill and luck were needed to succeed. By encouraging such striving, the society itself reached hitherto unimaginable heights of prosperity. Meanwhile, its citizens lived under a system of extraordinary liberty and stability compared to almost everywhere and every time else in human history.

That life was not some perfect fairy tale, of course, and some very bad events disfigured American history. Yet even at the worst moments and in the most difficult issues there were many to stand for the right. For example, the struggle over slavery went on for a half century before the Civil War began and in that war the North made tremendous sacrifices to prevent the existence of a separate country built on slavery. Afterward, the country made a serious attempt to redress wrongs and treat citizens equally, an effort that failed partly due to racist resistance and partly to the excesses and corruption marking that Reconstruction effort.

Only much later did the civil rights movement, with wide popular support in most of the country, and all that followed succeed in breaking down the previous walls of racism. The transformation came with amazing speed and comprehensive thoroughness.

On this as in other matters, American experience taught that a republic where citizens enjoyed strong individual rights, coupled with a reasonably regulated capitalism and a culture that provided the basis for pluralism, was capable of constant improvement.

In short, Communist countries were simultaneously highly repressive and economic failures, class societies ruled by a privileged elite. This was an unattractive model to most people in capitalist societies that were doing far better. By the 1970s, Communist movements were faltering in the West and Communist states were falling further behind; in 1991 the Soviet bloc collapsed.

And the United States succeeded most of all. In part, this was due to its large size, geographic insulation from foreign threats, and ample resources. But this triumph was made possible due to a constitutional system attuned to both stability and change, able to limit and balance the state, the power of private economic institutions, and individual liberties. Its history included many class, ethnic, and racial problems yet it was able to overcome them to a remarkable extent.

A lot had happened since Marx's day. Writing in the nineteenth century, Marx was describing genuinely awful social conditions and profound inequality. It was understandable for him to think these things inevitable as long as capitalism and "bourgeois democracy" existed.

Yet only after the Marxist-Leninist route's failure was clear beyond doubt would a new version of the left arise that would seize control over what might be called "the means of mental production" and use them as a lever to change the world. Marx simply didn't believe this was possible; in a battle waged on that front the revolutionaries would always lose. He wrote in *The German Ideology*:

The ideas of the ruling class are in every epoch the ruling ideas, i.e., the class which is the ruling material force of society, is at the same time its ruling intellectual force. The class which has the means of material production at its disposal has control at the same time over the means of mental production. . . .[3]

The Progressive era and the New Deal produced reforms redressing imbalances created by large-scale industrialization, things that required some regulation, a stronger government, and trade unions that could protect workers. Equally in sharp contrast to their sometimes reactionary and war-beset counterparts in Europe, conservative rule brought America repeated massive eras of growth and spreading prosperity, including in the 1920s, 1950s, and 1980s.

In America, this problem that had blown up European countries in violence and hatred had been successfully defused. Americans were entertained and horrified by the scandals and foolishness of those who were richer, thinking that such people, for all their privileges, were worse off in some ways than themselves. People were proud of personal independence and for having earned everything they possessed. Taking money from the government was, unless absolutely unavoidable, seen as shameful, as a serious lowering of status.

Religion provided a different yardstick for measuring achievement and one's personal standing. First and foremost, the emphasis was on making the pie ever larger. People could see that each generation did better and so labored for the sake of their children. Wanting their children to inherit everything they had earned meant understanding that richer people worked harder due to the same motive. They basically understood how capitalism worked. If a business did not make profits it could not pay salaries. And finally they hoped that they or their children would become rich, or at least wealthier.

This did not mean everyone was satisfied, by any means. But in structural terms, liberalism accepted this capitalist framework entirely. Liberals had limited goals: ensuring poor people did not suffer too much; keeping open the doors for advancement; ensuring a safety net for those who needed one, like the elderly and those temporarily unemployed; preventing monopolies that kept the system from working properly; and dealing with certain neglected problems such as the environment.

This relatively optimistic and generally celebratory—though also self-critical—school of scholarship, sharply contrasting with today's dominant anti-American narrative, was called liberal history. How could liberals argue that the United States in the late twentieth century was a bad system—still rife with racism and sexism, an environmental disaster and a moral shame, all organized around a failed capitalist system—when they had been the main factor shaping that society?

Since both liberals and conservatives shared a basic understanding and support for America's version of capitalism, the two groups could reach compromises. Nobody wanted to go too far into debt; neither of them wanted to strangle productivity. Class struggle was seen as a tool of the enemy, Communism, and class cooperation—rejecting the idea that prosperity was a zero-sum game—was a basic assumption. The arguments would be over the details.

In America, then, both sides contributed to the country's success. Liberal reforms were shaped and kept within bounds by conservative thinking that curbed notions that were unworkable, too expensive, or would have undermined the constitutional order. America's survival and prosperity owed much to folk who clung to guns and religion; had strong families and strong faith; worked hard and didn't expect handouts; were jealous of their liberty and suspicious of government; were entrepreneurial, built businesses, and made things.

There was, however, a longer-term problem. Much of the crisis of liberalism arose from its success. About 1900, American liberals concluded that the federal government must be strengthened to balance the rise of big corporations and big city-political machines. That made sense. But if the sphere of government kept growing endlessly, the system on which America's success was based would be destroyed.

Consequently, liberals were so successful that a once-weak government bullied by the big corporations, banks, and railroads became steadily bigger and more expensive in its own right. A country with no entitlements at all became a welfare state where the costs of such payments grew to unsustainable levels. To go on and on endlessly with bigger government, regulation, and entitlements—not to mention government-mandated inequality in the treatment of different groups of citizens—went far past the point of diminishing returns.

As part of that totalitarian oppression, Marx predicted workers would be treated like slaves:

> Masses of laborers, crowded into the factory, are organized like soldiers. Slaves of the bourgeois class, and of the bourgeois state; they are daily and hourly enslaved by the machine . . . and, above all, in the individual bourgeois manufacturer himself.[4]

Instead, due to the decline of factories, advances of technology, and the benefits of unions and labor laws, conditions improved. Another example of a capitalist development Marx expected as inevitable was that living standards would go ever lower: "The increasing improvement of machinery, ever more rapidly developing, makes their livelihood more and more precarious."[5] Yet progress has brought higher living standards and such nineteenth-century conditions have nothing to do with contemporary life. As a result of its projected deprivations, Marx asserted that the working class would be transformed into a revolutionary sector that completely rejected capitalism and bourgeois values. For example, they would have no more loyalty to their country: "Subjection to capital . . . has stripped [the capitalist] of every trace of national character."[6] Yet American working people were among the most patriotic of Americans. Marx predicted that they would become cynical about individual freedom in a society where that was reduced merely to "free trade, free selling and buying." Yet the people treasured their individual liberty, knowing personal freedom was very real and precious.

And he asserted that most would not get a fair shake or a real chance: "Those who acquire anything do not work."[7] Yet people who succeeded in America worked very hard.

There were, however, certain groups that did fulfill this list of characteristics that Marx attributed to working people. This was, however, quite a different class, one that would indeed reject religion, patriotism, traditional moral values, the fairness of the system, the value of technological progress, and the importance of individual liberty as against the state. And that class would form the early-twenty-first-century far left's leadership and shape its doctrines.

In sharp contrast to both Marxist predictions and to Communism's practice, the Western system of capitalism plus democracy fared far better. Since the United States was a new start in many ways, without Europe's feudal baggage—which included an all-powerful state and restrictions on individual liberty—it could devise a new system. The founders' careful research, thinking, and debates led to them to create a structure based on balance, maximizing the rights of the individual and restricting government as much as possible.

Nothing in the fate of Communism, or fascism for that matter, would have surprised them. Equally, the founders knew that every previous democratic republic in history had failed and that unless its people understood why this had happened and remedied it, the United States would soon become just another monarchy or dictatorship.

They found the answer in this principle: No individual, group of people, or governmental institution can be trusted with power; every individual, party, or group will inevitably abuse power. Having witnessed the effects of statism in Europe, they were strongly antiauthoritarian. Thus their solution was to divide up power and create limits, to ensure that nobody got too much. They did this in numerous ways:

Voters elected political leaders and could remove them from office, and laws constrained officials from doing as they pleased. Federalism divided power between the national and state governments. On both the national and state level, power was split among the executive (president or governor), legislative (Congress or state legislature), and judicial branches. Moreover, the Constitution limited the central government's power while also reserving certain rights for states and citizens. While government's powers were limited, a huge amount of freedom was left for individuals. The Bill of Rights further strengthened citizens' ability to protest and criticize governments while limiting government's ability to repress or order citizens.

In short, the founders considered government as a wild beast that could never be tamed but had to be penned and trussed up so as to use it for beneficial purposes without being devoured by it. The founders knew that the kinds of people who seek political power are so often eager to accumulate power, glory, and wealth for themselves.

As further safeguards, the founders protected diverse nongovernmental institutions such as newspapers, civic organizations, and universities so they could serve as watchdogs exposing abuses of power, corruption, and incompetence. As long as these institutions took different political lines and varied partisan sides, they would serve their purpose.

This combination of ingredients created a new system: a democratic republic that could actually endure without collapsing in anarchy or turning into a dictatorship and that permitted the unleashing of human potential and an opportunity for even the non-aristocratic masses.

Across the Atlantic Ocean, Communists considered European social democrats to be traitors. In the United Kingdom, the Labor Party was said to have been more influenced by Methodism than by Marx. By the early 1920s, social democrats had abandoned the Marxian view that capitalism should be overthrown. Instead, they worked within the system and patriotically rallied to their nations' cause during World War I. In succeeding decades, they had participated in bourgeois governments, embraced limited reforms, and even given up the idea of nationalizing industries.

After all, in Europe, the state had preceded society, democracy, and modern nation. In America it was the other way around. Europe was more statist than America largely because of the lingering traditions of feudalism, monarchy, and centralization rather than because of Socialists' policies. France's welfare state, for example, owed more to conservative Gaullist governments than to the few years of Socialist rule. The last time any considerable nationalization of industry happened there had been in 1982, when President François Mitterrand's Socialists took over some enterprises only to re-privatize them just four years later.

Thus, European social democrats often seemed indistinguishable from centrist or conservative counterparts, who accepted virtually all of the reforms the social democrats had made. Socialists simply were not interested in fundamentally transforming their countries. Even Communist parties had to present themselves as moderate reformists, in order to appeal to their own nonrevolu-

tionary constituency and membership, before disappearing completely when the Soviet Union collapsed.

When Western Communist parties sought alliances with liberal or social democrat groups it was only to infiltrate and fool
them, to recruit away their members and to alter their worldview
toward that of Marxism. To ensure their own unity and strength,
the Communists formed disciplined parties. And their role model
of course was the Soviet Union, whose supposed successes proved
their doctrine's validity.

This Communist strategy for making revolution had both
strengths and weaknesses. It ensured a strong organization, a clear
worldview, and a potentially inspiring role model. Supposedly,
the Leninist party could always outmaneuver its rivals. Yet these
same characteristics were also a source of failure, especially in the
United States. Americans didn't like ideology, authoritarian style,
or political discipline.

That was largely due to their history and experience as well as
the successes of moderate and democratic reforms. As America developed after the Civil War, corporations, banks, and railroads became so powerful that for the first time in U.S. history they could
boss around the government. This was the low point for American
democracy, roughly from around 1870 to 1910. The Republican
Party was dominated by the big capitalists; the Democratic Party
was dominated by the racist southern aristocracy and the big-city
political machines that bought the support of new immigrants to
make them reliable voters, indifferent to the corruption and com-
petence of those they supported.

The reform movement that came in reaction to these problems
was also present on sides liberal and conservative, Democratic and
Republican. That's why an ideologically based or partisan analysis
of history in either direction doesn't fit the facts. Among Republicans, there were upper- and upper-middle-class people horrified
by the corruption, waste, and fraud who formed good-government

movements. Among Democrats, there was the populism that ap-
pealed to farmers, especially in the West, and some of the new
working class.

While a detailed look at this history lies far beyond this book's
scope, the basic pattern is important to understand. There were
terrible conditions—strikes, racism, low living standards, and so
on—but these also provoked a reaction. And the American system was able to handle the problems. The issue was not capitalism itself but rather a transitional form of capitalism that could be
moderated by reformers, institutions, and organizations curbing its
worst excesses. These reform movements were also motivated by
fear that if the system were not improved there might be a bloody
revolution, a fundamental transformation, and a new, far more oppressive Marxist-style system.

Part of their solution was to strengthen the federal government
to preserve its power to control and regulate industry. But the
goal was not government control but to preserve fair competition
between companies (as opposed to monopolies); to protect con-
sumers (without taking away their choices); and to give employees
leverage in dealing with employers (unions and laws setting better
working conditions for them).

With these liberal modifications, capitalism not only brought
the greatest expansion of wealth in human history but also succeeded in spreading prosperity widely. Not everyone gets the same
proportion, but since everyone benefits from a larger pie and opportunity, that relative difference—short of pure envy—doesn't
matter very much. Some do better through making profits, some by
making higher wages and getting jobs, and some because wealthier
societies can pay more welfare and other benefits and provide better services and infrastructure.

The far left can never recognize this aspect of American history.
Whatever lip service it gives to American progress, the Third Left
has to insist that the level of racism, corporate power, oppression

of workers, ravishing of the environment, and so on has not greatly declined. After all, if that is true, there's no need for fundamental transformation, an ever-stronger government, or the granting of special privileges on the basis of race and other groupings.

For all these reasons, America had been largely immune to the radical left's appeal. How could leftists face this history of American success in contrast to the failure of leftist movements and regimes, yet still find some way to turn everything on its head? In short, their basic goal was to convince Americans the exact opposite of what their experience proved: that the country had fundamentally failed and that old leftist solutions were the answer.

Yet in, say, the year 1960 this seemed to be a mission impossible because few people would accept the ideas that a revolution was needed, America was terrible, and socialism was the solution. Nevertheless, the late 1960s and early 1970s was a period in which these three ideas once again flourished. And this crisis came about not because of economic problems but the twin issues of equal rights for African Americans and the Vietnam War, along with several other issues such as feminism and environmentalism. In the long run, this would signal the need for the left to switch from an emphasis on the proletariat to new emphases on race, gender, social issues, and American foreign policy.

In this process, the USSR's decline and eventual collapse, as well as the Communist Party's virtual demise, temporarily created a deep crisis but was ultimately liberating for American Marxists. The failures and crimes of Communism were quickly forgotten, especially by a generation that did not remember or learn about them.

An American left could arise that was no longer subject to Moscow. Instead of a single party that was easily identifiable, large numbers of groups came into being that could experiment and appeal to different sectors of the population. And in place of a rigid party line, a hundred flowers might bloom and schools of thought contend.

And thus in the 1960s the left made a partly fresh start, which is why it was called the New Left. At the time, though, it only partly succeeded. After the New Left itself disintegrated in the early 1970s it would take many decades for its determined survivors to transform its ideas fully and work themselves into positions of influence. At that point, in the early twenty-first century, the seeds laid down in the early period would germinate into a dense forest that would dominate the political and social landscape.

Back in the 1960s, the New Left activists vaguely understood that they would have to toss out a lot of Marx; imbibe a great deal of psychology, advertising, and community organizing techniques; use their class privilege to gain key positions; and subvert the proudest democratic institutions of schools, universities, and media.

One would naturally think it easier to provoke a downtrodden proletariat into activity than, say, someone writing on his laptop complaining of owing student loans after years of studying whatever he wanted at a university. That's what Marx thought and it makes sense.

The New Left was rooted in Communism but made adjustments in trying to deal with the legacy of failure and the changed situation. Because Stalinism had created oppressive societies, the New Left focused more on Marx's early writings, claiming to favor an allegedly humanitarian socialism. It vacillated in identifying the motive force for revolution. Would it be students and African Americans or would the more traditional proletariat get the nod as the vanguard force?

In contrast to the disciplined Communist Party, the New Left was much looser, multi-structured, and more diffuse than its predecessor. This made it more attractive and easier to join—though also easier to leave—since there was more than one choice and one political line available but, by the same token, it was also less able to do anything except hold demonstrations and write pamphlets. A liberal or social democrat might more easily be pulled into its orbit at least on some ideas.

The New Left did protest about real issues. Racial discrimination and mistreatment was still terrible, though by the late 1960s often it was combatted by U.S. governments. At times U.S. foreign policy was exploitative and the Vietnam War—whatever its intentions and strategic justification—had grown out of hand. The women's movement was challenging an unequal treatment as old as humanity's existence and seeking new arrangements made possible by the very technological progress and social development made possible by capitalism.

Yet hadn't liberal reforms solved these problems by doing away with racism, ensuring equality for women, dramatically removing barriers for homosexuals, protecting workers' rights, and cleaning up the environment? If so, there was no need for a radical movement, fundamental transformation, or far-reaching changes. All that was required would be relatively secondary adjustments. Moreover, it would have been obvious that the main problems were now coming from a different direction: the overgrowth of the government, regulation, and anguished self-criticism. In fact, the supposedly healthful medicine had been overdosed and was poisoning the patient.

Another central debate that might well have dominated American discussion during the early twenty-first century would have been whether everything identified as a social imperfection was susceptible to being fixed. The ordinary and inescapable corruption of life and abuse of power were actually being increased by attitudes and programs that made it harder to grow the size of the economic pie. Thus average people would have lower living standards with "equality" than in an "unequal" society.

Yet if these successes had been acknowledged, the demands

raised having been satisfied, it would be impossible to maintain a radical opposition with the dream of total transformation, of attaining utopian heights, and of rejecting the status quo. At any rate, enough progress had been achieved to ensure that there was no way the New Left could have taken over large sectors of American society or created large and lasting institutions without undergoing a far-reaching change and self-laundering process.

The New Left had no strategy to achieve victory. Most Americans either hated or laughed at this movement perceived as so alien to mainstream American beliefs or values, too bound up with long-failed ideas, too closely aligned with anti-American forces abroad.

While much New Left thought was delusional, it was hard for the more serious thinkers—especially over time—not to recognize this reality even in the late 1960s. At first these militants were angry that American society had refused to leap into the utopia they were offering. Consequently, they angrily saw the American public itself, or at least the white and male sectors, as the enemy.

If the motive force for revolution might not be found within capitalist society, there were revolutionaries aplenty in the Third World, including an "internal" Third World formed by African Americans. Abroad, China, Cuba, Vietnam, and a score of revolutionary movements were the New Left's heroes, replacing the boring, unhip USSR. These others were, at least, fighting. And if anyone needed a Marxist theoretical link for justifying this new thinking they could refer to Lenin's writing on imperialism as the way capitalism was able to survive.

The New Left could explain that revolution had indeed been bought off by consumerism, but only because that was financed by plundering the Third World. Instead of succeeding due to its virtues, Western civilization was a mere thief. Thus its success proved nothing about the superiority of capitalism to other systems.

Given the capitalist democracies' relative success compared to the miserable failures of Communism and other leftist movements, any American left established on these ruins would have to deal with the fact that its product was incredibly unpopular. It was thus necessary to change the product. Americans were relatively satisfied and happy, too, so this "false consciousness" had to be transformed into anger, intergroup conflict, dissatisfaction, and a false consciousness that America was, and had always been, an evil place. This certainly seemed like mission impossible.

The bottom-line reasons for the failure in America of the first, Communist, left, and the second, New, left can be summarized briefly:

Everyone is familiar with the idea that capitalist systems require inequalities of power and wealth. But the key point to understand—and which history has amply proven—is that this is also true of socialist societies. And the difference was that capitalist societies have proven to work far better. They even evolved socially more successfully, incorporating larger and larger portions of the population with greater and greater fairness and equality. Starting earlier but especially in the 1950s, Americans understood this. The later decline of the Soviet Union and its collapse in 1991 reinforced that lesson.

But that lesson would be overturned by a very strange sequence of events. On June 18–22, 1969, a bizarre drama was played out that improbably shaped the course of American history: the national convention of a small group called Students for a Democratic Society (SDS). That group had been born merely seven years earlier from the mildly left liberalism of pro-labor and vaguely socialist young people who wanted to perfect American democracy.[8]

During the brief period in the 1960s, however, that group had evolved at a rapid pace from do-gooder reformers into thinking of themselves as ferocious revolutionaries. They were also confused, pathetically disorganized revolutionaries. The question before them was how America would be fundamentally transformed. Their minds were split between the most hidebound, stale

Marxist-Leninist rhetoric and some new type of youth-oriented, social restructuring.

There were a multitude of factions among the roughly young two thousand people attending. The largest sector was the highly disciplined Progressive Labor (PL) Party, whose views were basically indistinguishable from the old Communist Party. Instinctively, the countercultural-oriented radicals understood that this would simply not work in America. Yet their own ideas were even more ridiculous, though they were feeling their way to something new.

The second faction was the aptly named Revolutionary Youth Movement (RYM), led by a child of Communists named Mike Klonsky. Somehow, he thought it possible to transcend social classes and exploit the innately revolutionary force of young people. And the third faction was the even more ill-defined national office collective led by Bernardine Dohrn, along with Jeff Jones.

The meeting turned into a festival of antidemocratic practices, putting the lie to SDS's name. When their opponents tried to speak, the PL cadre drowned them out with chanting. And when the PL leaders tried to speak their opponents chanted, "Smash racism!"

And as for PL's opponents, they called in the supposed ultimate arbiter of proper radicalism, the Black Panther Party. Since RYM and the national office deified African Americans and the Black Panther Party in particular, it would literally lay down the line.

As uniformed, tough-looking Panthers ringed the hall—in an effort at intimidation—a Panther leader named Bobby Rush denounced PL, though he made the mistake of insulting women, saying the proper position of women in the radical movement was "prone" while threatening the PL people with violence if they didn't surrender.

What nobody fully realized at the time was that this farce was also a profound confrontation between two ideologies. On PL's side was the historic, proletarian-based Marxism-Leninism led by a vanguard party based fully on Lenin. On the other side was the then-inchoate idea that race, gender, and youth must trump social class as the key elements of any revolution that was going to be made in America.

Seeing that PL had the majority, Dohrn led a walkout of delegates, who organized a separate meeting and then voted, with only about one-quarter of the delegates, to expel PL from SDS. Now there were two SDS organizations. The RYM–National Office group, in which the most prominent leaders were Klonsky and Dohrn, presented their key points.

First was support for the "black and Latin colonies" in the United States to be separate nations with the right to form their own countries if they so wished. Second was unstinting support for the victory of North Vietnam and its allies in the south to win the war against the United States. That act of proud treason—though, of course, not in the legal sense—was followed by even more provocation: explicit backing for North Korea, Albania, and China to battle America and also for any Third World people who wanted to fight the United States.

These declarations seemed ridiculously extreme, as if formulated to outrage and alienate the American people, and especially the generally conservative working class. Yet over the years the people who produced that statement would learn better how to polish, conceal, and revise their aims and their new revolutionary ideology.

The willingness to shout down opponents with insults and absurd allegations, indifferent to the truth, became political correctness. The strident manipulation of nonwhite Americans became multiculturalism. And the hatred for America's role in the world became one of apology, concessions, and support for new enemies.

Forty years later, remarkable as it might seem, the ideas born from those that were crudely expressed at that SDS meeting would be for all practical purposes running America.

To deal with these realities, those New Left veterans dropped or totally reversed many of Marxism's and Communism's basic premises. They did not do so on the basis of grand theory or the works of political philosophers but through a pragmatic rethinking of their ideology and experiences.

Marx and Lenin had spent as much time scorning radical viewpoints different from their own as they did critiquing capitalism. Marx ridiculed the naive and intellectual in *The Communist Manifesto*, those "[e]conomists, philanthropists, humanitarians . . . reformers of every imaginable kind," who never really understood society.[9] They were suspicious of anyone working within the system, horrified by those who claimed people would be transformed by ideas put into their heads, and laughed at any notion of using a "bourgeois" state as a mechanism for changing society.

A primitive reading of Marxism-Leninism would be refined over the years. An increased sense of maturity, realism, and impressive financial assets (from such sugar daddies as George Soros, and the radicals' own inheritances) transformed it into the hegemonic views controlling the intellectual production system's commanding heights four decades later.

And what did it teach? That the way to pull the rug out from America, to destroy a seemingly invulnerable system included indoctrinating youth; turning "antiracism" into a weapon; joining forces with anti-Americans abroad; and undermining American economic and cultural structures. That isn't a conspiracy theory; it's a description of what an initially small movement did achieve with the power of ideas and clever strategizing.

In the early 1970s, the New Left soon disintegrated into factions and follies. The PL retreated to its factory floors to try to persuade workers who had no interest in doing so to become Communists. The RYM went on trying to organize students who had moved past the radical times of a few years earlier. And a new group, the Weathermen, organized by the SDS national office group, led by

Dohrn, Jones, and Bill Ayers, played at being revolutionaries complete with an underground, bombings, and bank robberies. One would have thought that America had heard the last from all of them.

To begin with, the Weatherman manifesto stressed that America is evil. Rather than attribute the country's success to a unique political and social system, the Weatherman manifesto explained it by rapacious theft and oppression:

> We are within the heartland of a worldwide monster, a country so rich from its worldwide plunder that even the crumbs doled out to the enslaved masses within its borders provide for material existence very much above the conditions of the masses of people of the world. The US empire, as a worldwide system, channels wealth, based upon the labor and resources of the rest of the world, into the United States. The relative affluence existing in the United States is directly dependent upon the labor and natural resources of the Vietnamese, the Angolans, the Bolivians and the rest of the peoples of the Third World. All of the United Airlines Astrojets, all of the Holiday Inns, all of Hertz's automobiles, your television set, car and wardrobe already belong, to a large degree to the people of the rest of the world.[10]

By being so successful, the New Left's veterans disproved F. Scott Fitzgerald's maxim that there were no second acts in American life. On May 21, 1970, Bernardine Dohrn released the Weather Underground's first statement: "America's youth [should] use our strategic position behind enemy lines to join forces in the destruction of empire." Who could imagine that a quarter-century later, she and her husband, Bill Ayers, would host the first appearance as a politician of Barack Obama, who would come to run that "empire"!

But just as important—probably more important—they and others from the 1960s' leftist movements created a new way of using that "strategic position" to change the institutions and thinking of a country they hated no less over time. Thousands of such cadre obtained positions of power and prestige they could use for that purpose. Thus succeeded one of the most brilliantly planned and original revolutions in all of history.

After all, social experience had richly proven that Marxism, Communism, and radical Socialism didn't work in part because America provided a better political and economic system in very different ways. Moreover, the left had not incorporated certain realities of society into its theoretical scheme.

The first of these factors outside the left's consideration is often called "human nature." The left's argument has been that people are overwhelmingly the product of upbringing and experience. Change these conditions and you can totally alter the behavior of human beings, creating, in the words of the old slogan, the New Soviet Man. Thus, for example, those given power in the government or factory would be selfless, dedicated individuals who had no selfish self-interest to make them into a new set of overprivileged dictators.

For the Third Left and its ideological allies, the "Progressive liberals," this concept would be taken for granted. After all, even more than Marx and the Leninists, they depended on ideas and training to reshape society. They often advocated such ideas, for example, as the abolition of gender roles. Education was of vital importance to them because it was the key element in the remaking of the masses into the image of the radical intellectual and activist elite.

As a result, the deep-seated drives of some individuals for power, wealth, and fame; family, tribal, and national loyalty; and other things as well were pushed aside as mere fantasies. Nothing whatsoever had been learned by this movement from the rich and

bloody experience of the twentieth century, including their predecessors' failed experiments, most notably the Soviet Union and its
satellite states, which ignominiously collapsed.

Their deliberate blindness on humanity's foibles meant they
forgot a point so well grasped by America's founders: that a government, no matter who is running it, is a leading candidate to be
the most powerful, oppressive force in society. A dictatorship by
the "right" people—be they the proletariat (which in the real world
meant the party bosses) or the enlightened educated who know
what's best for you—is still a dictatorship.

Yet the movement's survivors still lived on and most of them
continued to adhere to the New Left's view of America as a profoundly evil society that must be ruined or revolutionized. They
knew that the inherited baggage from the Old Left—Marxism-
Leninism, Communism, openly extremist provocation, the worship
of dusty theories and enemy dictatorships, the whole proletariat-
based, rhetorically obsessed deal—had to be tossed into the dustbin of history.

Clearly, if the left wasn't going to become extinct, these gradually maturing and aging revolutionary veterans realized, it needed
to be fundamentally transformed. They debated and thought on,
through the 1970s and 1980s, largely unnoticed, realizing that the
United States was not the nineteenth-century Europe analyzed by
Marx, the early-twentieth-century Russia revolutionized so ruthlessly by Vladimir Ilyich Lenin, the mid-twentieth-century China
of Mao Zedong, or the Vietnam of Ho Chi Minh.

Suits and ties were more suitable dress than pseudoproletarian
garb; liberalism a far better pretense than rhetoric about killing
"pigs," overthrowing the government, and instituting a Socialist
paradise. After all, few Americans were "prisoners of starvation"
and a smaller proportion than in any other country in history could
be called "the wretched of the earth." Industrial workers became
rare and there was scarcely a peasant in sight.

Wholesale change would not be made by an alliance of proletarian and landless sharecroppers under a Marxist-Leninist party's leadership. Revering a foreign socialist motherland guaranteed alienating an American people immunized to the appeal of Uncle Joe Stalin and his successors, by decades of anti-Communism followed by that system's decline and collapse.

No, Americans had to be wooed by using their most vulnerable points: to be good and up-to-date people who helped the poor, detested racism or other bigotry, and on top of all this virtue got more material goods, praise, and personal advancement.

Those factors, along with America's allergy to extremism and especially the far left, along with the radicals' need to tame and revise traditional liberalism, meant, however, that this revolution had to remain a silent one.

CHAPTER 4

The Making of the Third Left

Many people don't believe that a far left can exist without the apparatus of red flags; Marxist jargon; a centrally directed, disciplined Leninist party; and all the other apparatus of history's Communists and New Leftists. These things were now not only unnecessary but actually fatal to success in twenty-first-century America. Instead, New Left veterans created the "Third Left" based on the understanding that they needed a totally different approach. Bit by bit, more by practical instinct than by written word or visible debate, the New Left veterans assembled their program and implemented it.

Only by portraying itself as liberal or "Progressive" could the far left adapt to twenty-first-century America. This is why critics calling the Third Left "Marxist" or even "socialist" met ridicule from most Americans, who didn't believe that it existed at all. Alternatively, denouncing the Third Left as typical liberals set off the defense mechanisms of many Americans for whom that standpoint had positive associations. What was wrong with being a liberal? Liberals were proud of it; centrists did not see that as a terrible sin. Check and checkmate.

Marx's *Communist Manifesto* had boldly declared: "The Communists disdain to conceal their views and aims. They openly declare that their ends can be attained only by the forcible overthrow of all existing social conditions."[1] But this principle had often been broken in practice. In the 1940s, for example, the Communist Party slogan claimed "Communism is twentieth-century Americanism." In its current incarnation, left-wing radicalism was said to be twenty-first-century liberalism. Millions of Americans accepted ideas without comprehending their origin or true agenda, thinking that these views were simply a continuation of historical liberalism.

Those who laid the foundations for the Third Left were influential and successful, while those who followed the old approach remained outcasts and cultists. For example, Mike Klonsky and Bob Avakian were leaders of America's rival Maoist parties. Klonsky's group, founded in 1971, was called the Communist Party (Marxist-Leninist). Avakian was founder of the Revolutionary Communist Party, begun in 1975. Decades later, Avakian remained an unreconstructed, old-fashioned left-wing sectarian heading a tiny cult without influence or respectability.[2] He fled to France in 1981 facing a criminal indictment. Thirty years later, he was still quoting Mao Zedong as his guru.

As the Beatles sang, however, "If you go carrying pictures of Chairman Mao / You ain't going to make it with anyone, anyhow." Or as the Third Leftist leader Van Jones put it, "I'm willing to forgo the cheap satisfaction of the radical pose for the deep satisfaction of radical ends."[3]

Thus, in contrast to Avakian's obsolete Maoism, Klonsky, and his friend Bill Ayers from the Weathermen abandoned such explicit extremism in the early 1980s and became key figures in the Third Left. While Avakian failed to adjust to the new approach, Klonsky and Ayers obtained doctorates in education and professorships.[4] By the 1990s they were both prospering and influential, receiving big foundation grants and later being leading figures in Progressives for Obama.[5]

Yet how different were the goals of Klonsky and Ayers from those of Avakian? This is not to say that they were still Marxist-Leninists in disguise, consciously seeking to impose a Communist system on America. But they were still trying to bring about a fundamental transformation of the United States along the general lines of what they had been advocating back in the New Left days.

Similarly, the former Weatherman Jeff Jones was head of Jeff Jones Strategies and a member of the well-funded—by the billionaire left-wing investor George Soros—and influential Apollo Alliance. The Alliance's founders including members of Congress, and its board members included the Marxist, Third Left activists Van Jones (who was briefly Green Jobs czar in the Obama administration) and professor Joel Rogers of the University of Wisconsin, an influential Third Left guru, as well as Robert Borosage, a former head of the New Left and later Third Left think tank the Institute for Policy Studies.

As Van Jones had said, the Third Left had dropped the radical posturing but not the radical ideas.

Although they had entered the system, tens of thousands of ideologically oriented professors and scientists or politicized journalists; environmental, feminist, African American, or Hispanic activists; foundation and think-tank officials; artists, filmmakers, and other cultural producers; government and trade union bureaucrats; and even politicians still remained radical activists. By entering into the system, they were not "selling out" or being co-opted. They still maintained their goal of thoroughgoing change.

And, as at the 1969 SDS convention, they were not going to play fair. They were certain that their side was correct and there was no need or room for discussion, no quarter or legitimacy to be given to opponents. Political correctness was merely the old party line dressed up as simple decency, the permissible borders of debate.

And, unlike in historical liberalism, one need not be ashamed of fixing the game to yield a single result.

The purpose of education, for example, was not to make students think better, see different sides of an issue, or make their own choices. Instead, it was deliberate indoctrination into leftist ideology. The same point applied to journalism and to any other institution where Third Left cadre gained power and influence. To paraphrase Mao Zedong, politics, not democratic processes, were to be in command.

Always and everywhere, the system was held to be fundamentally rotten, innately unfair, and profoundly illegitimate. Reform was insufficient; the most basic premises must be trained.

In other words, the point was not to teach kids that fresh food was healthy or that they could grow gardens but that the capitalist system ensured poor people didn't get proper nutrition. This approach seems to have been plagiarized by Michelle Obama, who, as First Lady, claimed the existing capitalist system deprived poor children by creating "food deserts."[6]

For Klonsky and Ayers, the priority was political indoctrination, with academic instruction merely supplying camouflage. And the Ayers-Klonsky position, pushed by many others, of course, gained hegemony in American grade school and university education by the turn of the current century. In this context, "social justice," with its soothing religious and humanitarian overtones, was a far more attractive slogan than Marxism or Communism could offer to twenty-first-century Americans.

Rather than organizing and agitating in its own name, the Third Left used the public school system to do the work as parents paid taxes and tuition for the dubious privilege of having their children indoctrinated. This new insight into "progressive" education was really not so original and certainly not at all liberal, having been practiced by radical dictatorships for decades. In short, single-minded politicization of education was nothing new but it was also contrary to American practice, liberalism, and democratic norms. For example, one counterpart of Klonsky and Ayers was the dean of education at Damascus University in Syria, who said:

> [W]e can teach the child the following mathematical problem: 25 [Israeli] tanks entered South Lebanon. The brave men of the resistance confronted them. They [burnt down] five tanks and damaged seven. How many of these tanks returned defeated back to where they came from?[7]

Where did all these ideas that set the course of the Third Left come from? It is easy to overintellectualize its sources. One could cite Marx's early discussions of alienation or Lenin's *Imperialism, the Highest Stage of Capitalism*, in which he asserted that Western capitalism prospered only by stealing from the Third World.

Parallels might also be found in the work of dissenting Marxists going back to the 1920s, from the Italian Antonio Gramsci through the Hungarian Georg Lukacs and the German Karl Korsch, as well as the Frankfurt School, whose best-known members were Theodor Adorno and Herbert Marcuse.

Of some importance in the 1960s was the German Marxist Andre Gunder Frank, who updated Lenin's imperialism theory, and such Third World radicals as Frantz Fanon, whose writings Obama expressed interest in.[8] Some read that all-American radical Saul Alinsky, with his focus on practical tactics and catchy slogans rather than theory. Both Barack Obama and Hillary Clinton were Alinsky devotees.

But such archaeology of political theories would be misleading. It would be a mistake to think that those who formed the Third Left were shaped by dusty books of forgotten dissident Marxist writers. Just as old-time Communists didn't plow their way through three volumes of Marx's *Capital*, contemporary Third Left leaders have probably read little other than popularizing books that endorse what they already thought.

No, the movement was based on original adaptations to America and direct experience. But if you want a single document that shows the foundations of the Third Left's critical new breakthroughs, it can best be found in a most unexpected place. The Weathermen favored violence and immediate revolution, a suicidal strategy that soon landed its leaders in jail or into hiding underground, but regarding the analysis of American society—and as to why traditional Marxist-Leninism didn't work—it had more in common with evolving New Left thought.

It would be this lunatic faction that would provide the foundation for the Third Left and, amazing as it might seem, the core thinking of an American president four decades later, filtered through his radical professors, unusual background, fellow students, and reading. The same would be true, though few of them knew it, for tens of thousands of other activists and literally millions of indoctrinated students.

These ideas can be found in the faction's June 1969 manifesto, "You Don't Need a Weatherman to Know Which Way the Wind Blows."[9] Three of the authors were Ayers, Dohrn, and Jones, the first two of whom played a direct role in promoting Obama's early career. There was no conspiracy involved but simply a situation in which like-minded thinkers helped each other.

It should also be stressed that the Third Left came a long way between 1969 and the time that Ayers, Dohrn, and Obama met. The former Weathermen had dropped their more overtly crazier concepts—which might be called Leninism on LSD—by the 1980s. In the transition to the Third Left they replaced deliberately outrageous positions and instant revolutionary attempts with an extremely patient campaign to take over quietly.

Seizing control of university buildings was replaced by seizing control over universities; creating alternative newspapers by staffing the big newspapers; railing against the power of big money by getting that funding for their own use.

Concepts like the idea that all wealth was not created by business and workers but stolen from poor foreigners and oppressed nonwhites, or that America was not a force for liberation but of imperialism, or that the United States was an irredeemably racist, sexist, homophobic, Islamophobic country in which democracy was a sham, religion disgusting, and patriotism distasteful, originated with the New Left and Weathermen.

Without the Weathermen's more dramatic rhetoric and crazy tactics, this is precisely what a generation of students would be taught. The idea that tens of millions of Americans could be, in effect, turned into anti-Americans seemed insane. But it happened, didn't it?

The Weatherman manifesto introduced many new ideas, though the Weathermen themselves did not at the time fully comprehend their meaning and, of course, these ideas developed further over the decades. One of the most important revisions of Marxism was that instead of the proletariat being the motive force for revolutionary change, that role belonged to nonwhite forces within the United States. In fact, the Third Left came to see race as the lever to build a mass base in two different ways.

On the one hand, the assumption was that African Americans would be the revolutionary vanguard. But—and this is all important—it would be white revolutionaries who decided which African Americans would truly represent that race and which demands were legitimate. In other words, the white radicals would harness the black community as its own tool, just as the founders of the Weather Underground tried to do at the 1969 SDS convention.

At that gathering, once the Black Panthers had spoken everyone else would shut their mouths because the Panthers "represented" the most oppressed group in America and out of fear of being called racists. That was the second element in the usefulness of race as a weapon. White guilt would neutralize opposition to what "African Americans" supposedly demanded. As the Weatherman Manifesto explained, "Any white who does not . . . [support "the blacks"] is . . . objectively racist."

The idea that this kind of thinking, much diluted and rationalized, would help bring about the election of a left-wing African American president was then, of course, beyond their wildest imagination. In the 2008 presidential race, Senator John McCain seemed terrified to criticize Obama lest he be considered racist.

Another key concept passing from the New Left to the Third Left was that racism was structurally permanent in America. Nothing could root it out and thus African Americans must be given special privileges, a practice extended to other groups: "Hispanics," women, Muslims, gays, etc. While racism against African Americans had often marked U.S. history, the Weathermen and later the Third Left wanted to reverse this process not by mandating equality—as the civil rights legislation did—but by creating a new type of permanent racialism.

After all, if race, ethnicity, certain religions, and social practices made for oppressed groups whose demands could never really be satisfied, that was a permanent justification for fundamental transformation. Nothing could have been more antiliberal than the idea that people should be divided along group lines by abandoning the principle of "equal justice under law," words inscribed over the U.S. Supreme Court building.

Those who could claim such status as a potential base for Third Left propaganda, recruitment, and as a base of support dwarfed the Communists' proletarian ranks. With 27.6 percent of the total population minorities and more than 50 percent women, if one adds another 2.5 percent for white male gays, then "oppressed minority" groups constitute about 75 percent of the citizen population, to which one can add illegal immigrants for an even higher proportion of the resident population.

The Weatherman Manifesto thus contained the seed of a central Third Left idea, that claiming to remedy past or nonexperienced discrimination could be a lever to destroy the basic American principle of equality for all citizens in favor of a system of special rights and privileges. To this, the Third Left added an entire list of proffered special privileges.

Groups offered or given privileges could then be expected to have an incentive to support the movement while those being made to give up such things—"white skin privilege," in the Weathermen's jargon—would be intimidated into silence or won over by the psychological (being fashionable, a good and nongreedy person) and material benefits, such as crony capitalists or other elite elements (teachers, journalists, intellectuals, etc.). Moreover, as an additional benefit, the fear or accusation of being called racist, sexist, homophobic, or Islamophobic suspended logical discussion or factual evidence.

The first to hurl an epithet won the argument, roughly in the way that *atheist* might win arguments in the nineteenth century and *Nazi* or *Communist* could do so in the twentieth century. The difference was, however, that the Third Left's version was far more effective since the accused almost automatically seemed to be judged guilty as charged.

In addition to these various racial, gender, religious, and sexual orientation groups, the other key revolutionary force for the Weathermen and later the Third Left was young people. The manifesto explained:

> In general, young people have less stake in a society (no family, fewer debts, etc.), are more open to new ideas (they have not been brainwashed for so long or so well), and are therefore more able and willing to move in a revolutionary direction.

The key phrase in that passage was "more open to new ideas," ideas shaped in school and cultural products. The Third Left would not just complain about "false consciousness" but would do a better and more systematic job of brainwashing the next generation than any nineteenth-century conservative patriot and religious believer ever imagined.

The manifesto continued:

> In jail-like schools, kids are fed a mish-mash of racist, male chauvinist, anti–working class, anti-communist lies while being channeled into job and career paths set up according to the priorities of monopoly capital. At the same time, the State is becoming increasingly incapable of providing enough money to keep the schools going at all.

The excuse of reversing alleged capitalist indoctrination in the schools—which did not prevent generally left-oriented campuses previously—was thus rationalized as justifying systematic left-wing indoctrination. Ironically, of course, "being channeled into job and career paths" turned out to mean being taught something useful for making a living. Instead, they would be educated "according to the priorities" of radical politics, which needed convinced cadre more than productive citizens.

As the abandonment of the educational basics or efforts at meritocracy resulted in schools being dumbed down, the proposed solutions were more spending and slanted content that only deepened the decline. This strategy did, however, ensure a strong Third Left constituency among teachers' unions and young people.

Thus the left solved its predecessor's problem of how to recruit activists and supporters. When asked why he robbed banks, the holdup man Willie Sutton had replied, "That's where the money is." Similarly, the youth were in the schools. As educational theorists, administrators, bureaucrats, and teachers, left-wing cadre would be paid by the public to brainwash its children. This objective was such a high priority that Klonsky and Ayers chose it as their personal specialty.[10]

More generally, the Weatherman Manifesto recognized that young people were ripe for revolutionizing because the traditional American order of religion, community, family, and patriotism was breaking down; the society's antibodies had been weakened. This raised tremendous opportunities for radicalization and recruitment:

> The family falls apart, kids leave home, women begin to break out of traditional . . . roles. There develops a "generation gap." . . . Our heroes are no longer struggling businessmen, and we also begin to reject the ideal career of the professional and look to Mao, Che, the [Black] Panthers, the Third World, for our models. . . .

Though not in all details, this idea prefigured the cultural contours of later decades. To replace "the ideal career of the professional," that of a government employee, a journalist going after the proper villains, a "public interest" group official, or a community organizer might have greater appeal. In film, literature, television shows, and many other places the antihero and anti-American hero prevailed. The businessmen were villains, struggling against the interests of the public. The symbolic culmination came in 2013, when the film star Robert Redford released a movie, *The Company You Keep*, glorifying the Weathermen themselves.

Aside from the focus on women and minority groups as well as youth, the Third Left's other main innovation was to change the definition of class struggle from that between Marx's property owners and wage slaves into a battle between two vaguely defined groups: the powerful rich and the suffering middle class.

There would not be, however, a disinterested struggle to raise the living standards of the poor and downtrodden. This should not be an end in itself, but rather was only positive if used to promote revolutionary ideas: "Probably the American Friends Service Committee serves more children breakfast, but it is the symbolic value of the program in demonstrating what socialism will do for people which makes the Black Panther Program worthwhile."[11]

The implications of this self-interested approach were enormous. First, as noted above, assisting the poor was merely a way to promote the movement. Second, help must be given in a way demonstrating the value of accepting Third Left goals. Third Left leaders and groups themselves provided no direct charity or assistance, nor did they materially improve the poor's situation. Its money and energy went into political persuasion. What was important was to give the appearance of working on behalf of the downtrodden. As the Third Left ripened, that would mean encouraging dependence on government largesse.

The Weatherman Manifesto predicted the 2008 financial crisis, which helped bring Obama to power. Yet, ironically, what the Weatherman Manifesto identified as the supposed causes of that crisis would actually be the solution provided by the Third Left after it happened.

The manifesto claimed the crisis would be caused by "[r]ising taxes, inflation and the fall of real wages, the collapse of state services like schools, hospitals and welfare." What they could not realize at the time was that their elder selves would be the ones favoring higher taxes, more debt, an inflation provoked by printing more money, strangling regulation, and constantly growing burdens on state services.

The manifesto also began to shape the kind of argument the Third Left would use for its economic policies and against critics of the Obama administration forty years later:

[There is an] urban crisis around welfare, the hospitals, the schools, housing, air and water pollution. The State cannot

provide the services it has been forced to assume responsibility for, and needs to increase taxes and to pay its growing
debts while it cuts services and uses the pigs to repress protest. The private sector of the economy can't provide jobs,
particularly unskilled jobs. The . . . inability to provide decent wages and working conditions for "public" jobs is more
and more a problem.

But in their later incarnation it would be the Third Left demanding more state entitlements, increased taxes, and growing
debt. What the Third Left learned, but which was not understood
in the Weathermen era, was that controlling the behavior of banks
through regulation was more comfortable, profitable, and successful than robbing them.

Equally prophetic was the Weathermen's definition of their enemies. Of course, this included the "rich." Yet the revolution's most
energetic opponent was identified as the "petit bourgeoisie," those
who were

[o]pposed to both monopoly power and to socialism. . . .
Small capital—both business and farms—and self-
employed tradesmen and professionals . . . gives it a political character of some opposition to "big government,"
like its increased spending and taxes and its totalitarian
extension of its control into every aspect of life, and to
"big labor." . . .

Finally, the manifesto took up the all-important issue of how to
break false consciousness, the ideas people held that didn't agree
with those of the left. While things would change later, the Weathermen chose the traditional Marxist approach, which inevitably
failed, of head-on confrontation:

On the whole, people don't join revolutions just because
revolutionaries tell them to. . . . People are brainwashed and
at present don't understand it; if revolution is not raised at
every opportunity, then how can we expect people to see it
in their interests, or to undertake the burdens of revolution.
We need to make it clear from the very beginning that we
are about revolution.

Why battle the American elite if you can persuade many of
its members to put the yoke around their own neck? Instead of a
priority on infiltrating the means of material production, the Third
Left put its emphasis on infiltrating the means of idea and opinion
production. This enabled it to indoctrinate young people, shape
the flow of information, and channel opinions. The Old Left went
to work in factories, the Third Left in foundations and NGOs;
popular culture (music, film, television), publishing, and journalism; cushy, high-paying, high-prestige jobs.

Marx didn't believe this was possible. He wrote, "The individuals composing the ruling class . . . among other things rule also as
thinkers, as producers of ideas, and regulate the production and
distribution of the ideas of their age: thus their ideas are the ruling
ideas of the epoch."[12] But in line with modern advertising, social
sciences, psychology, and public relations techniques, the Third
Left assumed human behavior to be infinitely malleable and they
were going to manipulate it. The Third Left argued that the radical
opposition could change society by turning its ideas into the ruling
ones without holding political power through other kinds of "soft"
power.

By such methods, the Third Left proved Marx wrong. It convinced people by a cultlike total immersion in its own doctrine.
The children of corporate executives could be turned into revolutionaries in the classroom. Ideas could overcome material conditions; getting people to read the right books might have more

effect on them than the surrounding reality because the surrounding reality would be interpreted through the left's ideas.

The cultural-intellectual battle was the base from which leverage would be applied to transform society. Historic Marxism had the exact opposite view. Class interests were immutable; ideas were useful but fragile. The state and bourgeoisie would always have the upper hand in this department, spreading false consciousness to persuade the masses that life was as good as possible, revolution impossible, and fundamental transformation bad.

Now, however, the Third Left turned the left's old problems on their heads. It would manufacture false consciousness as an asset for the cause. A false picture of America had to be built up, a mirage so powerful that people would be smugly certain it was true and base their lives on that assumption. America was a bad, not good country; a failure, not success; a land that should be divided along lines of ethnicity, race, and gender, not a highly integrated society. And these opinions would be made to appear not only fashionable but in fact the only opinion a decent high-status individual could hold.

Marx and Lenin had argued that it was an illusion to believe changing consciousness could transform society; they spent as much time ridiculing this notion as they did excoriating capitalism. Yet as a dialectical materialist—believing that ideas and material conditions did interact, albeit material conditions were more important—Marx left the door open for some followers to develop such notions. He explained, in *The German Ideology*:

> The materialist doctrine that men are products of circumstances and upbringing, and that, therefore, changed men are products of changed circumstances and changed upbringing, forgets that it is men who change circumstances and that the educator must himself be educated.[13]

A critical point was the Third Left's abandonment of materialism—a position that had been shared by modern liberals, conservatives, and Marxists alike—for philosophical idealism. As noted
above, the concept had been that real conditions and experiences
determined people's consciousness. If the economy was a disaster,
people would vote against the incumbent government; if some policy damaged one's own interests, that individual would oppose it.

Thus people were expected to act "rationally." They could not
be brainwashed—except under the most rigid conditions of isolation and intimidation—into thinking something that was "obviously" untrue or to abandon the society's most cherished precepts.

But in contrast to all the main leftist movements of the past
150 years, the Third Left abandoned a materialist philosophy for
that of philosophical idealism. What could be more appropriate
than the fact that the Third Left mega-guru Noam Chomsky was
a linguist while many other leading intellectual figures denied the
existence of truth and focused on the manipulation of words?

Philosophical idealism means deriving conclusions about the
world from the mind rather than material evidence. If one simply asserts that certain ideas are "fair" and "just," these must
take precedence. Therefore, the fact that the left's program had
failed so miserably and that liberal programs weren't working becomes irrelevant. What's important is that they should work and
eventually—with enough time, money, and effort—they will do so
because they are right. That's why the phrase is *political correctness*
and not *factual correctness*.

The Third Left version of radical strategy amounted to saying
that capitalism would not be overcome by deep structural reasons
forcing workers to revolt but because people became convinced
that it was icky and unfair. In Marxist terms, this amounted to the
heresy of philosophical idealism, trying to control the economic
base by ruling the ideological superstructure rather than the other
way around.

Such philosophical idealism dominated the Middle Ages, when it closed down free discussion and scientific progress with a politically correct line. It was against this dictatorship that assumed it possessed absolute truth that the great Western philosophers and scientists had battled. Communism in its implemented form, Stalinism, revived this kind of medieval system. In contrast, the modern university and media system, as well as liberalism in general, rested on defending freedom against a monopoly for dictatorial certainty, against certain answers and areas of inquiry being declared off-limits.

Like twenty-first-century Third Left ideologues, conservative medieval monarchs, churchmen, and their intellectual supporters insisted that their own views were obviously correct and best served humanity. No challenge to them should be taken seriously or given freedom to compete. Any critic was a heretic who should shut up or be shut up in prison or even burned at the stake.

But the Third Left, like the medieval authoritarians and the twentieth-century totalitarians, sought to roll back the great liberal democratic revolution in human society. Anger, hysteria, and class warfare replaced pragmatism and logic. It did not expose and correct its own failures.

As Francis Bacon, one of the greatest Enlightenment thinkers, put it in denouncing philosophical idealism:

Men have sought to make a world from their own conception and to draw from their own minds all the material which they employed, but if, instead of doing so, they had consulted experience and observation, they would have had the facts and not opinions to reason about.[14]

It is often assumed that the academic-cultural caste, if one can call it that, must inevitably be liberal, democratic-minded, and favoring open, honest debate. Yet this forgets the fact that these forces have often played a reactionary role in society. The Enlightenment and scientific revolution were largely waged in conflict with the academic and intellectual establishment of their day, which had fear and contempt for anything not politically correct under the contemporary standards. Bacon complained that universities were strongholds of "degenerate learning" whose faculties, "having sharp and strong wits and abundance of leisure . . . and knowing little history," spun cobwebs to destroy the search for truth.[15]

Ironically, one factor that helped revive such a situation was Marxism's failure, which discredited materialism on the left. In 1963, the Chinese Communist revolutionary and ruler Mao Zedong had explained Marxist dialectical materialism as follows:

> Where do correct ideas come from? Do they drop from the skies? No. Are they innate in the mind? No. They come from social practice, and from it alone; they come from three kinds of social practice, the struggle for production, the class struggle and scientific experiment. It is man's social being that determines his thinking.[16]

This approach had failed for Marxism in the West even while pragmatism—based on historical experience, science, and technology—had let liberal capitalism succeed so brilliantly. In its place, the Third Left embraced philosophical idealism, arguing that it was man's thinking that determined his social being. It would defy the fact that the Western industrialized world had delivered more freedom and prosperity than any system in history. Indeed, such a step was inescapable for anyone who sought the fundamental transformation of those countries. No Western left could survive in the twenty-first century if it paid too much attention to material evidence.

The Third Left's philosophical idealism accorded well with its class base: social groups that dealt in ideas and paperwork rather than producing material objects. The growth of these sectors was the outcome of what has been called a "postindustrial" society in an era when information—and control over it—was said to be primary. These people aspire to be the new ruling class, seeing themselves as the font of all that is good precisely because they are above grubby materialism.

In this context, members of the Third Left elite were rebelling against the West's material success. The original Marxist left demanded that everyone share in higher living standards, only to discover that this goal, which they wrongly thought capitalism and "bourgeois democracy" were incapable of achieving, drained the masses' revolutionary motivation. Third Left cadre, who live very nice lives, want to denounce materialism and consumption without giving it up.

They usually solve this problem in daily life by trying to lead a "higher-quality" lifestyle involving, for example, nonpolluting cars and healthier foods. These things are more expensive and tend to be upper-middle-class tastes. The people who follow this path have less and less in common with the poor, working class, and even much of the middle class. And naturally they think they are superior to all the others.

As a result, social snobbishness is transformed into political virtue. Wealthy people, intellectuals, and movie stars want to be simultaneously a pampered elite and heroic strugglers for a better world. Isolated from what has to happen to keep them supplied with goods, paying others to protect liberty in battle, not having to meet a payroll or manufacture a three-dimensional product, this caste naturally tends to believe that ideas are everything and reality is subordinate to what's in the mind.

Accordingly, the Third Left was entitled to its own version of truth, the manufacture in good conscience of a new form of false consciousness under which scholars have no obligation to pursue truth and journalists no duty to communicate the best possible approximation of it. Freedom was an illusion; manipulation was the reality. The innovative Marxist political philosopher Herbert Marcuse developed the idea of "repressive tolerance," that America's apparent liberty merely camouflaged a system in which the rich imposed capitalistic ideology, making sure its ideas always won the debate. The Third Left guru Noam Chomsky cowrote a book titled *Manufactured Consent: The Political Economy of the Mass Media* to demonstrate this point that the game was rigged.

Societies are not built, according to the left, but consciously "constructed" by plans in the ruling class's heads. If nations do not grow organically and logically based on the original situation, their own structural needs, and human nature, then the left can succeed in rebuilding society any way it pleases. Here the Third Left returns to a Marxist concept that the rules by which society is run or the procedures by which the economy works are not absolutely necessary to maintain prosperity but merely class-based deceptions cooked up to fool the people.

This intellectual imperialism, transmuting leftists into medieval reactionaries, thus saw the citizenry as an inferior, childlike race that must be ruled for its own good by the superior elite. Supposedly, the ruling class tells the masses what to think and fools them with false information. Rather than conclude that it offered failed and unreasonable solutions the people didn't want, the left blamed its unpopularity on the masses being tricked. Its solution? To trick them in the opposite direction.

The difference between the New Left and Third Left, however, was that the latter needed to convince the public that it had nothing to do with revolution. Indeed, the left's transformation also did follow broader social changes and attitudes. As the scholar Andrei S. Markovits writes in his brilliant analysis of the Western left's modern evolution, historically the radical movement had been "sociologically anchored in the male, industrial, mainly skilled working class; ideologically . . . ardent advocates of growth at all costs."[17]

Now, however, all of this changed as a result of postindustrial society and cultural changes as diverse as birth control and environmental awareness. According to the German leftist Joschka Fischer, who rose from clerk in the Karl Marx bookstore to become his country's foreign minister, Bob Dylan had more influence on his thinking than did Marx. The civil rights and anti–Vietnam War struggles became models for activism. The revolution seemed to be becoming from students instead of workers.

Some young rebels, Markovits noted, "went into unions many of which had [previously] been conservative and anti-Communist, turned them into motor forces for the movement but certain privileged unions representing the new forces SEIU [Service Employees International Union] and teachers especially."[18] Once-beleaguered unions were, however, now powerful organizations that expected to get most of what they wanted from employers, often with the government's help, not embattled underdogs.

Instead of impoverishment—exhausted workers, starving slum-dwellers—being the incentive for revolution, prosperity would be the spur. All was possible, everyone could be well-off, successful, with a college education and excellent health—not only in the Western but magically in the Third World—if only the greedy, superstitious, and conservative who opposed any project that claimed to feed hungry children, stop global warming, save obscure species, and block evil oil wells and coal mines were swept aside. If patriotism was once the last refuge of the scoundrel, false do-goodism was the late-twentieth- and early-twenty-first-century equivalent.

Consider the example of environmentalism, a much-needed movement to fix the abuses of industrial society once technology made such improvements feasible and economically possible. Yet once the air and water were cleaned up, demands to do more kept escalating. Ever-tighter regulations had an ever-smaller positive effect on the environment but an ever-larger disastrous effect on jobs, the economy, government spending, and freedom. By the early twenty-first century, vital industries could be shut down, tens of millions of dollars spent, and hundreds of jobs sacrificed to secure some obscure subspecies.

As Markovits summarizes:

> Being left and progressive [had once] meant building dams and steel mills. . . . It now implied saving little fish and rare birds from the destruction wrought by those very dams and mills. The universalism of class as a primary political identity was superseded by the particularism of groups. Faith previously placed in technology, centralization, and the state was now conferred upon localism, decentralization, and community power. The left moved from growth, state, class, economy, and politics to identity, gender, empowerment, and deconstruction.[19]

Essential to this transformation was, in effect, the standing of Marx on his head. The crisis of twenty-first-century America and the grievances demanding change were quite different from Marx's predictions. Yet sometimes Marx's prophecies merely seemed premature and were ultimately correct because of capitalism's successes and not failures in raising living standards.

Consider, for example, religion, which Marx saw as the sworn enemy of Communism. In the nineteenth and even well into the twentieth-century Western world, Christianity remained too strong. He claimed "[t]he bourgeoisie . . . has left no other nexus between people than naked self-interest. . . . It has drowned out the most heavenly ecstasies of religious fervor . . . in the icy water of egotistical calculation."[20] This was in part true, but materialism replaced religion by the twenty-first century not because of the people's desperation but because of their material satiety.

Marx would have been astonished to see how the expectations

for high living standards in exchange for little productive work had risen so high. It was among the elite—the motive force for Third Left revolution—and not the masses where this was most true. Similarly, that same elite was no longer willing to accept the grubby realities of capitalism or even the contradiction that prosperity required getting one's hands dirty sometimes, whether with war or coal mines.

And so the Third Left movement would follow suit, empowering sections of the upper middle class, dressed up in self-serving revolutionary garb, against the rich and much of the rest of the middle class. It had been a New Left joke that the Weatherman group was composed of the most spoiled kids from the wealthiest families.

Actually, it made sense, since it was an elitist-led movement that most benefitted this elite's interests, even while it fooled many of the masses (and also benefitted the parallel self-selected racial, gender, union, and immigrant elites) into thinking that it benefitted their interests. For example, they were when necessary exempt from the most civilized fairness, the most deliberate slurs, and rewarded with most cynical success.

At any rate, the irony was that, except for the reversal of philosophical idealism and materialism, the Third Left followed the most classical reactionary pattern. It was off the liberal-conservative continuum.

Why was this "instantly unjust" America so quickly accepted? Because it was backed by an accepted, unprecedented, all-media, all-educational blitz.

Marx was always contemptuous—as the twenty-first-century Third Left would be—of those who believed ideas, rather than material conditions, played the key role in shaping society. How, he would have asked, could revolutionaries win power by changing people's thinking, which was irredeemably determined by their social class? And if people were not that badly off, indeed much better off than their parents' generation or—in terms of freedom and material well-being—any society had been in history, then why would they possibly adopt radical positions that might undermine those benefits?

Yet this was the mission that the Third Left undertook and succeeded at: that tens of millions of Americans could be convinced that their country was evil and needed fundamental transformation even if that was not objectively true, and even if this conclusion was against their ostensible class interests. This set of fabrications seeking to stir up hysteria and class and racial hatred, and to portray America as systematically, historically unjust, has become the ruling social and economic philosophy's basis. It was a picture corresponding more closely to the Weathermen's fantasies than to either historical liberal doctrine or the real world.

According to this dramatically transformed vision, America was a place where rapacious corporations sought to pour poisons into the air and skies; where oil and coal companies held back wind power and solar energy by sheer malice; where doctors cut off people's feet to make more money;[21] where police salivated to round up Hispanic families taking their kids to the ice cream parlor because they might be illegal aliens;[22] where those waging a "war on women" wanted to deny them the right to buy contraceptives; where workers and a beleaguered middle class knew their children had no fair chance; when brave Third World revolutionaries and regimes battled for liberty against America or even blew up American civilians in murderous but justifiable attacks; and where a heroic left was the underdog of a well-financed, powerful right-wing steamroller.

This was not merely criticism but systematic demolition. The Third Left's stance was that capitalism itself was evil and profits made no sense. America was not a meritocracy but a colony ruled by older white males in which women, nonwhites, and the young generally were second-class citizens. Therefore, stoking hatreds and conflict made sense. Cooperation with Republicans or conservatives became impossible because they were not merely people with a different view but autocrats and enemies who deserved to be destroyed. All the old limits and balances accepted by liberalism were to be tossed into the dustbin of history.

The first principle, then, was that the United States was an unsuccessful society; the second that America was an unjust society. But that failure and injustice were due to a fundamental flaw that went to its very roots. Property is theft, said the early Socialist Pierre-Joseph Proudhon in 1840. Nothing had been clearer since the mid-nineteenth century than that capitalism created new wealth. The Third Left reverted to the view that capitalism was a zero-sum game. Yet how had enough been stolen without impoverishing the working class, enough to buy off the masses? This is the third point: that the money had been stolen from other countries through imperialism, which generated guilt. Success was not won by a good system and proved nothing. All of these apparent achievements were in fact bad things, and since "excluded" or unborn younger people weren't responsible, they could redeem their guilt while still enjoying their possibly unearned lifestyles.

U.S. foreign policy is given the same treatment as evidence of the system's sinfulness. Certainly, at times, the United States acted in a wrong or imperialistic manner, albeit far less than its European, third world, or Communist counterparts. Yet here, too, the Third Left must focus on every negative incident and use it to make a systematic case for America as evil, aggressive, and greedy. The dropping of nuclear weapons on Japan in 1945, for example, becomes not a difficult decision to avoid the millions of deaths on both sides that would have resulted if a full-scale military invasion had been required to end the war, but rather an act of horrible racism or indifference to human life.

Among American society's other victims were said to be those in foreign countries who had been exploited by U.S. imperialism.

Instead of teaching them how to make internal reforms in order to develop their own societies, they should merely be doled out redistributed American wealth originally allegedly stolen from them. They, too, were to be made permanent victims succored on welfare.

If you give a man a fish, you feed him for one day; if you give a man a fishing pole you allow him to feed himself, if you steal a fish from someone else each day to give to the man, you haven't made any progress. And if you tell the man that the only reason he doesn't have a fish is that a capitalist American stole it from him, what do you do? Hand him an AK-47 and tell him to get revenge?

Remember that the Weathermen in the 1970s had seen the main purpose of revolution in America as being to take away the American prosperity obtained by making the rest of the world suffer. Who would believe that the Third Left could sell to millions of people that old line? Thus, in retribution for Americans international exploitation, a global redistribution of wealth and power away from the United States was both just and necessary. Rather than, as liberal development strategy had tried to do, helping the Third World succeed by using the Western model, underdeveloped societies were defined as permanent victims of the West, to be treated as welfare recipients and given its wealth and power as entitlements.

But if the United States was the bad guy in international affairs, who were the good guys, the role models and heroes in the war against imperialism and to build a just society? This no longer meant Communist regimes, which were deceased (the USSR), gone capitalist (China), or the obviously repulsive (North Korea). Michael Moore might make a film about the glories of Cuban medical care as superior to America; Obama romanticized the Venezuelan dictator Hugo Chavez, but this kind of dictator chic wouldn't appeal to most Americans.[23] (Although to show the left's progress, it elected as New

York City mayor an openly repressively pro-Communist [Sandinista] without noticing in 2014.)

But in the early twenty-first century, the left's problem was that the world's only remaining revolutionary ideology was Islamism. This seemed a dangerous liaison, yet the Third Left and later the Obama administration certainly embraced it, supporting Islamists into power in several countries, minimizing the danger of their radicalism. Antagonistic to Western religions, leftists, out of romanticism for fundamental transformation of societies and a shared hostility to the one in America, became apologists and enablers for forces that an old-fashioned Marxist-Leninist would not have hesitated to call "clerical-fascist."

The Third Left pressed the issue of class struggle but in a different way from the past. Marx had warned that the proletariat faced extinction; now this claim was ludicrously made by the Third Left on behalf of the middle class. True, the idea of milking the rich to give to the middle class was an idea received with favor by many of the potential recipients. Marxism had a more reasonable narrative, however (though one less likely to appeal to Americans), since at least it purported to show some link between fat, cavorting, top-hatted capitalists and underpaid workers whose sweat was transmuted to the wealth of others.

Without this zero-sum game—some link between the prosperity of some and the misery of others—there can be no class struggle. Yet America, and capitalism, had been built on the theory that the enrichment of someone else doesn't hurt others and might even help them, since that person could thus hire people, produce useful products, or provide philanthropy. America had long since broken through this zero-sum barrier because of its size, resources, newness unbound by tradition, openness to change, freedom of the bonds of government, technology, and opportunity for small business, among many other factors.

The real class struggle was between this group and those owning the means of production. In the Leninist model, the new class had merely been handmaiden to the proletariat. Now, however, it could explicitly take the lead against those it saw as greedy, ignorant capitalists abetted by hypocritical evangelists and buffoonish militaristic generals. The goal was no longer a dictatorship of the proletariat but that of the beautiful people, superior to an old ruling class and its supporters too steeped in patriotism, religion, bigotry, and false consciousness to see the truth.

Whereas in the past, revolutionaries had traditionally emerged from socially and economically unsuccessful sections of society, in the United States more than a century later, the traffic went in the opposite direction: The failed revolutionaries of the 1960s and 1970s became personal success stories, leading their movement from positions of privilege to those of power.

As early as 1942, the political scientist Joseph Schumpeter had accurately predicted the emergence of this sector. Attending college, he explained, might not qualify a person for professional work, but it would make him forever after reject lesser employment. Those who inevitably could not find work or occupations they felt were theirs by right of diploma would be

[i]n a thoroughly discontented frame of mind. Discontent breeds resentment. And it often rationalizes itself into that social criticism which [is] the intellectual spectator's typical attitude toward men, classes and institutions especially in a rationalist and utilitarian civilization.

. . . Here we have . . . a well-defined group situation of proletarian hue; and a group interest shaping a group attitude that will much more realistically account for hostility to the capitalist order. . . . This hostility increases, instead of diminishing, with every achievement of capitalist evolution.[24]

Those who became part of the successful new class thought of themselves as rightful rulers of the country; those who failed were bitter and eager for fundamental transformation. Along with these factors came the chronic psychological factors that have always produced radicals and revolutionaries, even when there was much greater injustice to rebel against: boredom, guilt, a superiority complex, a snobbish preference for the exotic, and revolutionary romanticism. Intensifying this hostility was the Western elite's loss of confidence over its own system: guilt over enjoying high living standards, disgust at materialism, shame at historical injustices, and doubt about the virtues of their society.

Together these combined into a new set of ideas: Is this as good as it gets? Can't we enjoy all the advantages of the current system but with far more social justice and equality, a pristine environment, a guilt-free foreign policy, recompense for past mistreatment of minorities—in short, everything we want? Wasn't this all good and fair and just and possible? No decent person could oppose such a program. Since it was right, the assumption concluded, it had to be possible.

Of course, to achieve political success required a much broader political base, built of overlapping elements for which Third Left policies brought material advantages. The Third Left sought to create a system that for certain strata of the population systematically reduced the rewards for hard work and increased them for dependency. Those who refused to work or could not find a job were to be paid off. Communism tried to build an effective economy and failed; the Third Left–"Progressive liberal" ideology consciously sought to foster a nonproductive economy.

One of the most amazing transformations was the reversal of the traditional American and Marxist suspicion of government. The system designed in the Constitution was built around the theme of limited government, and the American Revolution had been largely fought against an overbearing regime. After all,

Americans had left Europe in the first place largely to get away from authoritarian governments, rigid class systems, and stagnant economies that told them how to live and held them back from improving their lives. How even more astonishing that such an attitude might be reversed into a rationalization of dependence, that Americans might proclaim—no matter how concealed and prettified the phrase had become—"We love Big Brother!" How could any movement dream of achieving such a Herculean task?

Yet Marxists, and especially Marxist-Leninists, and certainly the New Left, had been totally suspicious of the government in a still-unrevolutionized capitalist system. Government was the enemy, and working within the system was seductive, the social democratic treason. Here, too, transformation was required to turn government from the enemy of counterrevolutionary reaction, the fortress of the bourgeoisie, into just another institution that could be taken over and transformed.

In the Third Left formula, the state became, in effect, the "people's friend," requiring ever-greater power to protect the people from capitalism's alleged ravages. The state was a saint, above institutional interest just as those who ran it were above personal interest. Like God, the state was a source of pure justice. The government should hold the whip hand not only when that power could be strictly justifying but in fact over pretty much everything. Those who were successful enjoyed their ill-gotten goods because they were achieved because of government's bounty and stolen from others.

In fact, though, the government was made of flesh and blood, being merely the instrument of those who ran it, along with all their own ambitions, greed, and personal views. Since when was creating a state obsessed with increasing control over society a successful formula for either liberty or prosperity, especially at the very moment European welfare states were collapsing under their own weight? Why should government be deemed innately superior at a time when evidence of its failures was overwhelming and its power over citizens and the private sector was already at the highest level in U.S. history?

But that was precisely the point. One thing the Third Left approach had going for it was that the power balance between state and big corporations had long since been shifted in the former's favor by a century of liberal reform. So the Third Left's strategy could succeed precisely because its analysis was a lie. Since ravenous capitalist domination didn't exist, the companies could be intimidated by bad publicity and wrapped around the government's regulatory finger. Since racism had plummeted, it would be manipulated as a weapon to permit unlimited illegal immigration and fear of risking being called a racist. And since public workers could have their way, taxpayers were powerless to lower the size of taxes, government, or regulation.

Indeed, the Third Left approach was a self-fulfilling prophecy for making the state the master and breaking the power of the private sector permanently. By taking in more money to pay for more programs, the Third Left expanded its power to give rewards, buying both ideological loyalty and electoral support. Robin Hood stole from the government, which had stolen from the poor. The Third Left would steal from the rich and give to the government, which then gave a lot of the funds to its government worker and crony capitalist constituencies and crumbs to the poor.

But since stealing from the rich yielded insufficient funds to pay for everything, the Third Left also had to steal from the middle class, borrow at interest, print money, and in effect eat the seed corn of capitalism that is the money used to invest, build companies, and hire people. In other words, the economy would decline, constantly adding to unemployment payments, food stamps, and other government programs, which in turn gave the Third Left more reasons to blame capitalism and the greedy rich for not having met society's needs; to demand even higher taxes; to raise taxes; and to increase government spending.

These structural shifts in America had been predicted by the Communist turned conservative James Burnham in the late 1940s. Burnham had pointed out that Socialism in the traditional sense was not the only alternative to capitalism; there could also be what he called a "managerial society," which he saw as undemocratic. He noted that the critical factor was not formal ownership but real control.[25]

While Marxism had understandable appeal at a time of grinding poverty, in predicting that workers' living standards would decline and force revolution, the Third Left assumed the opposite. In its mistaken view, America was so rich that it could afford unlimited entitlements, special privileges, and socially mandated luxuries as a permanently sustainable strategy. If the rich paid their "fair share," there would be enough money to fund this system forever. The grateful constituencies of the Third Left would be happy, the rich would still be rich, and there would be no ill effects on the society.

And as long as material and psychological benefits kept flowing they were not easily moved by high unemployment figures, inflation, mounting government debts, higher taxes, or strangling regulations that hurt other people.

On one level, this expectation was based on a utopian ignorance. Having departed from Marx's attempt to scientifically understand the nature of society, the Third Left merely saw the productive sector as a cow that never stopped giving milk and a goose that never stopped laying golden eggs no matter how much it was abused. They were certain that any burden could be placed on it—for the "public good"—and things would still work just fine.

On the other hand, the movement sought to bring about revolutionary change and wanted to break the existing system, since it assumed humans were infinitely malleable and could be endlessly manipulated. Such expectations, of course, were not purely imaginary. After all, the movement did succeed because they were also based on structural changes in American society.

Its politicized social engineers, foreseen by Burnham but not by Marx, were trained to think government decision making was superior to the market and that capitalism without ever more intensive regulation was on the moral level of a jungle; now they held key jobs throughout the society. They demanded, as their diploma-based right, prestigious jobs and high pay rates as administrators; regulators; officials in federal, state, and local government; anti-bias police and sensitivity instructors; checkers to ensure institutions complied with new laws; teachers of useless skills; liaisons to government and with each other; and form filler-outers.

They had read carefully selected books and were ignorant of alternative worldviews and woefully short on practical knowledge. The economy was like an army with too few fighters and too many bureaucratic generals and clerks whose priorities dragged down productive efforts and wealth creation. Who cared if cars wouldn't sell or production moved overseas, as long as the vehicles conformed to ever-tightening environmental standards? What did it matter if small businesses shut down because they couldn't pay higher overheads required in fulfilling regulations? It was silly to let coal mines operate or oil pipelines be built if there was the slightest possibility of the most minor environmental damage, or to think that giving farmers enough water was more important than protecting some obscure fish's habitat.

The twenty-first-century left would abandon traditional Marxist thinking that strengthening the state in a "bourgeois capitalist" society would make fundamental transformation impossible.

From the feudal context and his own era, Marx was familiar with governments that were too restrictive, trying to regulate everything and control social behavior. He would have been astonished to hear that the twenty-first-century left had reversed this point by being both statist and anti-development. Yet in the age of the iPhone and personal computer, the new, post-Marxist movement, the Third Left, seemed to conclude that the liberation of people now required complete equality; the right to government-paid (that is, taxpayer-provided) free university education, free Internet, and free condoms; open immigration; and other such desirable things.

This basic idea of the state as a machine whose workings were undistorted by human characters or institutional interests would still be held by the twenty-first-century American left and by its offspring. Good citizens with lots of education would be, in effect, philosopher kings, telling everyone else how to live and making decisions in their best interests for the common good.

That is the mechanism implanted in the brains of about half the American people. And the "smarter" the individual, the more powerful this dumbing effect on those deeply fried in indoctrination, immersed in media hypnotism, and dizzied by intellectual double-talk.

This was a very strange left indeed. No wonder so many people found it difficult to grasp that such a movement even existed. Thus one of the most amazing stories in political history remained largely hidden, even as it transformed a country and as those supporting this transformation energetically denied that it had taken place at all. Marx had hoped there would be a withering away of the state. Instead—like Lenin—there was a deification of the state.

CHAPTER 5

A New Political Philosophy in Power

As a graduate student in the 1970s, having seen the growing politicization of universities, I became fascinated by a historical question. Did Communist and pro-Communist professors of the 1930s and 1940s, a time when they felt confident, indoctrinate their students in class? Did they use their lectures to feed them the party line and try to turn them into revolutionary cadre?

I researched this issue comprehensively, including reading the transcripts of anti-Communist congressional investigations that had every motive to publicize and exaggerate such activity. The results were clear: There was hardly a single incident in which radical professors politicized classes. Professors were attacked for being members of the Communist Party, not for indoctrinating students or trying to destroy the integrity of the university itself.

Why did these professors not bring their politics into the classroom? Fear of losing their jobs was one motivation, a concern that obviously doesn't exist today, when such behavior is often employment enhancing. Yet even those open about their Communist views and involved in public activities did not betray their profession.

They actually believed that the democratic free marketplace of ideas and a sincere pursuit of truth would bring Marxism's victory. But when that didn't happen and the contradictions between ideology and reality, professional principles and political stances, became inescapable, their scholarly integrity would lead them away from Communism.

The profound contrast of contemporary academia with that earlier era was amply symbolized by an announcement I read in 2008 on an email list of scholars. The chair of a history department at a major eastern university had died and one of his colleagues wrote a very nice tribute. Among the virtues listed was that the deceased professor ensured everyone hired in the department was a Marxist.

I was shocked for two reasons. First, it amazed me that professors would so violate professional ethics and the university's very purpose by making politics the main criterion for hiring. But the real shocker was that this would be done openly before hundreds of colleagues. The author had no fear that his colleagues would react in horror and denounce him, or that some journalist might investigate this situation. Such behavior was now accepted as normal and acceptable in the academy.

When I spoke on campuses it was clear how far this same process had gone on the student side. It was not that everyone held radical views; far from it. But the hegemony of the Third Left forces was clear, with dissenters too intimidated to speak out. On one famously radical state college campus, an apolitical student told me that everyone knew papers must focus on the evils and imperialism of the American system in order to receive a good grade.

Radical hegemony and indoctrination were pervasive. In 2010 my son took a computer course in a summer camp that rented space from a swank Anglican private high school in Potomac, Maryland, a wealthy Washington, D.C., suburb. On parents' day I went to see the presentations, which just happened to be screened in a class-room used during the school year by the history teacher.

In this random classroom in a random private school, on dis-play were fifteen short quotations up on the walls around the room, virtually all from radical thinkers, including three by Noam Chomsky and one each from Cornel West and Howard Zinn. The theme? History was just a construct made up by those who ruled. Consequently, the battle was not to find the truth but to use this narrative as a weapon for promoting one's own political views.

Also hanging in the classroom: a poster of Malcolm X with the quote "By any means necessary," which meant, of course, the use of violence to bring down the evil United States; a poster of Che Guevara with a Cuban flag and revolutionary slogans; a poem by Allen Ginsberg about how America is evil; a collage called "A Needless Sacrifice?," about how America's wars are evil; a collage of the anti–Vietnam War movement, with a big peace sign; and several posters and cartoons ridiculing the "traditional" role of women based on some stereotype of 1950s America, one of which claimed that wives always had to agree with their husbands and that a woman's main job was to have dinner ready when her hus-band got home.

There was nothing to balance all this indoctrinating mate-rial. The only thing in the room that didn't reinforce the teacher's radical themes was a card with a humorous quote from Lyndon Johnson about how hard it was to be president. Even the George Santayana quote was of the "history is bunk" variety. No, there were no pictures of the founding fathers or anything about the Constitution or Declaration of Independence.

The message of all this was a tribute to indoctrination written on the blackboard by grateful students on the last day of school: "Thank you, Mr. ——— for teaching us to think independently!"

So I had accidentally happened on a scene that showed how wealthy parents from the Washington-area elite were paying lots of money to have their children indoctrinated into being left-wing radicals to the exclusion of all other ideas or worldviews, left so naive that they were grateful to receive what they took to be well-balanced wisdom. Hundreds of such situations can be recounted by parents.

With the Third Left attaining intellectual hegemony, institutional control, and even a degree of political power, American public life was transformed. Many people noticed no difference, yet roughly half the population understood that there had been a sharp change of course that bore little resemblance to what liberals had advocated.

Understanding the situation was difficult, however, because the new order had to be differentiated not only from liberalism but also from the past Marxist-dominated radicalism. Yet given the state of public debate—leftist denial, liberal surrender, and conservative siege—there was little systematic discussion of these issues.

Of course, trying to implement such a notion is going to lead to a stagnant society, as Obama's first term proved. But such a failure, if one can dominate the sphere of ideas and build a coalition of those who benefit, need not produce defeat, as Obama's victory in 2012 demonstrated.

Since, for example, the mass media are just the tool of the bourgeoisie, the radicals have a right to seize this instrument and manipulate it for their own benefit, too. This is the exact opposite of the liberal position that the mass media should be as independent and as honest as is possible.

The same cynical approach applies to the Third Left's strategy toward both culture and intellectual life. Any writer's intention is less important than how the text can be twisted without reference to its context. All American history, and that of Western civilization, falls short because it is less elevated than today's thought, rather than being seen as the basis on which the current world's achievement stands. There is an element here of the spoiled ingrate who has inherited a great fortune, which he enjoys while demeaning those whose labor, daring, and sacrifice let him live so well at so little effort of his own.

In all of its elements, the Third Left coalition was brilliantly constructed. Some people's humanitarian desire to help those less fortunate was manipulated; others were won over by appeals to self-interest or from indoctrination. Still more could be recruited simply because going along would help their careers and make them seem fashionable and sophisticated.

One huge advantage for the Third Left over its predecessors was that Communists could offer only what they themselves called, when referring to religion, "pie in the sky." Join a risky revolution and after we win we will give you lots of stuff. In contrast, the Third Left offered material benefits immediately through government checks, privileges for minorities, and higher social prestige, along with more successful careers for those whites who went along with the program.

One of the Third Left's most original, spectacular, and seemingly invulnerable creations was an elaborate system to defend itself by discrediting alternative views as being racist, sexist, greedy, homophobic, Islamophobic, and—equally potent—unfashionable. To hold certain ideas makes you cool; to hold others makes you cruel. To avoid being called nasty names made toeing the party line attractive even though there was no party and no official line.

Stubborn critics could be destroyed; the less courageous, intimidated; and shaky adherents kept from defecting. Those who boasted of their bravery in defying social taboos, who would laugh at being called "enemies of the working class," cringed and surrendered at any hint of being labeled with one of these new isms. Politicians trembled; intellectuals capitulated; average people censored their speech lest they give rivals or enemies any opportunity to twist their words into hate crimes.

Another major innovation was getting the image of an evil fantasy America accepted as reality by tens of millions of Americans. This was an America that had lost its way, where the American dream was dead and the middle class going down the drain.

Yet this set of fabrications seeking to stir up hysteria and class and racial hatred and to portray America as systematically, historically unjust has become the ruling social and economic philosophy's basis. This is a picture that corresponds more closely to the Weathermen's ideas than to either historic liberal doctrine or the real world.

Yet the Third Left approach also raises an incredibly important question that has never been publicly debated: If they believe that America was so bad after a century of liberal reform—in Barack Obama's phrase, had never worked; in Michelle Obama's phrase, never worth being proud of—how could the Obamas and their supporters claim to be the heirs of Teddy Roosevelt, Woodrow Wilson, Franklin Roosevelt, Harry Truman, John F. Kennedy, Lyndon Johnson, Jimmy Carter, and Bill Clinton, presidents who had collectively governed; not to mention Democratic domination of Congress, and numerous liberal Supreme Court decisions during half of the previous century?

Had all these hundreds of laws, dramatically changed attitudes, and new institutions failed to solve the problems that the Third Left claimed were so bad, or had they even made the situation worse? Wasn't the system they railed against in twenty-first-century America far more the creation of liberals than conservatives?

In fact, this idea that the enrichment of some brought about a worse situation for other Americans—"a world in pain run for white folks' gain," as Obama claimed, quoting Jeremiah Wright—was a reactionary notion. America had long since broken through this zero-sum barrier because of its size, resources, newness unbound by tradition, openness to change, freedom of the bonds of government, technology, and opportunity for small business, among many other factors.

One feature of Third Left thinking that mirrored their view of American capitalist society was the idea of an international zero-sum game. The wealth of those at home was stolen from the Third World. In Obama's writing this view took the form of the Cruise Ship Theory of Economics. Obama took this image—there is a direct relationship between passengers on luxury cruise ships throwing away food and people in Haiti starving—from Wright.[1] The concept basically amounts to arguing that people in Haiti are poor because people in America are rich.

Yet this wasn't true. People in Haiti were poor because the country lacked some natural resources, a democratic system, and a leadership that cared about the people's well-being. The problem of Haiti, and other such countries, was not capitalism but, in a real sense, the lack of capitalism. It was not having a government that was too weak but having one that was too strong and strangled the society.

The Third Left's proposed solution, that Americans be forced to transfer wealth to others, would mainly result in financing ruling classes far greedier and less productive than the American capitalists the Third Left loathed. It would also ensure that Third World countries remain impoverished and repressive either under traditional-style dictatorships or the new-style autocracies of people like Chavez or the Islamists.

How does this Third Left movement neutralize those who might be expected to offer the most opposition, that is, those whom Marx would have called the ruling class and its chief lieutenants? By making those ideas fashionable so that expressing them certifies one's high status. Advertising agencies sold cigarettes and cars by associating them with romance, sexiness, success, popularity, and wealth. To sell the Third Left version of leftism you do so by making it proof of one's intellectuality, generosity, purging of the sin of being wealthy, and moral purity.

There have always been wealthy men, and more often their

children, among the revolutionaries. Friedrich Engels, Marx's closest colleague, was a factory owner. The U.S. Communist Party had
Frederick Vanderbilt Field and others who assuaged their guilt by
campaigning for their own extinction. But these were rare individuals. In the 1970s, the joke was that the Weathermen included
so many rich kids that an affluent background was a precondition
for membership.

Convincing a large portion of the affluent, whites, and males
that they have been evil and lived too well not only added useful
cadre to the Third Left's ranks and helped finance its campaigns
but also reduced the opposition. In the past, if such individuals
supported radical positions they could face social censure and im-
pediments to their career. By controlling both institutions and the
debate, however, the Third Left could now offer them rewards.

Indeed, a critical element in the Third Left is the detachment
from any concept of the relationship to the means of production.
Anything was possible. There was no need to produce wealth, because it was just arbitrarily stolen after being produced by something close to magic. And to share it through the state one did not
have to produce (like the Marxist proletariat) but merely to exist,
and thus have a right to demand not just a safety net but a full share
as any major productive person would rate.

No previous Marxist left had ever conceived of such a brilliant
mechanism. The Third Left taught people to feel guilty about their
privileges yet offered them not only redemption but also material
benefits. You could enjoy a big house, a well paid job, and expensive material goods while still being a hero of the virtuous revolution, sort of like Che with an SUV. Beyond that, you were more
likely to get that good job in a glamorous line of work if you toed
the line.

Ironically, the Marxists had been fair-minded in comparison.
When they spoke of class struggle they were against the entire
bourgeoisie, since their class standpoint was thought to be virtually

inevitable. Far more effectively, the Third Left let the bourgeoisie make a choice. It could support the movement's agenda, lose nothing, and gain a lot.

Finally, there is the transference of blame and snobbishness toward the lower orders as the Third Left absorbed the historic haughtiness of the rich. Historically, the left had delegitimized and ridiculed elites. The Third Left, however, ridiculed the masses. The "enlightened" upper-middle-class left-liberal viewed his mission as transforming others to be just like himself, the enlightened epitome of history, in terms both of beliefs and behaviors, down to the very foods he prefers.

With good conscience they look down on those from most small towns and rural areas; big or small businesspeople; and lower-middle-class and blue-collar workers. They have put the hip social elite and yuppie upper middle class in place of the proletariat. They romanticize distant peasants—or terrorists—while jeering at anyone who shops at Walmart.

There is a strongly snobbish tone in Obama's April 2008 speech to upper-class Democratic Party contributors in San Francisco, implying that cosmopolitan atheists are superior to those bigoted, paranoid, stupidly religious inferiors in the benighted Midwest or small towns, people who "get bitter, they cling to guns or religion or antipathy to people who aren't like them or anti-immigrant sentiment or anti-trade sentiment as a way to explain their frustrations."[2]

But Marx said something similar in *The Communist Manifesto*: "The bourgeoisie has subjected the country to the rule of the towns. It has created enormous cities, has greatly increased the urban population as compared with the rural, and has thus rescued a considerable part of the population from the idiocy of rural life."[3]

Obama and his cohorts viewed the big city as the seat of all that is good and civilized. America's founders, of course, appreciated

the agrarian and small-town side of the argument, too, understanding that the United States had a chance to be democratic precisely
because the sturdy independent farmer and pioneer also had virtues not seen in your average university town.

But that's precisely why the current leftism worked so effectively. It allowed one to have a high living standard, believe oneself
exceptionally virtuous, and flaunt supposed superiority. Obama's
behavior was consistent with this approach as he luxuriated in his
rich and Hollywood connections in a way that would have brought
massive media ridicule and criticism to any counterpart of different
political views. Nothing illustrated the administration's snobbish,
"let them eat cake" attitude better than his opulence-drenched
fund-raisers, glamorous costly vacations to luxury spots, and endless rounds of golf.[4]

And nothing could surpass the marvelous appropriateness in
this context of the British-born editor of *Vogue* magazine, Anna
Wintour, as cohost of a highly publicized New York fund-raiser
during the 2012 election campaign. Wintour was notorious as the
title character of *The Devil Wears Prada*, the very symbol of the exploitative boss who treated workers terribly. So contemptuous was
Wintour of Americans in the "flyover" heart of the country that she
sneeringly described most of Minnesota's residents as being as fat
as "little houses."[5]

Yet just as Obama and his supporters could never be called
racist because they were on the left, they could never be accused
of class arrogance, for the same reason. In fact, though, the Third
Left had put both phenomena at the cornerstone of their new doctrine.

And so this ideology is essentially a reactionary, snobbish, and
anti-diversity philosophy. The radical elite loves itself as it saves
the world by staging a no-risk revolution, at considerable benefit
to itself, while looking down on the backward, inferior gun-and-
Bible-hugging little people.

Liberals and conservatives can argue that they want everyone to play by the same rules; the Third Left cannot honestly do so. On the Supreme Court Building in Washington, D.C., it is written: "Equal justice under law." That is an example of fairness.

Western democratic civilization was based on Deuteronomy 16:19–20: "Thou shalt not wrest judgment; thou shalt not respect persons; neither shalt thou take a gift; for a gift doth blind the eyes of the wise, and pervert the words of the righteous. Justice, justice shalt thou pursue." But this was not, as many would have it, a paean to what is now called social justice; rather, it was the opposite: an insistence that whether one is rich or poor, black or white, female or male, there should be equal treatment. And a gift (bribe) need not be merely monetary in value.[6]

This ideal has usually not been practiced, but that does not justify throwing it away, especially at the very moment in American history when it has come closest to fruition, just as it is disastrous to throw away the ideals of fair news reporting and honest scholarship. After all, liberalism had been based on the very demand that this precept be fulfilled.

Fair, one of the Third Left's favorite slogans, was a strange word to use in politics because, of course, it has no specific meaning. Who is to determine what is fair? Of course, the Third Left view is that this is to be done by itself and by the government. Moreover, the hypocrisy of talking about how everyone has to obey the same rules rings hollow as the Third Left coalition reaps rewards by establishing special and different rules for its own coalition members, whether labor unions, racial or ethnic groups, or crony capitalist companies.

There is also a completely different issue here. Effective economics are not based on sentiment. What if "fairness" undercuts productivity and incentive to work? If the pie becomes smaller everyone suffers. Isn't the most "fair" system the one that has the largest ability to grow and thus offer more for everyone?

Finally, there is also a hint in the Third Left's propaganda theme of a mob-inciting demagoguery, a protection racket. In April 2009, Obama told a meeting of bankers, "My administration is the only thing between you and the pitchforks."[7] Yet those mobs, if there were any, were being created and incited by his own supporters.

Thus, the Third Left has been a master of both carrots and sticks. At the onset of the New Left in the 1960s, Buffalo Springfield sang in "For What It's Worth" about the fear of that generation's young rebels: "It starts when you're always afraid / You step out of line, the man come and take you away." In a half century, the Third Left reversed that process. Now they were "the man," and while they couldn't literally arrest you, they enjoyed the power of intimidation, being able to take away someone's reputation and career. In contrast, if you didn't step out of line you would prosper.

How quickly the much-vaunted courage of intellectuals, professors, and journalists vanished! When Annie Hall, in the 1977 film of that name, mused before Woody Allen's character about how she would stand up under the Gestapo's torture, Allen responded that she would tell all as soon as they took away her Bloomingdale's credit card. The Western intelligentsia did no better. Any potential loss of status was enough to make them turn stool pigeon, and the slightest hint of radical Islamist intimidation made them fold like a lawn chair.

Who are the people today who hate those different from them? In the past, it had been conservatives who behaved in this manner. That's one reason liberals detested conservatism and continue to do so today, long after such behavior patterns largely ceased to exist. Calling someone un-American, atheist, homosexual, a Communist, or labeling them with an ethnic epithet, was a terrible weapon to smite any dissident. Liberals fought to eliminate such stigmas; the Third Left simply added new ones to its arsenal, turned them against opponents, and reintroduced all the old patterns of intimidation.

Instead of being condemned as unpatriotic, people were ridiculed for being patriotic; instead of being shunned for being atheists, they were mocked for being religious. Rather than being persecuted for opposing capitalism, they were barred from jobs for not being sufficiently to the left. They were told what permissible words might be used; what opinions could be held. Even the Hollywood blacklist has been turned on its head as conservatives had to hide their views or face discrimination.

The new, fashionable hatred was not to look down on other races or nations or homosexuals. This had been replaced by hatred of the truly religious, non-big-city, and nonleftist people who don't think the right things.

The Third Left's diffuse power in changing the most basic attitudes was revealed by hundreds of developments. Take, for example, the political label *progressive.* As pointed out earlier, since the early 1920s the main use of that word was as a cover for Communists.[8] In the late 1960s, for example, then SDS vice president Carl Davidson came up with "new working class" theory. The cultural-psychological dissatisfactions of professionals and technicians, not the proletariat's economic grievances, would be the motive force for change. That prediction was proven as the Third Left seized power in the commanding heights of cultural-intellectual production.

In 2008, Davidson headed Progressives for Obama, the explicitly radical component in supporting Obama's campaign. All those involved in the group were radicals. At that time, nobody else was using the word *progressive.* Now the controlling forces in the Democratic Party as well as the defining powers in academia, popular culture, the mass media, and fashionable folk generally used that label to describe themselves, though many did not understand the full implications of that choice. What better symbol of the far left's triumph?

The adaptation of the label *progressive* today was a rare example of Third Left bravado, almost daring an exposure of its true nature. On one hand, the Third Left maintained the pretense that it was heir to normative American liberalism. Yet on the other hand it was flaunting its extreme left-wing orientation. I have never seen any liberal academic or mainstream media outlet point out the radical hint contained in this name.

More out of opportunism than conviction, Hillary Clinton, too, announced she was a Progressive. Yet a few years earlier she and her husband had been the First Family of an administration that was self-consciously striving to be at the center, the very model of a moderate liberalism that would have been horrified by the world-view she was embracing. At that time, anything as radical as what Obama and his supporters would successfully market a few years later was rightly considered political poison.

In 2007, though, Hillary Clinton could claim:

> I consider myself a modern progressive, someone who believes strongly in individual rights and freedoms, who believes that we are better as a society when we're working together and when we find ways to help those, who may not have all the advantages in life, get the tools they need to lead a more pro-ductive life for themselves and their families.[9]

Yet these three statements were at odds with reality. The Third Left wanted to reduce individual rights; advocated bitter class, racial, and gender conflict; and did little for the poor. Moreover, the Third Left and "Progressives" were trying to buy the masses today with taxpayer money. And Obama himself is the product of the last of the corrupt big-city machines that mistreated the local power, stole their money, and provided them substandard services.

Like the loaded term *progressive*, another indication of the Third Left's true nature was its friendly relationship with what might be called the small "open left," those who hadn't got the memo that they were supposed to pretend otherwise. They still cling to explicit Marxism, anarchism, or anti-American slogans. Compared to the sophisticated Third Left, the Occupy folk seemed more like descendants of Abbie Hoffman's "Revolution for the Hell of It" crowd. And some people always do feel good to be shouting slogans, parsing ideology, and scandalizing the bourgeoisie.

The great advantage of the Third Left and Obama himself was concealment, denying extremism and sugarcoating their message. Many sophisticated people still believed Obama was nothing special and that it was ridiculous to think the left dominated the media and academia.

To protect its image, the Third Left could easily have denounced the Occupy Wall Street movement as a way to demonstrate its own "moderate" credentials. Yet it never did so, despite the fact that this alliance should have sent danger signals to those who had been fooled by these new-style radicals' professed liberalism. That judgment proved correct. The camouflage held.

Yet the Occupy movement provided a prime example of what the Third Left was really all about. Far from being oppressed or underprivileged, the Occupy movement represented a spoiled-brat brigade seeking more consumer goods and "free stuff." It viewed the American people as the enemy. Yet the new political elite's enthusiastic support for the Occupy demonstrators demonstrated the audacity of its hope that nobody would notice how much they were alike.[10]

What Marxism and fascism, as well as pre-democratic conservatism, most had in common was an insistence that they understood all of history and know what's best for people whether they want it or not.

Until the "Progressive" takeover, liberalism did not think that way. In its far left version, liberalism has joined this antidemocratic club. This is why the great democratic philosopher Karl Popper explained in his two-volume work, *The Open Society and Its Enemies*, that the enemy of democracy was those who thought they knew everything, that they were absolutely right, and that since they could predict the direction of history they had the right to jump in the driver's seat and take everyone there whether they wanted to go or not.[11]

The Third Left abandoned Marxism's "scientific" and historical inevitability aspects, having learned that the promised revolution and subsequent utopia were not inevitable. Quite the contrary! That had been the losing side. So the twenty-first-century movement had to depend on acts of will, not forces of history, by using the new sciences of advertising, psychological manipulation, and propaganda.

With its adaptation to changing conditions in the West and its ability to create mechanisms to defeat opposition, the new ideological system was simultaneously elegant and horrifying. The meaningless word *fair* implies that opponents are meanies. A costly program labeled with the proper humanitarian name is excused failure, because the intentions behind it were good. Diversity is trumpeted as those hired or extolled all totally agree with each other. Next to the Third Left ideology, Marxism looks like an abacus beside a computer.

Marxism was a do-it-yourself movement. It organized its own party, publications, and tiny party schools, at one of which Frank Marshall Davis, Obama's mentor, taught.

In contrast, the Third Left understood success could only be achieved by skill and stealth. To promote its power it took over a large, popular, established political party. To publicize its ideas, it manipulated large portions of the mainstream media. And to teach its thinking it indoctrinated students in the huge public school system and universities financed by others.

It is not hard to figure out which approach would be more effective in the United States. Those strategic choices made the difference between an obscure sect that might have received less than 1 percent of the votes and a movement that could twice elect Obama as president despite his terrible record in office.

CHAPTER 6

The Conquest of Institutions

The contrast between the New Left and Third Left era was well illustrated by a tale of two parties. In 1970 the music conductor Leonard Bernstein held a fund-raising event for the Black Panthers at his expensive apartment in Manhattan, attended by several dozen famous actors, writers, artists, television personalities, and other cultural luminaries. The panhandling Panthers there explained, "This country is the most oppressive country in the world, maybe in the history of the world." Those present then showered them with big guilt-assuaging donations.[1]

Three decades later, in 2012, another fashionable event was held not far away, to combat "Islamophobia," chaired by newly coined network television personality Chelsea Clinton, daughter of the current secretary of state and previous president. That audience was, like their Bernstein predecessors, made up of, in the writer Bruce Bawer's words, "upper class" New Yorkers engaged in "narcissism and self-congratulation, shameless social climbing . . . and a truly repellant condescension toward the purported prejudices (read: legitimate concerns) of the lower orders."[2]

Yet while the Bernstein party was ridiculed by the contemporary media, most notably by the novelist Tom Wolfe, the celebration of radical movements three decades later had become a mainstream phenomenon and Wolfe's article probably would not have been publishable at all.[3] America had become one big radical chic party.

It was not a composer throwing a soiree in his penthouse apartment but the president of the United States throwing a party in the White House with rappers like Jay-Z, whose lyrics advocated violent abuse of women, or the South Korean star Psy, who advocated the murder of American soldiers in Iraq and their families.[4] It was not the invited guests who were making contributions of a few thousand dollars but the uninvited taxpayers who were forking over trillions for the federal budget.

Wright, a minister who sounded like the Black Panthers, was the chief executive's mentor, while Obama chose another minister, Joseph Lowery, who proclaimed that all white people were going to hell, to deliver prayers at his first inauguration and later to receive the Medal of Freedom.[5] Jim Wallis, still another minister, who was Obama's current spiritual guide, openly proclaimed his view that Christianity was socialist, even as the 2012 Democratic convention voted down the mention of God in the party platform.[6]

And the perfect parallel was that the very same Black Panthers in their new incarnation enjoyed the attorney general's patronage and protection as he dropped a criminal action against them considered certain to result in a conviction. In 1970, the Panthers were complaining about police harassment. But in 2008, under the protection of the nation's chief law enforcement official, they were allowed to threaten voters at Philadelphia polling places openly and get away with it. In 2012, they repeated that performance, now enjoying immunity from the law altogether.[7]

You don't need a Weatherman to tell which way the wind blows, or a Black Panther, for that matter. To hear that the United States "is the most oppressive country in the world, maybe in the history of the world," is something you can do in almost every university—and quite a lot of secondary schools and even primary schools—throughout the United States.

The 1970 Panthers' claim that "the pigs have the weapons and they are ready to use them on the people . . . [and are] ready to commit genocide against those who stand up against them" is like a line from the Occupy Wall Street movement of four decades later, which enjoyed the verbal approval of the president of the United States, the "liberal" (that is, camouflaged radical) establishment, much of the professorate, and mass media.

The idea that wonderful saintly people were accused of being terrorist extremists whereas they are actually—as the Panthers claimed to be in 1970—just "a peaceable group" running "clinics and children's breakfast programs" was a narrative now applied to the Muslim Brotherhood and other revolutionary Islamists by the mainstream media, experts, and even high officials in the U.S. government.

The Third Left had not abandoned the traditional Marxist-Leninist approach in vain. It proved that the main idea-manufacturing institutions could be taken over and its big guns turned against the system. Public schools, universities, mass media, cultural and entertainment "factories," trade unions, mass organizations, think tanks, and civil society groups were so turned in astonishing numbers. And the new management need not fear criticism or exposure for its misuse of them, since the mass media would not cover this story, far less explain how such behavior betrayed the very nature of the institutions involved, which included the media itself.

As one former Weatherman leader accurately wrote: "Becoming a knowledgeable participant and innovator in any field of work takes years and tens of thousands of [19]60s activists dug in to do the work." In order to lie low and infiltrate mainstream institutions, however, they had to resist "[t]he lure of easy, Leninist solutions [which] was still strong."[8]

To achieve these goals, the Third Left was flush with well-trained, highly educated cadre; large amounts of money; and an extremely tolerant society. Thus, to borrow a radical phrase from the 1970s New Left, the Third Left's way was clear to make a revolution in the revolution. The New Left cadre, largely on an individual level and a few small groupings here and there,[9] began the "long march through the institutions"[10] and "working within the system," a strategy that would succeed beyond their wildest dreams.

By turning entertainment into propaganda, education into indoctrination, and mass media into thought-directing rather than news-providing organs, the Third Left achieved miracles. By demonizing those who disagreed, intimidating the fainthearted into silence, and recruiting opportunists onto what seemed the winning side, a small group of Third Left supporters, say 5 percent of the population, came to control a larger liberal base of around 30 percent by persuading them to be "Progressive" liberals, and another large segment of centrists or those without strong views by convincing them that they were merely holding mainstream views while their opponents were crazed reactionaries.

Granted that a large body of people existed who had this ideological and class profile. But how could such a massive change happen without being thoroughly reported, questioned, and discredited? That development was possible due to a successful Third Left strategy implemented independently by thousands who without orders or instructions simply pursued their careers as professors, teachers, journalists, officials in foundations or nongovernmental organizations, and in other such professions that influenced opinion and policy.

It is not uncommon in history for a group of people, a movement, an ideology, or a party to try to transform the meaning of the most basic human and political concepts. Nor is it uncommon for them to have some success. What is rare, if not unique, is to succeed so fully as to drive from people's memories the displaced reality and to discredit in advance any criticism. Repressive dictatorships closed off their countries and severely punished anyone challenging their monopoly on truth. But to achieve that effect in a democratic society was surpassingly unique.

Lenin was quoted as saying, "The Capitalists will sell us the rope with which we will hang them." In the equivalent modern version, the Third Left did even better by not only getting their opponents to finance its plan but also recruiting their children and persuading them to place their necks in the noose.

These efforts were no coordinated conspiracy. Indeed, one of the post-Communist left's greatest assets was its lack of centralization. The Leninist-Stalinist model—a single disciplined party at home, an idealized Communist motherland abroad—had been a big handicap. Having a party or party line would raise suspicions and opposition. Having a foreign model—as the USSR had been—was counterproductive for the left when that society was so horrible, and loyalty to it seen as disloyalty to America.

With no party, hierarchical leadership, or even coordinating organization, the movement could become invisible, portraying any claim that it even existed as a conspiracy theory. The battle was carried out by like-minded cadre and loose networks. They simply advanced the movement by advancing their careers and using their higher posts to channel funds to movement interests, take the proper political stances, and hire only those who shared their ideology.

This invisibility and camouflage equally ensured there could be no organized opposition, no systematic critique of its ideas, and no resistance to its takeover of mass media, universities, grade schools, and popular culture. To claim such a process was even happening—despite the massive information available from daily life—would be to court charges of paranoia. And so tens of millions of Americans could conclude that nothing had changed from previous decades or liberal practice as universities and mass media institutions were transformed until they taught the same radical ideas and put the same spin on the same stories. A mighty mechanism had been created that had the power to transform clones into cadres.

To have any credibility with the public for their ideas, left-wing academics, journalists, and other influential persons had to erase the history of why the radical left, and especially Communism, had always failed while capitalism—especially when modified by liberal reforms—had succeeded. The Third Left had to erase the actual history of Communism in the USSR and elsewhere. Students simply didn't learn such things, while popular culture didn't show them.

An anecdote shows how far this process had gone. A college student explained in conversation that "terrorism was the contemporary equivalent of Communism." At first she seemed to be saying that terrorism was the major threat today. But the student explained that she meant that both Communism and terrorism were phony dangers invented by the American ruling class to sustain its rule. The party line on the Cold War, following the New Left historians of the 1960s onward, was that the conflict had been largely or totally America's fault, a view that came to pervade the universities and sometimes the mass media.[11]

Ironically, of course, the Third Left's own experience belied its ideological claims. If America was the kind of country they claimed, its institutions would have discriminated against radicals, not let them take over. Yet no influential job was closed to them, nor was any argument banned. Clearly America was not a country prone to revenge or ideological discrimination. The Third Left, however, would not prove so generous when it took over institutions.

Historically, Marxists defined the capitalist state as innately bad and unchangeable from within. The state and the glittering prizes its society could offer would seduce the revolutionary into selling out long before he could bring about real change. Reforms undercut revolutionary energy. Marx defined revolution as a struggle in which one class overthrew another. Since the bourgeoisie would never give way voluntarily, the masses must be mobilized for open struggle that might well involve violence. To think otherwise was to commit the sins of opportunism and reformism.

In contrast, the Third Left viewed the capitalist state and mainstream institutions as the best base for furthering its agenda. There was no need for any general strike, massive demonstrations, civil disobedience, or armed uprising. That is why "fundamental transformation," so subtle and rationalized as to persuade millions of people that it wasn't even happening, was so different from "revolution."

From Hollywood on the Pacific to Harvard on the Atlantic, a curtain of ideas has descended across the United States. In the universities, schoolrooms, media newsrooms, cultural fountainheads, nonprofit and advocacy organizations, and often in political institutions in many of the famous cities and the populations around them are in the Third Left's and "Progressive liberal" sphere of influence.

No matter what scandals or misdeeds became public, Obama was not held responsible for them by the political elite or mass media. This included the Internal Revenue Service political discrimination against conservative groups applying for tax-deductible status; the Benghazi affair, in which four American officials were murdered in Libya while Obama slept soundly and the causes of the attack were covered up; the administration's wiretapping of journalists; the outreach program favoring largely Islamist radical organizations and even terrorists; and most of all the continuing economic depression. Nor were the ideas and practices leading to such abuses examined critically.

How was this silent revolution accomplished? Most generally by a conquest of institutions through the following four stages:

1. Institutions were flooded by the left's cadre or by people who were sincerely persuaded that there was no other legitimate way of thinking. They became professors, teachers, journalists, politicians, artists, filmmakers, trade union officials, foundation officers, leaders of nonprofit and advocacy organizations, government bureaucrats, leaders of ethnic, racial, or gender-based groups, even religious ministers, and ultimately even business managers, politicians or judges, too.
2. The implicit rules of these organizations and institutions were changed from open-minded liberalism to permit the pushing of narrow political agendas, indoctrination, the slanting of news, and other ways to become tools of a single set of ideas and attitudes in a political and ideologically partisan manner.
3. Opponents were declared illegitimate, were demonized, and were forced out. Opportunists and careerists drew the proper conclusions on how they could benefit or be punished.
4. Like-minded people were hired and promoted until virtual monopolies existed, or at least the different views were neutralized and became impotent. Lavish funding was obtained from the institutions themselves and the foundations so colonized or family fortunes inherited. Those who held them would tone down their criticism and outspokenness so as to be permitted to remain. They were also rendered ashamed at not joining the consensus, being put on the permanent defensive.

The conquest of foundations supplied the Third Left with virtually unlimited cash. For example, the Joyce Foundation, founded by the heiress of a family whose fortune came from the lumber industry in the Midwest and South, originally focused on hospitals and other health facilities but under leftist control moved into the massive backing of Third Left groups and causes.[12] Foundations distributing the wealth of conservative businessmen were taken over by leftist staff members who channeled tens of millions of dollars to finance the movement. As a result, the Third Left was far better funded than their conservative rivals, despite all stereotypes to the contrary, and, ironically, used conservative-origin foundations' funds.

And now "Progressive" postmodernism took the same road. A lot of effort went into this revolution on campuses, including the cooperation of foundations, as in the Ford Foundation's 1990 Campus Diversity Initiative, with programs at 250 universities to create racial-gender-ethnic studies' programs, preferential hiring and admissions policies, and "sensitivity" training. These programs, including the one Michelle Obama helped supervise as a student at Princeton, were almost always controlled by radical professors and doctrine. The training sessions took on the style of a political reeducation camp, cramming what was in effect Weatherman ideology into students' heads.

> The demand for open admissions by asserting the alternative to the present (school) system exposes its fundamental nature—that it is racist, class-based, and closed—pointing to the only possible solution to the present situation: "Shut it down!"[13]

As the Third Left took over many schools and universities—with former SDS leaders Bill Ayers and Mike Klonsky, among others, posing as educational philosophers—they did advocate indoctrination and lower standards. Preferential admissions as students and hiring of professors based on race and gender criteria were surpassed by the hidden radical political qualifications required in order to get a job. Grade inflation took care of ensuring that unprepared students did not flunk out, and if university tuition became ever more expensive—thus profiting a key Third Left sector—the movement could demand that the resulting student loan bills be forwarded straight to the taxpaying public.

Another institution distorted for that purpose was the public school system, which had not done such a great job of educating children in recent years. It would take on the additional burden of expanded breakfast, lunch, and in some places even dinner services. And it would also be assigned the task of nudging children into eating what government bureaucrats decided was healthy for them. That would really demonstrate that the state was the people's real friend and savior. Yet none of these efforts would bear fruit unless there was a situation conducive to creating a revolution.

They had to believe that America was structurally racist, sexist, homophobic, and Islamophobic; whites or males or non-Muslims must accept whatever the other group wants or be guilty of thought-crime.[14]

Thus there was talk of the need to fight "false consciousness" in which members of subordinate groups accept the capitalist ruling class's worldview. At Columbia University, new students were encouraged to get rid of "their own social and personal beliefs that foster inequality." The assistant dean for freshmen at Bryn Mawr announced that the school's freshman orientation helped students free themselves from "the cycle of oppression" and become "change agents."[15]

Hugh Vasquez, a so-called diversity expert, in his study guide for a Ford Foundation–funded film, *Skin Deep*, discussed "white privilege" and "internalized oppression" while urging whites to become allies of the oppressed by rejecting privilege and supporting such groups.[16] One can easily imagine what would happen to any student—or employee in the many parallel programs conducted by corporations—who openly dissented from these programs' claims and premises. They would suffer intimidation and punishment for

exercising free speech or thinking for themselves, the very qualities universities are supposed to promote.

Those who have had experience know about the remarkable
closing of the American academics' and journalists' mind.[17] Early-
twenty-first-century Americans were naive about ideology, having
been so long protected by an open society, few domestic threats,
and high living standards. As a European journalist explained, in
his country every newspaper had a clear political line and even
party affiliation. No one could infiltrate and change them. But in
America, where every newspaper was nominally fully open and
had no formal allegiance, it was easy to do so while still keeping a
pretense of independence.

The result was not, as the Old Left imagined, a revolution from
below, but rather a takeover from above. As the liberal Democrat
John Roche, former head of Americans for Democratic Action,
prophesied in 1984, "talent, messianic energy, intimidation . . .
have given the new class a role utterly disproportionate to its size."[18]

He continued: "Moreover, while their whole sybaritic lifestyle
rejects the Marxist-Leninist notion of a militarily organized cadre,
they have absorbed the key lessons on the route to power: locate
the fuse box and identify the crucial circuits." Thus one could both
be prosperous and comfortable (more comfortable even) and simultaneously prosper and be rewarded.[19]

"The consequence," Roche concluded, "is the emergence of
'mandarinates.'" Using a Russian rather than a Chinese reference,
however, the Obama administration would call them "czardoms."

In addition to taking over institutions, the Third Left and its
"Progressive liberal" allies—the two groups distinguishable by
whether its members were consciously radicals who sought to
destroy the system, or thought they were still liberals—formed a
powerful coalition on the basis of the components' diverse self-
interests.

This coalition consisted of six elements:

Third Left ideologues among the managerial sectors of society, who hated capitalism and wanted to fundamentally transform the American system into some blend of statism, socialism, corporatism, communalism, and socialism. They were aware of their goals, strategies, and methods and concentrated in academia, media, foundations, nongovernmental organizations, and intellectual and cultural-artistic circles, often under liberal cover.

Trade unions, usually led by Third Left cadre whose hidden agendas were those of the ideology and movement rather than their members' interests. Many of them were in public employees' unions for reasons explained below.

Crony capitalists who sought to base their wealth and success on government grants, contracts, regulations tailored to their interests, and special privileges.

Organized racial-ethnic-lifestyle-gender groups, usually under Third Left leadership that defined their grievances, methods, and goals in radical ways. Rather than seek equality, as they had under generally liberal leadership in the past, they sought specific privileges in exchange for real or alleged past sufferings.

Entitlement seekers, who often do have justifiable claims to benefits like Social Security, Medicare, pension funds etc., but faced the fact that the money was simply not there to further fund or expand them. To get the help they want or need, they are pressed to demand high government spending, high levels of taxation, and indifference to debt or the draining of investment capital from productive enterprises.

The lumpenproletariat, that is the genuinely poor, especially dependent on government help. While they had genuine needs they also wanted to maximize benefits and minimize their responsibilities. Told that they were poor because the wealthy were stealing from them and that they had a right to the wealth—rather than that society was showing good faith in helping them—they became angry and felt justified in antisocial behavior.

A key element in the new worldview of this coalition was that of previously neutral institutions as a partisan tool. The mass media, universities, schools, and government would be the weapon wielded by those smugly certain they were right (politically correct), and anyone who disagreed was wrong and thus their views did not deserve a fair hearing. In short, it was the abandonment of the liberal open marketplace of ideas.

Consider, for example, the evolution of the mass media. While radical or "Progressive" liberal journalists denied such accusations, it was obvious on a daily basis that for political reasons some stories were ignored, others were played up, facts were hidden, distorted, or highlighted for political-ideological gain, and reporters routinely used politically charged language that would have gotten them fired in earlier times.

Despite its decline in the face of Internet and social media, the mass media remained enormously powerful in setting the views and agenda of early-twenty-first-century America. It was able to define good and evil; praise or damn individuals and causes; turn someone into a hero or a pariah; and secure or destroy anyone's reputation in history. Consequently, most of the elite was desperate to please the mass media and avoid its wrath. He who lives by celebrity can also die by it, a factor especially important in the highly competitive, pressure-cooker world of Washington, where the mass media can determine the fate of anyone's career.

Thus radical ideas have achieved true hegemony and shape both the debate and the resulting policy. The mass media was generally out to protect the image of anyone on the left side of politics and destroy that of anyone else even when this required ludicrous contortions. To cite just two examples, Bill Clinton's terrible treatment of women, risking his presidency's effectiveness and even perjuring himself under oath, and Ted Kennedy's involvement in the death of Mary Jo Kopechne did not prevent the media from presenting them as heroes on women's rights, while others, who had done nothing, were being accused of waging a war on women.

This use of the media to reward and punish, to channel and indoctrinate, thus shaped the behavior of the ambitious. When the wealthy journalistic dilettante Arianna Huffington was a conservative, *Time* magazine ridiculed her, in 2001, as a "fund-raising cultist" pretending to be an "intellectual." But when she turned to the far left, the same publication extolled her in 2006, publishing a glowing tribute.[20] Such lessons put across the point that those who cooperated with the Third Left would be rewarded; those who crossed it would be destroyed.

The opposition and indeed any reasoned criticism were discredited. While the Obama administration benefited greatly from virtually total media support, the transformation from watchdog to lapdog did a serious disservice to the country. If the mass media had been critical, Obama might have been pushed toward more moderate policies that would have worked better.

At the same time, the bias—so obvious to many, though invisible to others—undermined the mass media's credibility, accelerating the loss in readers and viewers already trending due to the growth of Internet and social media. Yet as with academia, many journalists were indifferent to these costs because their overwhelming priority was to push their political agenda. This new journalism rationalized reporters' personal views into stories, behavior previously considered unacceptable and subverting the purpose of a free press. The "do-good" approach held that the journalists' political line was so obviously right that they had to push it for the good of everyone.

A prime example of this pattern was JournoList, a confidential discussion list whose members included hundreds of liberal journalists. When some messages were leaked they showed that systematic bias was now taken for granted as virtuous. Many in the profession practiced it; none within the establishment criticized it.

One JournoList poster, for example, Spencer Ackerman of the

Washington Independent, told colleagues to deflect attention from Obama's relationship with the Reverend Wright by picking one of Obama's conservative critics, "who cares [which one] and call them racists." Sarah Spitz, a producer for National Public Radio, boasted that if she saw Rush Limbaugh suffer a heart attack she would "[l]augh loudly like a maniac and watch his eyes bug out" as he writhed in torment.[21]

"Is anyone starting to see parallels here between the teabaggers and their tactics and the rise of the [Nazi] Brownshirts?" asked Bloomberg News reporter Ryan Donmoyer. "Esp[ecially] now that it's getting violent?" In fact there was no such violence. Others spoke of how to be most effective in ensuring Obama's election victory in 2008.[22]

In some ways, what was most disturbing of all was the defense of the list by its leader, Ezra Klein of the *Washington Post*: "What would be disturbing is if people came to a conclusion together, and you looked the next day and it appeared in everyone's blog or everyone's column."[23] This was still another instance of the Third Left activist's arrogant self-confidence in being able to get away with anything because they would not be challenged by anyone who counted. After all, virtually every day on key issues these journalists did sing in harmony, with little or no effort being made to hide the existence of a consistent party line.

Many examples exist of the absurd contrasts involved. A huge story appeared in the *Washington Post* during the 2012 election claiming that as a teenager, the Republican presidential nominee Mitt Romney had once bullied a schoolmate with long hair, implying the student was allegedly gay. During the 2008 election a clearly false story was circulated by the *New York Times* that the Republican candidate John McCain was conducting an affair with a lobbyist.

Yet not a single serious investigation was conducted about Obama's earlier life or in many cases about the implications of ad-

_____

ministration policies and scandals. The media's massive resources stood by and rusted rather than dig into the dramatic, strange story of the man in the world to whom those resources most assiduously should have been applied.

Professional scholars and journalists failed because they jettisoned their proper, job-doing curiosity about who Obama was, what he had done, and what he believed. This same point also applied to the seemingly invisible Third Left elephant in the room. Journalists were supposed to be eager to break news yet instead put politics in command. They flaunted double standards while simultaneously denying them, convincing roughly half the population—often the more "educated" and "informed" part—because they were the people most influenced by that same mass media.

Alongside the mass media, the other main institution forming people's views about politics and the world was education. With so much one-sided indoctrination going on, the results were a massive shift in the worldview of young people. Asked in 2009 whether they preferred socialism or capitalism, 53 percent of adults said capitalism, 20 percent socialism, and 20 percent didn't know. But among young people between ages 18 and 30, respondents were evenly divided.[24] Where had this penchant for socialism suddenly arisen, since there had been no explicitly socialist movement to push people in that direction, nor any dramatic incentive in society for young Americans to think that way?

This was no natural process but in fact a deliberate, concerted effort to make them think that way. Indoctrination was all-invasive and easy to document, reinforced by class curricula and readings, defined as coolly fashionable, cheered by campus groups and freshman orientation programs, strengthened by films and mass media, and protected from criticism. Lacking were not only conservative professors but also liberal ones who adhered to the professional ethics of balance, open debate, and keeping their partisan opinions out of the classroom.

Students persuaded of Third Left ideology and those who were not were both also deprived of a good education. Many were left with a certainty of belief but an ignorance of alternatives, accurate facts, and even how to reason. That is why different views could only be met with the merest caricature of scholarship.

Dumbed down, they resorted to slogans and name-calling, with huge gaps in their knowledge. They could honestly not comprehend how others—except due to greed or deceit—could possibly disagree with them. This was far worse than anything that had happened from normative Marxism, which gave young people the intellectual equipment to discover someday that this ideology was false. With twenty-first-century Third Left indoctrination, however, such a future escape seemed far less likely.

Then, too, this fundamental transformation was just as hurtful to institutions so distorted as it was to the victims of their wrath. Both the quality and credibility of the mass media and academia suffered accordingly. Poorly informed people made bad decisions; inaccurate information damaged the society and economy; young people with useless degrees, self-reliance, and the ability to think for themselves would do a great deal of damage.

This system ironically revived, even outdid, nineteenth-century conservative patterns of control against which liberals had once rebelled. Conservatives had invoked tradition or religion as a basis for restricting freedom and asserting these claims in place of reasoning. Now the left did the same in the name of alleged good intentions and struggle for "social justice." If conservatives had once subverted the free functioning of media and academia, so now did the left. As conservatives had once discriminated against dissenters, so too now did the left.

The power of the monopoly of ideas and information required by the left's domination of education was necessary precisely because of the weakness of its arguments. As Galileo Galilei, a professor who once rebelled against a parallel conservative monopoly, said, "I understand very well that one single experiment or conclu- sive proof to the contrary would suffice to overthrow both these and a great many other probable arguments."[25] He provided the ev- idence, but because he offended contemporary religious beliefs— again, close to becoming a crime in the Third Left era—he was threatened and forced to recant.

In contrast, as mentioned previously, when the history depart- ment chair at a well-known university died, one of his colleagues wrote a glowing obituary on a closed historians' email list that in- cluded as one of his accomplishments that he had ensured that only Marxists were hired in the department. None of the hundreds of historians pointed out that this was a basic violation of academic freedom. Even the booklets to study for the SAT college entrance exams contained numerous politically slanted questions, all in a leftward direction.[26]

What makes the situation worse is the decline of professional ethics, sense of fair play, and other factors constraining the con- version of America's "referee" institutions into propaganda organs. Moreover, the level of power attained by those who would use such institutions for political goals is far more complete than ever be- fore, and, unlike their predecessors, they have no sense of guilt or entertain any sense that they might be wrong. In other words, there is less permissible political diversity today in elite institutions than ever before.

Part of this campaign was the rewriting American history to make these claims convincing. If the United States was a sinful na- tion of class and other oppression, a place where the economic sys- tem never worked and only favored the wealthy, then it could only be saved by fundamental transformation. Thus history becomes a series of crimes—imperialism, sexism, class exploitation, racism— and failures.

The new version drew heavily on Marxist historians from the Communist era—like Howard Zinn—and the New Left generation. Rather than show how well the society had progressed and how the system really functioned, history became a revolutionary tool for discrediting it and thus showing it is unworthy of continued existence. The techniques used were similar to those employed more broadly in the media and academia.

One of them was to find or create discrediting deeds taken out of context, besmirching heroes, and creating an endless inventory of victims. In *The Victims' Revolution*, the conservative gay dissident Bruce Bawer writes:

> Once, the purpose of the humanities had been to introduce students to the glories of Western civilization, thought and art—to enhance students' respect, even reverence, for the cultural heritage of the West; now the humanities sought to unmask the West as a perpetrator of injustice around the globe. Once, the great poets, authors, philosophers, historians, and artists of the Western canon had been heroes whose portraits and statues adorned university campuses; now they were to be viewed with a jaundiced eye for most of them were, after all, Dead White Heterosexual Males, and therefore, by definition, members of an oppressive Establishment.[27]

Thus, in his series *The Untold History of the United States* for a cable television network, the director Oliver Stone explains that the United States was responsible for the Cold War and that the USSR was relatively innocent in the clash. This is a staple of university history courses despite the fact that the documents show a very different story. Stone's series also suggests that Henry Wallace would have made a better president than Harry Truman.[28]

Up until the recent revision of American history, Wallace was regarded as a well-meaning man but a Communist dupe nonetheless. But he was, after all, the 1948 candidate of the Communist-dominated Progressive Party. While Stone's series was called *The Untold History of the United States*, it was a version told quite often, in many places exclusively, at Third Left–ruled education systems.

Students have been taught that their work is always good as long as it expresses themselves or the proper political line. They become incapable of serious self-evaluation and are disoriented if they ever have teachers who hold them to high standards. Upon graduating, many in the liberal arts and humanities are left with large tuition debts, a sense of entitlement, a propensity to accept the Third Left line that the system was innately unfair, and relatively few marketable skills. Whether the conditioning will wear off is still to be seen.

As for the faculty and administrators, despite the pose of being heroic intellectuals speaking truth to power, many are cowards or opportunists who cling to a fashionable consensus. Once brave intellectuals who defied tyrants who shouted "Off with their heads!" now dare not say anything that might jeopardize grants or bring criticism from their peers.

Yet when someone does express a contrary opinion—and academia is supposed to exist for the purpose of open debate without fear of retribution—intimidation or repression quickly followed. Thus when Naomi Schaefer Riley, a columnist at the *Chronicle of Higher Education*, wrote an article pointing out with detailed examples the low quality of Black Studies programs, she was quickly barred from the publication.[29]

Meanwhile, colleges raised tuition sky-high without incurring government action or media criticism. As the Obama administration took over student loans, the system seemed developing toward one in which universities could charge whatever they wanted and students, parents, or ultimately taxpayers would pay whatever they demanded. In effect, the middle class was being forced to subsidize the future upper middle class. Thus a waitress or small businessperson or mechanic would pay for better-off kids to study art appreciation, feminist studies, conflict management, philosophy, etc. and then these same kids would complain that capitalism was treating them unjustly. That wasn't socialism; it was a class struggle in reverse.

When my son went to an upscale elementary school in Washington's Maryland suburbs, the curriculum included multiple readings on the internment of Japanese during World War II, man-made global warming, and math taught with Obama for President campaign playing cards. Pro-American material was systematically excluded, even down to singing the national anthem; the anniversary of the September 11, 2001, terrorist attacks was ignored except for a short book glorifying a Kenyan man for marking the occasion.

While all such stories are anecdotal, there are so many examples from so many places in the country that the conclusion that wide-scale political indoctrination is taking place is inescapable.

Second, there was a stress on the history of specific groups—women, workers, African Americans, gays, etc. The problem was not in putting such previously neglected people at center stage but rather the presentation of their story in a crude Marxist-style narrative. As the Weatherman manifesto had posited, they were portrayed solely as oppressed groups struggling against a hostile society in order to show the injustice and hypocrisy of democracy and capitalism. In fact, without leaving out the negative parts, the principal story should have been American society's remarkable and successful advance within a successful system toward both greater justice and more prosperity.

At my son's elementary school, students became obsessed with racial distinctions, and charges of racism embittered recess quarrels. One young man became enraged and charged racism when a salesman said to him that he probably liked soccer—he did—in trying to sell him some equipment. The student interpreted this as a negative stereotype toward Latin Americans. Foreign-born students voiced their hatred of America as an unjust and prejudiced place, based neither on what their parents told them nor on personal experience but due to the instruction they were receiving.

Third was "historicism," up to then considered an academic sin, which meant reading the present into the past and failing to understand those eras and their people in their own context. Instead, complex and hotly debated issues were transformed into conspiracies in which a vicious ruling class sought to keep down the masses.

In his remarkably prescient book from 1989, *The Closing of the American Mind*, the professor Allan Bloom foresaw how an end to teaching classic works and the evolving philosophy that governed Western civilization would produce students ignorant about their own society and its virtues, thus easily falling prey to extremist ideologies.

The abandonment of the Western canon in higher education, the rejection of the classics, has meant that students remain ignorant of how Western civilization actually developed and works. The result was to produce universities that trashed the very values of free inquiry, honest debate, and maximum depoliticization on which Western intellectual discourse flourished.

Fourth, while Western capitalism's real or alleged sins were highlighted and exaggerated, Communism's massive crimes and Marxism's failures were hidden from students. The same point applied to the reasons why Third World societies lagged behind the West, ignoring their own internal problems and putting near-exclusive blame on Western behavior. It also meant celebrating those Third World demagogues and revolutionary movements who looted and oppressed their own societies and then blamed the inevitable result on imperialist oppression.

A few journalists, artists, and intellectuals in Western Europe and America had fallen for fascism in the 1930s and 1940s; a lot more backed Communism; while some briefly embraced the new Left in the 1960s. But nothing compared to the Third Left's ability to brainwash and mobilize such a massive proportion of these groups.

One of many campaigns involved in this effort was the assignment of pre-interpreted radical books as required reading. For example, incoming students at Brooklyn College and other schools were assigned Moustafa Bayoumi's anti-American book, *How Does It Feel to Be a Problem? Being Young and Arab in America.* The book depicts Arab-Americans as victims of bias after the September 11 attacks, even though there is scant evidence such bias took place. The goal was to transform the event from an attack on America into one more proof of American perfidy.

Another year's featured book was about a Haitian victim of mean-spirited immigration policies and U.S. imperialism.[30] This developed the narrative about the United States being a thief rather than a success story and the blaming of suffering in other countries on America.

And this book was followed by Rebecca Skloot's *The Immortal Life of Henrietta Lacks*, alleging that a poor black woman in 1951 was exploited when some cancer cells taken from her, instead of, as usual, being thrown away, were used for research that benefited others. The faculty ensures that such books will not be discussed critically or in a diverse way but point to the only proper conclusion. What would happen to a student who openly challenged the indoctrination?

The book was presented by a biology professor, who explained on the Brooklyn College website, in language closer to that of the revolutionary agitator than to any scholarly examination:

This is a story of evil and good, poverty and wealth, selfishness and altruism, racism and love, capitalist exploitation and self-sacrifice. . . . We see in this book the human cost of denied access to decent education and health care, and also the amorality of science and medical research. Lacks' daughter is described as "filled with psychological insights about how white elites functioned in a racist society."[31]

Many issues were so reduced to "evil and good" in contradiction to the honest search for truth and understanding reality in all its complexity, which is what scholarship should be. Institutions supposed to be self-correcting and self-critical lost those attributes. Once again, the radical stance contrasts with the liberal academic approach of openness, balance, self-criticism, and the search for truth, replacing it with an a priori, ideologically determined, single-minded emphasis on pushing a party line. Whatever the truth of man-made global warming, science handled the issue in a highly politicized, unscientific manner determined by political pressure, economic incentives, and media demands.

When problems became obvious, radical forces mobilized to ignore evidence, declare discussion unnecessary ("the science is settled"), and vilify those raising questions. This was the same pattern of cultural-intellectual repression that conservatives used in the pre-democratic era.

Marx was quite familiar with this phenomenon. In the "illusion" of his day, Marx charged in *The German Ideology*, history was seen as only "the political actions of princes and States, religious and all sorts of theoretical struggles. . . ."[32] The contemporary illusion is that history must be judged on whether it contributed or interfered with the creation of a new utopia of absolute equality of everyone based on the systematically unequal treatment of different groups.

To become a political force, the Third Left had to organize a broad coalition. Perhaps the most revealing definition of this strategy was given by Van Jones, an open Marxist and the former Obama White House green jobs czar, speaking at a June 10, 2010, forum of the Campaign for America's Future. This group itself was a left-wing Democratic Party think tank headed by Robert Borosage as a better-camouflaged place after he headed the openly New Left, Marxist think tank the Institute for Policy Studies. Borosage introduced Jones as a "central leader of the Progressive movement that is transforming America."[33]

Borosage joked that Jones had gone to Yale Law School but "risen above it." Yet that joke was in the context of concealing that the Third Left's leaders were the most highly privileged, and not the most downtrodden. After all, Jones had gone to Yale Law School, like Bill and Hillary Clinton; Obama had gone to Harvard Law School, Michelle to Princeton. Jones now worked at the Center for American Progress, the Obama administration's most favored think tank.

Jones proceeded to define the "Progressive movements" strategy as "top down, bottom up, and inside out." Clearly it was top-down. Jones even said that the battle was to contest control of the federal government. The "Progressive" liberals would include by 2012, for example, about one-quarter of Democrats in the House of Representatives, who were members of the party's Progressive Caucus. All of these people would publicly ridicule—and many would do so in their own minds—any idea that they were extreme left-wing, much less supporting retreaded and revised Marxist concepts.

The top-down nature of the Third Left's plans—taking over institutions—was its biggest innovation. And it was certainly inside out, by populating those institutions with cadre to the point that one could begin to speak of a virtual monopoly.

Yet it was not at all bottom-up. Lacking were the mass protests—Occupy Wall Street was a tiny movement, for example—but there was the appearance of bottom-up efforts through an organization's leadership ordering members or supporters into action. Yet if compared by the grassroots activism of the Communists and even of the New Left, the mass movement aspects of the Third Left were pitiful.

A Communist militant would be organizing workers on the factory floor; a Third Left militant would be a high official in the union. New Left militants were scruffy, impecunious students; Third Left militants on campus were the professors. The Communist or New Left militants worked for tiny radical newspapers handed out on street corners. Third Left militants dominated the main newspapers and television networks in the country. If a Communist or New Left radical worked at a university, union or factory, or regular newspaper, he would have to fear being fired every day. In contrast, the Third Left cadres were the ones doing the hiring and firing.

Why should the Third Left put the priority on organizing those who were too poor and downtrodden to do much when they could, in the phrase of Saul Alinsky, the proto–Third Left socialist theorist, "organize the organized," those who were well placed to exercise influence, were more articulate, and knew how to work the system and use its privileges? A single member of the new technological-intellectual-managerial elites with education, power, and money was better able to affect society than one hundred workers on a factory floor. And who else would be paid money far above the wages of a hardworking proletarian to write the reports justifying such policies and the articles persuading others to support the Third Left agenda by claiming it to be wonderful, necessary, just, and chic?

This, then, was the first and most important element in the Third Left coalition: the managers of idea and information creation: the educators, journalists, entertainment and publishing industry figures, government and trade union officials, the leaders of ethnic or single-issue groups, and others of that new class. They were in large proportion the cultural-intellectual elite that resented corporate power and thought it could run society better. This included professors, intellectuals, and people with degrees in social sciences, community organizers, indoctrinated students, journalists, artists, government-linked scientists, and a wide range of other professions. These people ran and managed Third Left–controlled institutions.

Some years ago, a former college classmate contacted me for help in getting a government job. I had no intention of recommending someone who I knew had written a doctoral dissertation celebrating Joseph Stalin and who was still an avowed Marxist-Leninist. Nevertheless, and despite a lack of expertise, he was hired by the Environmental Protection Agency and had a long, high-level career writing and imposing regulations on businesses he despised and wanted destroyed. There were many such cases among leftists, those on the left fringes of liberalism, or people simply pumped full of Third Left ideas.

Here was the intersection with the second element in the coalition, the union movement and particularly the government bureaucracies. Of course, with the expansion of federal, state, and local government, a much larger sector than ever before did so on some level, a group including teachers, for example.

Indeed, those who worked for the government or for those servicing its needs had become a huge sector of the population and the core of the labor movement. Their interests lay with a larger, better-funded government employing the maximum number of employees and paying them the highest possible money and benefits.

The trade union movement, once the bulwark of Democratic Party moderates, had been fundamentally transformed as a generation of radical activists had taken leadership positions not because they had been workers themselves—mainly dedicated to improving working conditions and wages—but because they intended to use them for political ends.

Many Americans still held to the myth of the powerless blue-collar union struggling against the autocracy of greedy capitalist employers, but the reality was quite different. More than 8.7 million public employees were in unions during 2011, compared to less than 6 million corporate employees. That same year, 37 percent of government workers were union members, a proportion five times greater than those in the private sector. Only 11.8 percent of American workers, 14.8 million people, were members, down from 20.1 percent and 17.7 million in 1983.[34]

This means that almost 60 percent of all union members worked for government. The National Education Association had 3.2 million members; the Service Employees International Union, 2.1 million, the American Federation of Teachers, 1.5 million; the American Federation of State, County and Municipal Employees, 1.6 million; and the International Association of Fire Fighters around 300,000.[35]

More taxes and regulations directly benefited them, and even if the economy did badly these people were insulated from those problems. Shrinking government, using resources more effectively, cutting taxes, or pumping funding or power into the private sector is against their interests.

In other words, unions were increasingly composed of workers whose demands are paid for not by profit-making corporate moguls but by the taxpaying public. Corporations have limited amounts of money, which must come from profits, and they face competition that prevents them from raising prices too high or letting quality fall too low. Thus corporation executives have a strong incentive to bargain toughly and not make too many concessions. The unions, far weaker in the private sector, know they must compromise so that companies don't cut payrolls or close down entirely.

In contrast, government can raise taxes, revise regulations, and—in the federal government's case—even print money. Thus government officials have an incentive to give unions what they want. The results were generous fringe benefits compared to the private sector, ever-growing costs, pressure against reducing the public workforce, and massive government deficits.

The system became one of institutionalized corruption. Compliant politicians use other people's money to raise salaries, pensions, and number of employees while they get paid off by large campaign contributions and votes for themselves. And if the existing local, state, or national government does not cave in, unions elect a different one. The real conflict in this case is between the public sector employees' unions and the public.

From 2005 through 2011, unions spent $4.4 billion on political activity. While corporations tend to contribute almost equally to the two parties (seeking future favors from both), unions gave almost exclusively to Democrats. In 2008, Democrats received 55 percent of the money given out by corporate political action committees and companies; unions gave 92 percent to Democrats. Far from being David with a sling, unions had become Goliath with a proportionately enormous checkbook.

For example, the radical SEIU's spending on politics grew from $63 million in 2005 to $150 million in 2009.[36] The AFSCME almost doubled its political spending from $75 million in 2005 to $133 million in 2009.[37] Union employees also furnished armies of campaign volunteers and turned out members to vote, though not all of them backed the Democrats.

The priority for education unions and their militant members was not better quality schools but better-funded, larger-staffed schools. But while it is in the teachers' unions interests—and those of other government workers—to advocate that the solution to everything is to hire more employees, pay them more money, provide larger budgets, and give them more benefits—that was far from being true.

Between 1970 the public school workforce almost doubled, from 3.3 million to 6.4 million people. One-third of those hired weren't even teachers and thus made little or no contribution to improved education in the classroom. Since enrollment grew by only 8.5 percent, that meant the number of employees increased eleven times faster than the number of students. Surely, that would have produced much better schools if the strategy being pursued was correct?[38]

No, it didn't. In fact, test scores showed that the level of reading, math, and science stayed the same or even declined during that period. Thus taxpayers had three million more mouths to feed, at more than double the cost, and got nothing in exchange. In comparison, private schools produced better results at 33 percent less cost.[39]

Most government employees and the powerful unions that represented them were leading supporters for the Third Left and its priorities. The problem was that this program was detrimental for the interests of the overall society.

A third element in the coalition are a set of racial (particularly African American and Hispanic), gender (women's), and sexual orientation (gay) groups. It is important to understand that just as with the members of labor unions, the members of these groups have not necessarily chosen to be part of this coalition. Rather it is the group leaders—NAACP, La Raza, the National Organization for Women, etc.—who are such cadre. The groups' budgets, political positions, and public statements are thus in line with the broad views of the Third Left–"Progressive liberal" forces. The same is true of groups like those working on scientific issues, senior citizens (AARP), environmental groups, etc. If dissidents exist, they are not quoted in the mass media. The leadership sets forth what this bloc believes.

For example, Third Left views on race—rooted in the Weathermen's concepts—focus on conflict and special privilege rather than integration and equal justice. Even successes do not bring satisfaction to the beneficiaries, making them love and praise America, since the agenda is not for winning battles but for using those battles to launch further campaigns. On the contrary, the result was anger, a sense of unlimited entitlement, intolerance to debate, and endless additional demands.

In addition to direct goals, the blocs can also be used for other offensive activities by branding any opposition to what they want as racist, sexist, Islamophobic, etc. Moreover, any member of the group—say a conservative African American or woman, an anti-Islamist Muslim—can be defined as illegitimate, unrepresentative, so as to be isolated and ignored.

Another goal is to seek special privileges in exchange for support. A poster woman for this process was Elizabeth Warren, a privileged person who used the system to gain even more advantages.[40] Claiming to be part Native American entitled her to preferential hiring in a system that re-racialized American society. True, America had been racist, but that did not make it a brilliant idea to, under the guise of being antiracist, be racist in the exact opposite direction. And so on through the other constituencies.

Warren was another radical recipient in what amounted to a reparations welfare program. She obtained her job at Harvard Law School as an alleged Native American without even having to provide any material evidence for this claim. The university benefited from not investigating Warren's assertion so it could brag about hiring her on that basis. The whole affair was a massive subversion of everything America was supposed to stand for, and the fact that it did not set off a scandal and intensive soul-searching showed how completely things had changed.

This and many other events signaled the new rule of academia: People should display a superficial diversity of gender and color but all have the same basic political stance. True dissent was unacceptable. Ironically, the veterans of a New Left movement that wanted students to ask questions had now itself become the establishment and demanded that students and faculty fall into line behind a single viewpoint.

The radicalism of academics had a big effect on national policy far beyond the ivory tower.[41] For example, court decisions and legislation were very much shaped by the "critical theory" taught in many law schools, which posited that the law embodies inequality and the ruling elite's interests. This was merely a dressed-up way of saying that democracy was, as Marx and Lenin had claimed, a fraud to hide the domination of rich people.

The Third Left innovation was merely to add the adjectives *white, male,* and *heterosexual.* This approach was a total rejection of the liberal philosophy that a merit-based society was possible and that the body of law built up over centuries did allow for real justice.

A specific example of this Third Left antiliberal revolution was how the situation of women in American society was evaluated. American society had moved to ensure equality for women. But the radical viewpoint insisted that this was impossible. The influential Harvard education professor Carol Gilligan said that women would not have equal opportunity for education due to the "patriarchal social order," and "Western thinking." Similarly, University of Michigan law professor Catharine MacKinnon wrote in *Toward a Feminist Theory of the State*:

> The rule of law and the rule of men are one thing, indivisible. . . . State power, embodied in law, exists throughout society as male power. . . . Male power is systemic. Coercive, legitimated, and epistemic, it is the regime. . . .
>
> [Consequently,] a rape is not an isolated event or moral transgression or individual interchange gone wrong but an act of terrorism and torture within a systemic context of group subjection, like lynching.[42]

She posited rape as "not an individual act" but "terrorism" conducted essentially by males as a group in order to subordinate females. Instead of being the deeds of bad men, rape or other attacks against women became the instruments of all men and, indeed, of all American society since they create a "climate of fear that makes all women afraid to step out of line." In other words, women as a whole are a permanently oppressed group that deserves special treatment.

Once this kind of thinking is accepted, American democracy disappears, the society is declared evil, and the people are broken up into permanently warring groups. MacKinnon's theories had a big effect on U.S. law, helping to shape the Supreme Court definition of sexual harassment law in the 1986 *Meritor Savings Bank v. Vinson* decision, the 1993 Gender Equity in Education Act, the 1994 Violence Against Women Act, and many other court decisions and laws.

This was also the concept behind "disparate impact," the idea that if fewer members of "protected classes" (minorities and women) are hired for any given job at less than their percentage of the local workforce, that automatically suggests deliberate discrimination and hence a need for legal action. If relatively fewer African Americans or women apply to a university engineering school or to become a firefighter, that doesn't reflect individual choice but social injustice. And the solution is to penalize the hapless institution and then lower or suspend standards until the proper quota is attained.

In other words, the United States has been transformed into a country of castes, something like a medieval society, while the goal of equal treatment of citizens and the attempt to reward individual merit were overthrown over in favor of special privileges. Every male and white person becomes guilty and can only attain innocence by backing the destruction of their own "privileges," that is, by backing the Third Left and "Progressive" liberal agenda.

The fourth element of the coalition are entitlement seekers, who can be divided into those who are middle class and those who are poor, members of Marx's lumpenproletariat. Both want government programs that benefit them and are exploited by left-wing populism. The middle-class entitlement seekers are relatively indifferent to the effect of their needed programs on the economy and on the budget. The poor also are likely not to care about tax levels since they don't pay taxes. The issue here is not how badly the entitlements are needed or how justified they might be, but how these desires overcome all other considerations and ensure a potentially permanent majority for a much broader agenda.

Finally, there are crony capitalists, which give the coalition additional muscle and money. Any capitalist who supported the Third Left agenda was freed of guilt over his status and could receive glorifying publicity and possibly government payments or competitive advantages. Thus, someone like Warren Buffett could simultaneously be a massive tax evader and, according to the president, a national hero and role model by allegedly wanting to pay higher taxes, even as he did everything possible to avoid paying existing ones.

The Third Left Center for American Progress did special favors for crony capitalist corporations that paid it money, a scandal unequaled by liberal or conservative think tanks.[43]

"Crony capitalism" has always been a feature of the system, but what exists today is somewhat different from the historic model of corruption. Historically, businessmen could benefit by getting special treatment from government, but in modern times this "carrot" of reward was joined by a "stick" to punish those who opposed government policies. Rather than just being looted by companies, government had become powerful enough to initiate deals. Executives and companies that collaborated (for example, General Motors, General Electric, "green energy" scams) reaped huge rewards (a good media image, social prestige, bailouts, contracts, a better deal on regulations) over competitors. Small business could not compete in this process.

The archetypal case was again that of billionaire investor Buffett, proclaimed virtuous even though his companies were refusing to pay $1 billion in tax bills. But Buffett had even more to gain by throwing his lot in with the Third Left. He had huge investments in two companies, Goldman Sachs and American Express, which received massive government bailouts. Another subsidiary of his company profited greatly from government-subsidized housing projects.[44]

Yet Buffett could be portrayed heroically by falsely accusing other corporations far more productive, job-generating, and tax-paying of being bad, greedy parasites on a beleaguered middle class. Indeed, the more a shady businessman had to hide and the less likely his enterprise was to be profitable, the more he needed to ally himself servilely to the state for its subsidies and protection from media criticism.

"Too rich," of course, was an accusation also made against those involved in business, that is, people who produce jobs and products. It is never applied to liberal politicians, tuition-grubbing universities, Hollywood stars, or entertainment moguls. The grubbiness of making things and taking profits has more to do with unfavorable image than actual greed or dishonesty. In effect, the wealthy could buy protection and approval, richly illustrated by the previously cited example of how Arianna Huffington went from object of ridicule in *Time* magazine—"Should the Huffingtons Be Stopped?" read one headline—to an acclaimed heroine and genius merely by switching sides.[45]

Al Gore may have a big house and a huge carbon footprint, despite his preaching the doctrine of man-made global warming, but that's okay because he talks about how these things are evil. And because he voices such views, Gore was made immune from the exposure of his hypocrisy in the mass media, just as his ideas were protected from criticism in academia. Indeed, even when Gore sold his failed television cable operation to the decidedly ungreen fuel sheiks of Qatar, he faced no questioning of his seeming hypocrisy.

Proper thinking and good intentions are the test of virtue rather than the results of one's actions. When the media, schools, and government want to make hypocrisy good, it is good. The outcome may be disastrous to the economy, the poor, the medical care system, and those living in countries victimized by one's wrong-headed foreign policy. But that's not important if you meant well. That's the implication of the term *political correctness*. Abandoning liberal pragmatism—changing to a radical measure by ideological standards rather than real-world effectiveness—is the start of abandoning successful democratic life.

Such was the coalition assembled by the Third Left. It pulled the Democratic Party sharply to the left and steamrollered traditional liberalism. It twice elected a president of questionable background, radical ideas, and incompetent performance. This alliance was tied together by material interests and overlaid with an apparent ideological consensus that followed the Third Left line.

These groups all did well in a poor economic situation as long as government spending remained high. To pay for what they wanted, the government reduced the amount of potentially productive capital through taxation; part of the money supported a large bureaucracy, contractors, and various institutions; the remainder was passed to the other constituencies as salaries, entitlements, or welfare.

The problem, then, was not that these forces were "stupid" in advocating things that hurt the country and undermined its future prosperity, or that they could easily be liberated from their false consciousness by seeing how bad conditions were. They simply supported policies and programs that benefited their interests, even if one argued that these were shortsighted solutions.

The basic American system had thus been changed, perhaps for a long time, possibly even permanently in that the interests of the political, cultural, and intellectual rulers and their electoral support base had become detached from the values, policies, and beliefs that had made the United States into a great, wealthy, and united country.

In all of its elements, though, the Third Left coalition was brilliantly constructed. Some people's humanitarian desire to help those less fortunate was manipulated; others were won over by appeals to self-interest or from indoctrination. Still more could be recruited simply because going along would help their careers and make them seem fashionable and sophisticated.

One huge advantage for the Third Left over its predecessors was that Communists could only offer what they themselves called, when referring to religion, "pie in the sky." Join a risky revolution and after we win we will give you lots of stuff. In contrast, the Third Left offered material benefits immediately through government checks, privileges for minorities, and higher social prestige, along with more successful careers for those whites who went along with the program.

The concealment of change and promotion of revolutionary idea-changing was a three-step process. The first was to gain control of information—education, university, mass media, lobbying, and nonprofit groups—by flooding these institutions with cadre who naturally gravitated toward such jobs. Once they gained positions of power as department heads, producers, editors, heads of academic departments, etc., they controlled firing, hiring, and the shaping of their institution's messages. In the 1930s, a Communist reporter for a mainstream newspaper knew he would be instantly fired if he engaged in slanting articles; now the editors themselves led the campaign and would give preference to such ideologues.

Second, once the movement took over prestigious institutions its views became the norm. Anyone who disagreed was the rebel against the establishment, and these rebels received far less consideration than their rival predecessors. Professional ethics disintegrated, to be replaced—since it was claimed that objective truth didn't exist, the modern version of the Marxist claim that "objectivity" was a bourgeois trick—by those who believed it their right and duty to push their ideology and to bury stories or ideas that contradicted it.

Of course, in a system as democratic and intensely pluralist as America, it was impossible to prevent alternative voices from existing and a large section of the population from heeding them. These included talk radio, a few mainstream print publications (notably the *Wall Street Journal*); a proportionately tiny sector of television (Fox); and large elements of the Internet.

But so what? Since the Third Left controlled prestige universities and publications, anyone who wanted to succeed and be praised knew what they needed to say and do. A large part of humanity is composed of opportunists, conformists, and people who just want to make a nice living. None of them will make waves. Possession of the idea-making institutions was nine-tenths of the battle for authority. If it was in the *New York Times* it must be true; if a Harvard University professor says something that must be accurate.

In contrast to Lenin, the Third Left did not seek to physically destroy opponents but merely to render them ineffective. Having enough votes at elections or control over institutions in which critics were shut out or shut up was sufficient for its purposes. Rather than the professional who felt guilty lest he wasn't taking into account all the information or being fair to differing views, a radical in the same job had no interest in examining alternative perspectives fairly or presenting them equally. If a tree falls in the forest and the next day newspapers and television networks say no tree fell, then no tree fell.

Third, dissent was discredited by defining it as evil, laughable, and unfashionable. The elite institutions' audiences would shut their eyes and ears to what others said, joining in the demonization of anything challenging the Third Left viewpoint. Such words were very effective. For while, as in the children's saying, sticks and stones might hurt their bones, people in American public life have encountered few such material assaults. But any aspirant to elite approval, rewards, and even membership would do anything to avoid being labeled a racist, sexist, homophobic, Islamophobic, reactionary, greedy, uncool person.

Alongside demonization was the power of fashion. The ability to bestow or withhold legitimacy is incredibly powerful, especially in Washington, Hollywood, and New York, where obtaining such a seal of approval is a matter of social life or death. As a snobbish movement of the "beautiful people" of high culture, good taste, and comfortable livelihood, the Third Left was like a caricature of those who historically opposed the left. For a movement seeking a mass base among the proletariat, such a contemptuous view would be suicidal. But for a movement shaped by an elite that already looked down on its own masses and deemed them hopeless as raw material for revolution, this concept made eminent sense.

The Third Left's method of suppressing dissent and persuading its constituencies that they had no choice but to support it against the raging reactionary hordes was superbly successful. The anti–Third Left view was presented as that of right-wing racist, sexist, homophobic, Islamophobic hicks clinging to guns and religion and waging war on women and others. In the 2012 election, millions of Americans were convinced that if Mitt Romney won he would end the possibility of having an abortion and suspend the civil rights of nonwhites.

Consider the simple case of the Tea Party movement. This grassroots citizen movement had clear and simple demands: smaller government, less government spending, lower taxes, and less government regulation. Yet this message was virtually never presented accurately by the Third Left–controlled institutions that determined pretty much everything large sectors of the population would know about the Tea Party. Instead, a massive demonization program largely succeeded on the basis of little or no evidence in portraying the Tea Party as the second coming of the Ku Klux Klan. Any debate over the actual issues or the opposition movement's real positions was shut off. This campaign was the exact equivalent of conservatives in past eras labeling their opposition as atheistic Communistic traitors. Thus, why should it have equal treatment by the Internal Revenue Service regarding tax-deductible charitable or educational groups, compared to properly thinking groups on the left?

Provoking hatred and anger against opposition figures and arguments went hand in hand with making people terrified of being identified with such evil forces. It would be unthinkable to listen to a monster's radio program or read their articles or listen with an open mind to their lists of facts. They must be ignored, just as, say, American Communists once dismissed information on Soviet purges and concentration camps as capitalist propaganda. Do you want to be considered a racist? Do you want to lose your friends and damage your career, and not be invited to Washington or Hollywood parties? Do you want to lose your credentials as a liberal, humanitarian, intellectual, cool person?

Every principle of modern advertising has been aimed at persuading people that buying a certain car or shampoo will deliver benefits. Often they were lying. But the Third Left actually could deliver on its promises to reward those who used its product or punish those who didn't.

None of this was accidental. The Third Left sought to jettison the principles of America's founders and historic liberals of open debate, fairness and balance, the honest search for truth and accuracy, and professional ethics. On orthodox Marxist grounds, the Third Left argued that such notions of liberty and objectivity were phony means of maintaining capitalist hegemony. Since schools, the mass media, and even courts were capitalism's class weapons, why shouldn't they be tools for anticapitalism?

In the spirit of the "postmodernist" philosophers, the Third Left claimed that since there was no such thing as truth and everyone was biased, there was nothing wrong with lying to serve the revolution. After all, these institutions had merely served as the tools of white male domination. Given these factors, a radical journalist could be proud to slant his article in the service of the cause; a professor pursued the greater good by twisting reality. Such people's highest calling was to indoctrinate others, a huge departure from liberal values.

A good look at the behind-the-scenes radical thinking that doesn't completely stay behind the scenes—it only seems so, given the mass media's refusal to cover such stories—was an April 2012 lecture justifying professors' indoctrination of students. The speaker to an audience of other teachers was H. Douglas Brown, professor emeritus in San Francisco State University's English department and longtime director of the university's American Language Institute.[46]

In his talk, entitled, "Teaching as a Subversive Activity—Revisited," Brown explained that radicals' goal of making the world a better place justified their teaching students that a radical standpoint was the only conceivable truth:

[O]ur motives are rooted in our desire to help people, to communicate across national, political, and religious boundaries and our desire to be "agents for change" in this world.[47]

Indeed, to bombard intensively their pupils with a single political message—in a course like English that had no actual connection with political issues—was a "moral imperative." Unless teachers did so they would be insignificant, failures. Only by being political activists in the classroom could they "be someone."

Does our zeal for realizing our own vision of a better world," Brown asked, "stand in the way of truly equal, balanced treatment of all issues?" By using straw men or at least blindness toward the opinions of others—a characteristic of the radical not liberal worldview—Brown said that no other viewpoint deserved to be treated equally. His examples of alternative standpoints:

justifying smoking, the Ku Klux Klan, racial prejudice, teaching American soldiers languages, and using English classes to preach Christianity.

None of these other views deserved fair treatment, he explained, including by implication the idea that the entire corpus, in its infinite variety of conservative and real liberal thought, was also illegitimate. Regarding conservatives, the influential distinguished professor explained: "Sometimes I think all of us wish that people didn't have so much freedom. I don't know how many of you listen to any syndicated morning talk shows lately, but there are some times when I wish that people didn't have that freedom. Ultimately because they disagree with me."

While presented as a joke, Brown admittedly conducted his work and ran his institute in that spirit. Radical professors unapologetically used the power of hiring, tenure, and grades to enforce their little dictatorships. As in a Communist country, obtaining and keeping a university job in the humanities or social sciences likely required meeting a political test. Some professors privately said they were "writing for their drawer," a phrase from dissident Soviet intellectuals who hid away their work hoping that a better day would make them publishable.

Alternative views in the classroom were not welcomed, whether expressed by other teachers or by students. If students objected, Brown said he responded: "We're trying to teach English, but we're trying to get you to think a little bit."

At any rate, he made clear that complaints had no effect on diminishing the classroom's use for political propaganda and recruiting. It says something about the state of American academia that the only audience member who challenged Brown's stance and defended the traditional view of the non-indoctrinating professor was an immigrant from India.

The reporter covering the lecture concluded, "This normalcy of radicalism [is what] makes it so alarming; people in the academic hothouse chat about the most disturbing ideas as if they were discussing the weather. The banality of subversion, as it were."[48]

Under normal conditions, such constructs would provoke laughter, yet with the same message blaring out of almost every loudspeaker, this method was quite effective. Remember that the most absurd lies can be told—even about public events, say a speech available in full text and on video via the Internet—and for those who accept the mass media version of what happened that lie will be completely accepted.

After all, the opposition, according to the Third Left, was defending a horror-show vision of America; they must be evil and had no right on their side. These claims were basically absurd. Were the paths to personal advancement closed, especially compared to the situation in any other country? Were corporations engaged in massive violations of the law by ruthlessly polluting the environment or viciously abusing workers, knowing the government lacked the power to punish them? Was there large-scale discrimination against Americans on the basis of race, religion, or national origin? Could only the rich start small businesses and build them up? Could only the rich become doctors or lawyers? Was home ownership restricted to the rich? Did the wealthy really pay at low tax rates?

Yet if children are taught such things in school, young people in the university, and adults from the media and politicians' demagoguery, how would more than half the population know differently? Remember, the alleged victim here was not just the proletariat or even the urban poor but the entire "middle class." The complaints and fiscal demands of everyone from welfare recipients to near millionaires supposedly could be remedied by beating up on the wealthiest 1 percent. How absurd, transparent, and yet nonetheless effective a trick this was. But it certainly wasn't normative liberalism.

For example, according to the Democratic Congressional Pro-

gressive Caucus, the Third Left's arm in the House of Representatives, and which includes about one-quarter of the Democrats
there, it is now necessary "[t]o protect the personal privacy of all
Americans from unbridled police powers and unchecked government intrusion"; "extend the Voting Rights Act"; "fight corporate
consolidation of the media and ensure opportunity for all voices to
be heard"; and "eliminate all forms of discrimination based upon
color, race, religion, gender, creed, disability, or sexual orientation."

This platform suggests that there is an incipient police state, a
right-wing monopoly on the media (rather than a left-wing one);
attempts to deny citizens the right to vote along racial lines (rather
than merely to eliminate fraud and illegal aliens from doing so by
the simplest precautions); and a tidal wave of racism.[49]

It is a horror-show America where trade unions have never
come into existence, much less command billions of dollars to
shape politics; where racism and sexism are still central features of
society; atheism and homosexuality are crimes; and where Republicans want to return to segregation or even slavery. It was a world
more akin to the late nineteenth and early twentieth than to the
early twenty-first century. And this is what students are taught in
many universities and increasingly in public schools.

This ideal has usually not been practiced, but that does not justify throwing it away, especially at the moment in American history
when it has come closest to fruition, just as it is disastrous to throw
away the ideals of fair news reporting and honest scholarship. Liberalism was based on the demand that this precept be fulfilled.

A lot of the transformation came out of the cultural interpretation that America was horrible, a change indicated by a wide variety of examples.

A clear expression of a mainstream Hollywood view was expressed by most openly and explicitly by Joss Whedon, a director
mainly known for *Buffy the Vampire Slayer* and *The Avengers*, at a
film fan convention.[50] Whedon stated:

I was raised on the Upper West Side of Manhattan in the 1970s, by the people who thought John Reed and the young socialists of the 1920s were some of the most idealistic people, and that socialism as a model was such a beautiful concept. And now of course it's become a buzzword for horns and a pitchfork.

Whedon did not mention that Reed's main political activity was as a founder of the American Communist Party, nor that while socialism might have been a "beautiful concept," the socialism advocated by Reed became a huge network of concentration camps, a totalitarian dictatorship, and an economic failure.

Whedon continued:

And we're watching capitalism destroy itself, right now. . . . I tend to want to champion the working class because they are getting destroyed. I write about helplessness—helplessness in the face of the giant corporations and the enormously rich people who are very often in power giving those people more power to get even more power.

We are turning into Czarist Russia. We are creating a nation of serfs. That leads to—oddly enough—revolution and socialism, which then leads to totalitarianism. Nobody wins.

It's really really really important that we find a system that honors both our need to achieve, and doesn't try to take things away from us, but at the same time honors everybody's need to have a start, to have a goal, to have a life, to have an income, to have a chance.

The fact is, these things have been taken away from us, sometimes very gradually, sometimes not so gradually, since the beginning of the Reagan era, and it's proved to be catastrophic for so much of America. . . . .What's happening right now in the political arena is that we have people who are trying to create structures or preserve structures that will help the working class and the middle class, and people who are calling them socialists.

The audience cheered. Obviously, not everyone associated with making films, plays, and television thought as Whedon did. Yet besides a tremendous political imbalance in the opinions of such people, which might have remained their own business, some of their cultural products were designed to make everyone think that way.

A key element in this process has been the Third Left's ability to make its positions fashionable. What Whedon said was eminently challengeable, yet no one at that meeting—or at thousands of other academic or social gatherings; newsrooms; or parties in Hollywood or Washington, D.C.—openly critiqued the favorite formulae of the "Progressive" liberals.

The Third Left's Cultural Revolution was also on display, though not so interpreted. Here are two examples of the transformation of worldview and values.

In 1962, the Hollywood film *The Manchurian Candidate* was released. American soldiers captured in the Korean War are brainwashed by evil Communists to assassinate an American leader and take over the country. In 2004, Hollywood remade the movie. Now, evil capitalistic warmongers brainwash American soldiers to take over the country. It was almost as if the Communists had brainwashed filmmakers to tout their old propaganda line. What is most shocking about this transformation is that nobody discussed these wider implications—they were so taken for granted that a 180-degree reversal of the original theme went unnoticed.

In 1951, Herman Wouk published his novel *The Caine Mutiny*, which won the Pulitzer Prize. In 1989, Aaron Sorkin, who would go on to write several Third Left–themed television series, saw his play *A Few Good Men* produced on Broadway. Both works were made into successful films. To understand how the West evolved in those years, consider the differences between these two versions of the same story.

Wouk's book is about the officers on a U.S. Navy minesweeper during World War II. The captain is unstable and one of the officers, Keefer, an intellectual with little military experience, ridicules him, persuading the others to join in. In the end, the captain cracks and the second in command takes over, but he is court-martialed as a result. The defense lawyer gets the mutineers off by showing the captain has serious mental problems.

But at the celebration party, the lawyer, Lieutenant Barney Greenwald, tears into his own clients. When they were having fun making money, playing football, and chasing women it was men like the captain who protected freedom. And if they had only supported him—as was their duty—everything would have been all right. Indeed, his clients were guilty:

> While I was studying law and old Keefer here was writing his play . . . and Willie here was on the playing fields of Princeton these . . . stuffy, stupid [people] in the Navy and the Army were manning guns. . . . Of course we figured in those days, only fools go into armed service. Bad pay, no millionaire future. . . . So when all hell broke loose and the Germans started running out of soap and figured, well it's time to come over and melt down old Mrs. Greenwald—who's gonna stop them?. . . . Who was keeping Mama out of the soap dish? Captain Queeg.[51]

The message of the book and film was that undermining honor and the democratic social order made things worse and that those who did so—despite the honor they received in intellectual circles—had nothing to be proud of. In an interview, Wouk explained his story as also an analogy for the relationship between people and God. The deity had not always done a good job lately, Wouk said, but this showed all the more the need for humans to act morally and energetically.

Now fast-forward almost forty years. Sorkin's play is about the marines at Guantanamo Bay, a location made retrospectively more significant by the fact that it later became the prison for radical Islamists trying to destroy Western democracy and to do the equivalent of the "soap dish" treatment for the Jews.

A marine is murdered by his comrades and the commanding colonel covers it up to protect the Corps' reputation. He is court-martialed and convicted, his career ruined. A friend of mine who was an actor in the play on Broadway—and had two brothers in the U.S. Navy—laughed out loud at Sorkin's ignorance about how the military actually worked.[52]

While drawn from Wouk's work, Sorkin's moral is the exact opposite: It is the colonel, Nathan Jessep, who is responsible for the killing by giving bad orders and hiding the truth. In the most famous speech, Jessep parallels Greenwald's outburst:

> You can't handle the truth! Son, we live in a world that has walls. And those walls have to be guarded by men with guns. Who's gonna do it? You? . . . And my existence, while grotesque and incomprehensible to you, saves lives. . . . You don't want the truth. Because deep down, in places you don't talk about at parties, you want me on that wall. You need me on that wall.[53]

But remember, Jessep was the villain and the speech comes across as one more example of using national security as an excuse for evil and antidemocratic behavior. Jessep was a stand-in for Richard Nixon, a defiler not a protector. Unlike in Wouk, it was not the mockers who should feel guilty but those who claimed to be protecting them from foreign threats. Wouk's respect for the military, the need for tough national security efforts, and even the readiness to use force came after World War II and from understanding the mistakes of appeasement that made conflict inevitable.

In Sorkin's revision of Wouk, it wasn't the failed Captain Queeg who was the hero but the iconoclastic writer who was trying to tear down the system, Keefer. Sorkin's was a post-Vietnam analysis coming from a left that viewed patriotism with the utmost suspicion, as the first, not last, refuge of scoundrels. Indeed, Keefer was the archetype for the kind of self-glamorized professor-teacher-cultural-figure who was a Third Left hero merely on the basis of his words, as opposed to the more proletarian-type Queeg, the man who did the tough job and received little reward or credit. It was the perfect embodiment of two worldviews.

Sorkin went on to become the highest-profile left-wing writer in television, working on *The West Wing* and other series, including the highly left-wing *The Newsroom*, and as a close supporter of Obama. "You can't handle the truth," wrote Sorkin, and neither—if it were going to succeed—could the Third Left let the American people find it out.

CHAPTER 7

Barack Obama as Case Study of a Third Left Cadre

Consider the kind of indoctrination a student, say one named Barack Obama, might have received at a typical university. This question was researched by a young man with no large staff or foundation grant who simply read the Occidental College campus newspaper for the period Obama studied at that Los Angeles school. A thousand full-time, well-paid journalists, hundreds of professors, and a dozen prominent, well-financed biographers writing books for major publishers might easily have discovered the same things. The fact that none bothered to do so makes the point rather effectively about the distortion of society's usual watchdog institutions.[1]

While Obama claimed the Occidental faculty was "diverse and inspiring," many of his professors were radical. The political science professor Larry Caldwell called Reagan's policy on the Cold War—which, of course, won the conflict—"myopic" and warned that the policy of confronting the Soviet Union was "bankrupt, devoid, and bound to fail."[2] Caldwell said: "The lesson that I learned from Vietnam was 'never again to have unmitigated loyalty to my country.'"[3]

There was also Lawrence Goldyn, a gay activist and political science professor under whom Obama studied. "[Goldyn] was a wonderful guy," Obama said in 2009. "He wasn't proselytizing all the time, but just his comfort in his own skin and the friendship we developed helped to educate me on a number of these issues." In fact, Goldyn, by his own admission, "talked about sexual politics in all of [his] courses."[4]

When Reagan was shot by a deranged loner in 1981, the Democratic Socialist Alliance held a colloquium in which three Occidental professors—Norman Cohen, Mike McAleenan, and Goldyn—spoke. Cohen blamed the shooting on the "capitalist system itself" and said he refused to stand for the national anthem. "To do so would be to support all of the American activities in El Salvador and other third world nations."

McAleenan blamed the shooting on the "so-called American dream" and our "never fail-always-succeed society." Goldyn assailed the "patriotic propaganda" designed to portray Reagan as an American hero, and seriously wondered, "If those who subscribe to the American Dream can be shot, then the lives of dissenters must be in even greater danger."

The political science and history departments, where Obama was studying, jointly presented a film on El Salvador, *Revolution or Death*, along with the Democratic Socialist Alliance. The film claimed the Revolutionary Democratic Front, a revolutionary Communist group, had as its goal "an end to terror . . . a redistribution of land, and true democracy."[5] Caroline Boss, Obama's friend and an Alliance leader, and several of Obama's professors were there. In a letter to the editor, still another friend of Obama's, Hasan Chandoo, his self-described "brother" and roommate, blamed America's desire to save the "capitalist order" for killings in El Salvador.

Obama was taught international affairs by Alan Egan, an Argentina-born Marxist who at teach-ins sponsored by the Democratic Socialist Alliance criticized American policy in Latin America.

Barack Obama's favorite professor was Roger Boesche, who spoke of Marxism's superiority to American democracy in an April 1981 lecture given while Obama was a student. According to the campus newspaper's report, Boesche said:

> Gradually [Marx showed] the vast majority will recognize their [own] power, recognize an "utterly umimbelishable [*sic*]" need to transform the world, and bring a more sophisticated form of democracy than Jefferson's world of shepherds and yeoman farmers could offer.
>
> [Marx's socialism] offers a democracy suited to the modern world of cities and technology, in which the producers or workers control the workplace, in which those who work reap the benefits. . . . I choose to value democracy in its broadest sense—democracy of the community and neighborhood, decentralization of centralized cities and states, democracy in unions and schools, and factories, and workers who control the enterprises in which they work.[6]

James Lare, an Occidental comparative politics professor and another teacher of Obama, extolled the virtues of 1970s Communist China, a country of maximum repression and minimum achievement in that time, and accepted all the claims made by the dictatorship there:

> The fact that the Communist regime, has, during its thirty years in power, virtually eliminated starvation from both city and countryside as well as reorganizing economic and political life in a way that has drastically reduced foreign exploitation, the most extreme forms of corruption, and

such social ills as prostitution, gambling, and petty theft, is itself a major achievement. Indeed, I view it as one of the masterpieces of social and political engineering of the twentieth century comparable in some ways to such technical achievements as the development of nuclear energy and the exploration of outer space.[7]

And these are only some incidents we know about; they don't include private discussions between Obama and these professors or other students. How much more influenced was he—or any student who went through college since the 1980s—subject to? And how few counterarguments did any student hear in the classroom or from speakers and conferences on the campus?

In his autobiographies and policies, Obama never showed disagreement on any major point with the ideas he was taught and developed through his campus experiences. The same point applies to tens of thousands of less-known people who also influenced society. Producing one indoctrinated student who became president of the United States was an unintended outcome; the mass production of such people to play a role in fundamentally transforming America was the conscious goal of an astonishingly high proportion of university professors.

Back in 1970, during the wave of New Left activism, Daniel Patrick Moynihan, a moderate liberal and Harvard professor who would later become a U.S. senator, wrote:

In the best universities the best men are increasingly appalled by the authoritarian tendencies of the left. The inadequacies of traditional liberalism are equally unmistakable, while, no less important, the credulity, even the vulgarity of the supposed intellectual and social elite of the country has led increasing numbers of men and women of no especial political persuasion to realize that something is wrong somewhere. These persons are [our] natural allies.[8]

But of course they lost. In the 1960s the campus rebels were students; in the next generation they were most of the faculty, at least in certain departments. And this professoriate had lost their liberal predecessors' idea that political indoctrination was something shameful that didn't belong in a university. Warning about the trend that was to produce such an outcome, Moynihan had explained in 1970:

America has developed . . . in Lionel Trilling's phrase, "an adversary culture." . . . The "culture" is more in opposition now than perhaps at any time in history. . . . As Richard Hofstadter recently observed, some really surprising event . . . is going to have to happen to change the minds of the present generation.[9]

The literary critic Trilling and the historian Hofstadter were both strongly liberal academics who didn't like what they were seeing. Things were to become far worse. It might have seemed that the "really surprising event" to bring a return to moderation might have been September 11, 2001, but that was widely reinterpreted within a narrative of American guilt that fit the Third Left's ideology. But it was not some specific event but largely the long, patient work of radicals burrowing into key institutions that ensured much of the following generation would be cloned by the New Left veterans.

In addition, this outcome arose from broader social-intellectual trends. As he did so often, Orwell nailed it:

. . . Western civilization has given the intellectual security without responsibility. . . . It has educated him in skepticism while anchoring him almost immovably in the privileged class. He has been in the position of a young man living on an allowance from father whom he hates. The result is a deep feeling of guilt and resentment, not combined with any genuine desire to escape.[10]

How could these intellectuals handle this stress? Orwell continued:

But some psychological escape, some form of self-justification there must be. . . . These creeds have the advantage that they aim at the impossible and therefore in effect demand very little. . . . The life of an English gentleman and the moral attitudes of a saint can be enjoyed simultaneously. . . .[11]

This describes why a radical opposition to its own society was this problem's solution. Many intellectuals, like other members of the elites, sought a set of ideas that simultaneously justified their privileges and let them play the role of noble rebels in a good cause, but cost them nothing.

The Weatherman group had demanded people become full-time, unemployed revolutionaries dealing out violence, suffering deprivation, and facing arrest every day. In contrast, the Third Left approach asked them merely to prosper in their careers, go about their daily affairs, have high living standards, and take no risk. On the contrary, holding and propagating radical views would benefit their careers, win them praise, and garner them the glittering prizes of the society they were bashing, all while being able to praise themselves for having deep moral and high political virtues. This combination proved irresistible.

This combination of guilt and redemption through a radical viewpoint was amply illustrated by the three key New Left principles that were taken up by the Third Left, Obama administration (often explicitly expressed by that president), and large parts of the academic world, mass media, and cultural and entertainment industries.

If Barack Obama had never been born, everything described up until now in this book would still be valid. Obama was not part of a conspiracy, but he was part of a movement, albeit a recipient rather than architect of its doctrines. With Obama, conspiracy theories aren't needed; what's required is just to examine his associations and doctrines in plain sight.

His thinking was largely developed in places where the traditional American system did not apply: in other countries, academia, and radical circles passionately opposed to the historic liberal-conservative political spectrum.

There is nothing surprising or extreme in this observation. After all, the Third Left's purpose was to create thousands of Obamas and seed them throughout the country's influential institutions and positions. Obama was shaped by the same influences—books, classes, professors, elite mass media—that formed so many others' thinking in the same direction. Obama is the product of this system just as medieval times shaped fervent Catholics and twentieth-century Europeans with intellectual pretensions might become Communists.

Moreover, Obama was far from the movement's centerpiece and certainly not its institutional leader. Nevertheless, he followed his own views, which were in accord with Third Left ideology, when possible, which meant, of course, that due to political considerations he did not go as fast or far as some of the radicals wished. But they were certainly on the same road.

Assume if you wish that Obama was not even a leftist. The problem is that he was deeply imbued with many of the movement's beliefs, assumptions, and proposed solutions. In other words, he like hundreds of thousands of others had been subjected to leftist indoctrination efforts in schools, universities, the media, groups, and even in the conversations of the people with whom he most often associated.

And even without him, the Third Left controlled a huge part of American civil society and still engaged in a long-term effort to transform America by changing consciousness and attitudes, setting permissible options in the national debate. What Obama did do, though, was to give the movement a great leap forward, to accomplish things that otherwise might have taken decades more.

With an adherent in the White House, along with the election of scores of supporters to Congress, the movement enjoyed a massive multiplier effect. It didn't even have to win backing from a majority of elected Democrats, because they would follow the lead of Obama and the dominating figures in the Senate and House of Representatives. Thus the left could restructure the party and use all of its assets, not least of which were its credibility and role as the national flagship for liberalism.

On top of that, as president Obama had the power to appoint thousands of officials, who, in turn, could hire additional thousands of permanent civil service employees using ideological criteria. These individuals and the agencies they controlled then produced new regulations that had the force of law though never having passed any vote in the Capitol. Of the greatest value, too, were the opportunists and careerists—the most numerous of persuasions—who jumped on their bandwagon to obtain rewards.

The only disadvantage was that the opportunity might have come too soon. What if the high profile of the Third Left and its program antagonized too many people, what if its failures—especially in dealing with the economic depression—discredited its nostrums? The victory of Obama and his colleagues in the 2012 election proved that this had not happened. While the margin might have been narrow it was sufficient.

Much of America really had been transformed, accepting the new framework, while demographic changes reinforced the new order. Moreover, there was no serious challenge to the Third Left's control over institutions. There was no liberal antiradical movement challenging its hegemony over defining liberalism. Even the Supreme Court and many lower courts endorsed most of their stances. The enemy had been successfully stigmatized as consisting mainly of "old white men," conservatives, and the wealthy. Except for control over the House of Representatives, the stage was clear for the Third Left to do pretty much what it wanted.

Of course, whatever worries the Third Left cadre might have, there could be no doubt that such a remarkable, once-in-a-century chance must be seized and fully exploited. After all, when the Bolsheviks seized power in Russia—I make the analogy only for illustrative purposes, not to suggest the situation is equivalent—they did not throw it away merely because Marx had said the revolution should occur in an advanced country.

Opportunity trumped ideology. And this was all the more true because everything worked out so well. A majority of the American people twice disregarded the evidence about Obama, often because they never heard it in the first place. Those responsible for conveying this information did not do so, because their partisanship and passion trumped professional ethics. Yet at any previous time in history, the case for Obama's radicalism would have been easily proven.

An example of this denial is an article by Ben Smith on David Maraniss's biography of Obama, *Barack Obama: The Story*. While Maraniss supported Obama, he was enough of a conscientious journalist to show that aspects of Obama's story were false. What was important, however, for those less scrupulous was to explain why such shortcomings should be ignored, indeed even turned from criticisms into proof of Obama's virtue.

One key contention was that bad people would use such flaws in immoral ways to do evil things. Or, in Smith's subtle presentation, "Obama's conservative critics [have] taken the self-portrait at face value, and sought to deepen it to portray him as a leftist and a foreigner."

The idea of misrepresenting facts lest enemies use them is an old theme in the Third Left arsenal. Yet that notion is antithetical to the liberal concept of a society that benefits from open discussion and the battle of ideas and its replacement by one based on tendentious behavior rationalized because it was in a good cause. By lying about things concerning Islam, one might battle Islamophobia; by whitewashing America's enemies, one might promote peace. And so on.

In trying to defuse the flaws that tell so much more from Obama's unintentional self-revelations, Smith admits: "His memoir evokes an angry, misspent youth; a deep and lifelong obsession with race; foreign and strongly Muslim heritage; and roots in the 20th Century's self-consciously leftist anti-colonial struggle." But in fact, Smith continues, Obama did not really have a "foreign and strongly Muslim heritage." Nor did he have "roots in the 20th Century's self-consciously leftist anti-colonial struggle."[12]

Yet how can one simply erase his foreign, Muslim father and stepfather; his being abroad during impressionable childhood years; and his largely living as a Muslim in Indonesia, not to mention Obama's own expressed self-image? Are we supposed to believe that all these things had no effect on the making of the man?

What reveals the underlying problem is the reference to Obama's "conservative critics," as if he could have no liberal critics or, most important, undergo honest journalistic and scholarly scrutiny. The analysis of Obama's worldview is defined as forbidden territory, unless one wanted to be a conservative, that is, one who opposes all good things. For in the Third Left lexicon, equal treatment—to analyze Obama as any other politician would be—constituted racism; to do one's proper job as a journalist or a scholar reflected partisanship. To paraphrase two wartime slogans, "Loose lips sink ships" and "Shut up! The enemy is listening."

Again, however, there is a legitimate question that should not be, though it has been, ejected from the public arena: What were the effects on Obama's worldview and policies from his having so many foreign, Muslim, and radical factors in his formation compared to anyone else who has ever been president?

Instead, we are told that since Obama exaggerated personal connections to anticolonial struggle and black suffering, such a background did not exist at all. But isn't the opposite true? Obviously, Obama suffered psychologically from how he perceived his personal racial situation even if he did not suffer materially. The experience as interpreted in his mind ruled Obama's development. And if he chose to alter facts in order to fit an ideological design— whites mistreated him, America mistreated the world—that is a guide to what he actually thought.

Note also that all his altering of facts was in a single direction. Obama did not fictionalize his life story to exaggerate the opportunities America gave him; the failures of the left-wing radicalism his father, mentors, and professors spouted; his fair treatment by so many whites; his enjoyment of privilege in attending the best schools; and so on.

Finally, Obama never took the opportunity to refute radical ideology, policies, or perceptions. He did not with any passion, detail, or consistency defend America from charges of "imperialism" and "racism," nor point out the shortcomings of Marxism, Third World radicalism, or American leftism.

This, then, was Obama's own self-image. His views have the strong ring of intellectual formation even when they do not reflect his material experiences. And his actions show that the views outweighed the experience. To portray himself as "an angry, misspent youth" holding militant view on race, a romantic (not religious) engagement with Islam, and a deep belief in a leftist worldview is not the kind of thing an ambitious young politician would do in order to further his career. And that's especially true for an ambitious young politician who claimed that America was racist and hostile to the Third World and to Islam.

Ironically, if America was at all as Obama claimed it to be then his statements would be suicidal for his success. Yet in the Third Left–dominated era, such a self-portrait would turn out to be a ticket to success. It embodied the antiliberal concept of "political correctness" in that the intent is more valid than the facts. An Obama friend told Maraniss: "Everything [in Obama's life] didn't revolve around race." But everything in his worldview does.

For Smith, though, Obama cannot be a radical if his experiences did not match the beliefs that he said resulted from such experiences:

> Maraniss finds that Obama's young life was basically conventional, his personal struggles prosaic and later exaggerated. He finds that race, central to Obama's later thought . . . wasn't a central factor in his Hawaii youth or the existential struggles of his young adulthood. And systematically ignoring what Obama wrote in his own memoir, he concludes that viewing Obama through the prism of race "can lead to a misinterpretation of the sense of 'outsiderness' Maraniss puts at the core of Obama's identity and ambition."[13]

Yet this is not only illogical but also irrelevant in political terms. The problem is what Obama thinks, and his experiences rested less on a foundation of personal experience with racism and imperialism than with the mentors, teachers, and books that taught him about such things.

After all, few contemporary American radicals lacked "conventional" childhoods or directly experienced imperialist crimes, capitalist oppression, and racist brutality. So much of their world-view, as with Obama, came from what they read and heard in classrooms, on how they learned to interpret the world. The indoctrination of universities and other institutions pointed them all in the same direction. And on top of that, Obama had additional inputs from being of partly African parentage, living in Indonesia, and receiving extracurricular indoctrination from Davis.

This distractingly exotic personal history only intensified a background, including a life of privilege, that was otherwise typical of the Western intellectual imbued with radical ideology. Their experience was reshaped to fit a template of ideas in which America was the world's most evil force, where people didn't have a fair chance or fair shot in love, though the radicals' own lives—Obama went to Hawaii's fanciest private school, for example—showed the exact opposite as they were showered with rewards, opportunities, and upward mobility.

In part, this separateness forced them to imagine how the masses felt and lived, imagining or exaggerating their bitterness and resentment at not sharing in such good fortune. It was also a way of expiating guilt for the privileges enjoyed and, to put it bluntly, for Western intellectuals to exalt themselves on the pretext of helping the downtrodden. The formula was there as early as the Leninist party, which offered intellectuals and resentful members of the elite (or at least those offered entry into that privileged group) a mechanism for ruling in their own right.

Of course, this does not mean there weren't those who suffered or injustices to be remedied. But it does respond to two political mysteries: why those who suffer least are at the forefront of complaining about their own society and why Western intellectuals have been more extremist than people who supposedly have far more motive to be so.

Generally speaking, Americans whose lives have really been marked by struggle and disappointment think quite differently.

They had learned that life itself, not America, was unfair; were proud about what they have achieved because they knew it was earned; and feared dependency as the first step toward a totally hopeless dead end. Such at least was America before being transformed by Third Left ideology. And that, too, was why left-wing and anti-American slogans were found on the bumpers of luxury cars, and patriotic and pro-capitalist ones on the backs of pickup trucks.

This did not mean Obama was consciously cynical. He obviously did consider himself essentially alien to an unjust America as it had always existed, and sympathetic to the forces challenging it at home and abroad. Obama's exaggeration of his foreignness and "Muslim heritage" was based both on reality and Third Left indoctrination, which taught him how to interpret his life even at the price of distorting it. The fictional triumph over adversity, the phony battle against a racist society made Obama a hero, first in his own mind and then to millions of others'.

Obama, like so many other contemporaries, grasped the fact that claiming to be a victim of America was a resume-enhancing move. For example, while Obama was not theologically attracted to Islam, his attitude made him feel that he should, to use a leftist term, "privilege" Muslims, like other Third World peoples, as another victim of America. A refusal to put the United States first in his admiration and loyalties was in the context of his time a sign of being a cosmopolitan, sophisticated person.

And Obama's radical reading of history taught him that he must show sympathy to Islam in order to prove that he—and America—were breaking with the country's imperialist, aggressive, and bigoted past. Unfortunately, in the early twenty-first century's political context this meant in practice not some harmless concept of everyone understanding each other better but rather a disastrous policy of empowering an anti-American revolutionary Islamism in various countries.

What is most significant was not that Obama exaggerated or fabricated things but the direction in which he did so. Suppose someone were to write truly in an autobiography: "My parents were very poor, my father was underpaid and fired from his job for no reason and I suffered a lot because I came from a blue-collar family and other kids made fun of me for my tattered clothes and funny accent."

If that sentence were true it tells us nothing about the person's inner life, since this background could have turned him in more than one direction as a result of these experiences. But if someone makes up a story it tells us precisely how he envisions himself, in Obama's case as someone trying to convince others that their society is unjust.

Maraniss said that Obama's goal in his autobiography was to make himself seem "blacker and more disaffected" than he actually was. Yet this is a very strange choice. Historically, politicians—liberal or conservative—sought to show themselves as exalting America, to show their ultimate affection for its institutions and society. In Obama's case, however, the deliberately chosen theme was one of alienation and complaint. These are motives to transform an unsatisfactory system systematically. In other words, he openly expressed a radical and hostile approach. To pretend Obama was a typical liberal required that his explicit self-image be ignored.

If America had heroically overcome racism—due in large part to the courage of the civil rights movement of the 1960s—then it was now generally okay. But if it was still steeped in racism, the United States needed fundamental transformation. After all, this was a man who could be elected president of the United States by a large majority and then complain he was a victim of bigotry because not everyone voted for him and some criticized him.

It is not at all difficult to see the foundation of Obama's radicalism. While Barack Hussein Obama II can certainly not be assumed to share his father's political views, it's important to note that the two men, as judged by the son's statements and policies, share a number of ideas in common. Since Barack II took his father as something of a role model, this is not surprising. And it is especially important to note that the son did not critique any of his father's key political concepts. On the contrary, and in sharp contrast to American liberalism, Obama the son promoted his own version of them.

In July 1965, Barack Obama I wrote an article in the *East Africa Journal* titled "Problems Facing Our Socialism." In it, the father endorsed African socialism as the best way to solve his country's problems. While rejecting old-style Marxism and Communism, the father could never define his own ideology except generally as statist socialism, a government-dominated and planned society. The father saw nothing good in capitalism and never considered a liberal, mixed economy, or free market approach for Kenya.

Barack Sr. defined African socialism as "[b]ased on communal ownership of major means of production and sharing of the fruits of the labors, so expended in production, to the benefit of all. . . ."[14] Every member of the community had an equal claim on all of the society's wealth, an idea he saw as equivalent to the Communist precept of from each according to his abilities, to each according to his needs.[15]

Such a view—that society has the prior claim on everyone's wealth—was quite different from American liberalism, which does, instead, assert the rights of those who earn and create wealth to the fruits of their labors. In the liberal view, government should take resources necessary to help the worst-off in society and fulfill its duties. Conservatives place more emphasis on personal charity and smaller government. But both liberals and conservatives reject the idea that the state, as representative of the community, is the proper owner of the national income and decides what to let earners keep or chooses to redistribute the wealth generally. Obama's and the Third Left's stance, however, was like that of Barack Sr.

Also interesting are Barack Sr.'s views on Kenya's racial situation. He wrote that a large portion of Kenya's wealth was owned by Asian and European citizens:

How then can we say that we are going to be indiscriminate in rectifying these imbalances? We have to give the African his place in his own country and we have to give him the economic power if he is going to develop. The government speaks of fear of retarding growth if nationalization or purchases of these enterprises are made for Africans. But for whom do we want to grow? Is it the African who owns the country? It is mainly in this country that one finds almost everything owned by the non-indigenous populace. The government must do something about this and soon.[16]

Although he spoke of "assimilating these groups so we can build one country," Barack Sr. also called them a "small minority of people and worst still on a racial basis, who have high incomes. . . ." And it is in this context he remarks, "Theoretically, there is nothing that can stop the government from taxing 100 percent of income" so long as that benefits the people. Basically, then, Obama Sr. was advocating the expropriation of Kenyan citizens on the basis of both wealth and race, with the black African being the rightful owner of the country and hence of its property and nonblacks being interlopers who essentially had no rights.

In a real sense, too, Obama and the Third Left would teach that, like Kenya, America was a settler-colonial state based on oppression and expropriation. As we shall see, Obama explicitly spoke of his home state of Hawaii in such terms. How could such a society be good or even acceptable? And how could its system be seen as anything but illegitimate and based on racism? As in Kenya, then, a fundamental redistribution of power and wealth was imperative. Whether that policy would add to the country's prosperity and stability was not an important consideration.

The kind of problem faced in Kenya has been a knotty one in history. In Europe, the concept of the Jews as the wealthy "small minority" led to long hostility, discrimination, and bloodshed. In Asia, the Chinese and Indian minorities faced similar things in various countries. In Kenya's neighbor, Uganda, such a full expropriation was carried out by Idi Amin, while in Zimbabwe the forcing out of white farmers and breakup of commercial farms led to economic disaster.

While Barack Sr. favored milder methods he still supported a racialist policy for Kenya based on redistribution of wealth and what might be called an affirmative action society. His son favored a systematic redistribution of wealth in America to redress parallel racial grievances. This approach was only necessary, of course, if one viewed racial discrimination as systematic and endemic, a problem that could not be solved by time, good actions, and the intelligence of the country's citizens.

And this was also what Obama was taught by his radical anti-American mentor, who met the impressionable youth when Obama was only ten years old. A journalist by trade but also a poet and pornographer, Frank Marshall Davis bragged that he had recommended fellow radicals for government jobs during the 1930s and 1940s; he would say any moderate black was "no good," but if he "was officially militant [meaning, a Communist Party member?] I would praise them the highest. I would say he is completely in favor of the Constitution. . . ."[17] One can speculate what Davis would have said if he had lived long enough to be asked to evaluate Obama's fitness for political office.

An interesting detail of Davis's career is his involvement in Communist attempts to take over other groups, notably the Hawaii NAACP or African American newspapers. He was an expert at forming front groups where radical leadership and ideology was

hidden behind some innocuous or humanitarian-sounding program but the party line was always in control. As such, Davis was
not only the perfect mentor for Obama but a forerunner for key
Third Left strategies of ensuring that newspapers and interest, racial, ethnic, and other groups were "represented" and their agendas defined by left-wing leaderships.

In his 1995 book, *Dreams from My Father,* Obama mislead-
ingly describes Davis, an obvious Communist Party activist, as a
"Black Power dashiki" type, leaving out his Marxism entirely. It fit
Obama's narrative for Davis to have only a racial agenda, and one
easy to make fun of as irrelevant to Obama's choices and concerns.
The truth, however, was quite different.

Clearly, Davis did have a tremendous influence on Obama.
Indeed, many of the arguments, issues, and proposed solutions
that Davis presented in his columns for newspapers in Chicago
and Honolulu reappeared in Obama's later political life. Obama
recorded, though he never really analyzed or rejected it, how Davis
inoculated him in the belief that only radicalism—not liberalism—
was the proper stance.

According to Obama, Davis warned him not to "start believing what they tell you about equal opportunity and the American
way and all that sh—." Saying that America was not fair and the
system had never worked was a major theme for Obama, as was
Davis's friendship toward foreign radical forces, and hostility toward mainstream Christianity and capitalism.[18] While Davis did
not make Obama into a Communist or black nationalist as such,
he certainly helped make Obama a radical on economic, foreign
policy, and racial issues. And if Obama did not think this way,
where were his counterarguments as to why Davis was wrong?

The same points applied to the relationship between Obama
and the Reverend Jeremiah Wright, who taught Obama precisely
the same things. Wright was a religious figure while Davis was an
atheist, and yet the two men's political thought was quite parallel.

Both men, too, had no reason not to conclude that Obama had absorbed their message. "Barack knows," Wright explained, "what it means to be a black man living in a country and a culture that is controlled by rich white people."[19]

If that racial-capitalist dictatorship was the problem, then obviously power must be wrested from this ruling class; a fundamental transformation was needed and the existing rules—which got the rich, white people into permanent power—were no good. America's self-image as a democracy, a land of opportunity, and a relatively open and egalitarian society was fraudulent. If things are in such a bad state, then clearly liberal reforms have been inadequate. More liberalism was not going to suffice.

A liberal would certainly admit that America has been racist and acted badly abroad during times in its history. But only a radical would claim that such evil, racism, and imperialism had been systematic and inescapable because the whole system was fundamentally flawed. Consider the people you know. All of them, you would presumably say, have made mistakes and even done things wrong. Such people you can still love, like, and try to help with gentle corrections. But how different it is to consider someone a person who does things wrong because of a permanent flaw, someone of whom you could say—as Obama did about his beloved grandmother—that the evil impulse has "been bred" into her and doesn't "go away"?[20]

What's important is that this statement revealed how Obama thinks. It only follows logically to view America as a country in need of some kind of total change, a revolutionary transformation. What was significant for Obama as he considered his grandmother was that essential evil was always there inside. Good intentions don't make them go away.

Obama spoke often of the influence Wright had on him, saying that he "[s]trengthened my faith, officiated my wedding, and baptized my children."[21] So precisely what kind of "faith" did Wright give to Obama, for surely in this case we cannot speak about some vague, banal, well-intentioned generalities about loving everyone that might characterize many Christian denominations?

Was it a faith in the fatherhood of God and the equality of all people in His sight? Of forgiveness and love for all groups? No, it was not the type of liberal Christianity so prevalent today—and common in African American churches—but rather a radical faith, a Christian version of the racialist Nation of Islam, from which Wright had himself come. Wright's preaching was a message of hate, division, and desire for revenge, merely a continuation of Davis's counsels, dressed up in a robe for Sunday preaching.

The defense Obama offered on Wright was remarkable and unintentionally revealing:

> I can no more disown him than I can my white grandmother—a woman who helped raise me, a woman who sacrificed again and again for me, a woman who loves me as much as she loves anything in this world, but a woman who once confessed her fear of black men who passed by her on the street, and who on more than one occasion has uttered racial or ethnic stereotypes that made me cringe.[22]

So Wright, a man who is radical, anti-American, and anti-Semitic and who openly confessed his hatred of whites and Jews, was still Obama's spiritual parent. Might not Obama have found a different one in all the African American churches in Chicago? If Obama did want to distance himself from Wright philosophically he could have done so while still showing respect. Instead, as usual, Obama was allowed to get away without being asked awkward questions or having to pay any political price. Yet precisely because Obama was treated so leniently he enjoyed more freedom to act as he wished. The fact that he decided not to separate himself from Wright's worldview in real terms—and didn't even see the need to fake outrage at "discovering" Wright's worldview—showed far more clearly what Obama thought than if he had been intimidated into making some hypocritical denunciation of his mentor.

In addition, the contrast was clear between his decision to denounce his grandmother and call her a racist—when she at worst muttered a remark to her African American grandson, whom she loved and cared for every day. Wright, in contrast, taught thousands of people to follow a racist position and incited them to hatred. Obama attributed to his grandmother things "that made me cringe" but did not feel that way regarding Wright. Obama could better have found thousands of other African American clerics to emulate and admire, people who expressed a liberal view that combined pride with a constructive approach.

Thus Wright emerges as someone more precious to him than the woman who raised him. By continuing his embrace of Wright, Obama might be considered a man of principles, but what are the principles? Obama never criticized any African American group or individual anywhere on such grounds. Obama endorsed the extremist, openly racist Nation of Islam by involvement in its Million Man March, and his administration would excuse the New Black Panther Party from investigation over interfering in the 2008 election voting.

Criticism of an African American government official, U.S. Attorney General Eric Holder, in his administration was said to be racist. Seeking to check voters' credentials to prevent fraud was racist. And Obama personally suggested that two legal cases—one involving a radical African American professor in Massachusetts and the shooting of a black teenager in Florida—were racist, without having evidence for what had happened.

Obama's and the movement's philosophy was the old radical theme that whites are inevitably racists but that nonwhites are either never racists or, if they have any prejudices, could be excused on the basis of their experience. Obama would apply this principle along myriad lines of policy, both international and domestic. He was not someone who sought really to bridge racial divides; despite all his subtlety at doing so, he saw himself as an instrument of racial *retribution*. Charging racism, as the Weathermen had seen, had become a weapon in the Third Left's political battles.

Wright's ideas were fundamentally opposed to the historic liberal view since he rejected integration, the treatment of people as individuals, and the belief that America could overcome racism. These concepts taken together and laundered so as to seem mainstream are called multiculturalism, the division of American society into permanent semi-separatist blocs with separate rights and privileges. It was an idea that Obama and the Third Left also promoted.

What is astonishing in the face of this evidence that Obama so openly aligned himself with radical, racialist, and anti-American forces or ideas is that he was so easily able to get away with it. Any politician in earlier years who had attended even one such Wright sermon—or the Caucasian equivalent thereof—would have had to dissociate himself publicly from the sentiments expressed or else face severe censure. But Obama was given immunity from such scrutiny, which also meant that he did not have to alter such views, because he was protected by Third Left–dominated institutions.

For years, Obama had uncritically praised Wright and that stance never altered. In 1995 Obama called him "a wonderful man."[23] And thirteen years later, on the verge of having to jump out of his pew, Obama could still insist, "I don't think my church is actually particularly controversial."[24]

Yet when Obama grudgingly divorced himself from Wright to the tiniest extent possible, the *Washington Post*, which had tried to avoid covering the story at all, gushed:

[Obama] used his address as a teachable moment, one in which he addressed the pain, anger and frustration of gen-

erations of blacks and whites head-on—and offered a vision of how those experiences could be surmounted, if not
forgotten. It was a compelling answer both to the challenge
presented by his pastor's comments and to the growing role
of race in the presidential campaign.[25]

After so many years of silence, Obama finally said that
Wright's views "[e]xpressed a profoundly distorted view of this
country—a view that sees white racism as endemic, and that el-
evates what is wrong with America above all that we know is right
with America."[26]

Yet this was precisely the message of Obama's own book, and
if Wright's view was so distorted, why didn't Obama make that
clear in his own writings or say a word about such views, rather
than wait until he was absolutely forced to do so by his political
interests? Why did he not take part in a debate to move the African
American community in the direction Obama claimed he wanted
it to go? Why did his policies and speeches, even as president, to
African American audiences reflect a watered-down version of
these same ideas?

There was something very revealing here in how Obama explained away Wright's extremism as that of a victim whose rage
was justifiable:

"For the men and women of Rev. Wright's generation, the
memories of humiliation and doubt and fear have not gone away;
nor has the anger and the bitterness of those years." He added,
"But the anger is real; it is powerful; and to simply wish it away,
to condemn it without understanding its roots, only serves to
widen the chasm of misunderstanding that exists between the
races."[27] The "roots," of course, were white oppression, and so a
discussion that began with Wright's racial hatreds, according to
Obama, should be advanced by explaining that they were basically justified.

In addition, however, Obama chose a radical, racialist minister whose dreams seemed to include violent revenge not only against Jews and whites generally but also against America itself. "Obama could have picked any church," a 2008 profile in *Rolling Stone* reminds us. "He picked Jeremiah Wright. Obama writes in his autobiography that on the day he chose this church, he felt the spirit of black memory and history moving through Wright, and 'felt for the first time how that spirit carried within it, nascent, incomplete, the possibility of moving beyond our narrow dreams.' "[28]

But what proportion of African American preachers spoke this way, even from Wright's generation? What would the Reverend Martin Luther King Jr. have said about Wright? And what would he have said about Obama's attempt to characterize a former member of the extremist Nation of Islam sect who continued to purvey that crackpot ideology in Christian form as being a typical member of his generation? Obama was making a radical choice—not reflecting some normative African American view—to regard Wright as the normative voice of black authenticity. He made similar radical choices on every other issue.

Thus the American people, with all good intentions, did not elect a generic African American politician but a left-wing African American who championed a view of America that had more in common with the white Third Left than with the overwhelming majority of black churches.[29] That's why, ironically, the white liberal elite found Obama so authentic, just as it found radical Islamists or semi-Marxist Third World radicals more authentic: because they corresponded to their expectations and the narrative of guilt and retribution. Their own ignorance also made them swallow and then perpetuate the idea of Wright as a typical representative of African Americans.

Obama wrote in *Dreams from my Father* about a sermon of Wright that impressed him so much that he named his other book after it: "The Audacity of Hope." It showed that he was indeed listening to Wright's sermon and also had accepted its themes, which were, despite their religious garb, identical to those of Marxism, Third World radicalism, and the Third Left's hybrid ideology:

> Everywhere are the ravages of famine, the drumbeat of war, a world groaning under strife and deprivation.
> It is this world, a world where cruise ships throw away more food in a day than most residents of Port-au-Prince see in a year, where white folks' greed runs a world in need . . . !
> And in that single note—hope!—I heard something else. . . . I imagined the stories of ordinary black people merging with the stories of David and Goliath, Moses and Pharaoh, the Christians in the lion's den, Ezekiel's field of dry bones. Those stories—of survival, and freedom, and hope—became our story, my story. . . .[30]

Hope of what? Hope of overthrowing that "white" ruling class and the system it had used to protect its power, "greedy" capitalism? Those connections to Biblical stories were certainly inspiring but they were no innovation of Wright's. There were many other black churches that made those links with the Bible without being radical and racialist.

In this case, the question was who was Goliath, who Pharaoh, and who the lions? And the answer to that both in Wright's theology and in Obama's ideology was capitalism, imperialism, the whites, and the American system. Of course, Obama was no "black militant." He could ridicule Davis as a "Black Power dashiki" type but he never dismissed Davis for being a Marxist.

Wright used far harsher rhetoric, but the underlying message was not so different. Wright openly said, "God Damn America."[31] Obama said, in effect, America has been damned by its sins of capitalism, racism, and imperialism, but I'm going to save it by changing it completely. And that's why Obama could never explicitly say where Wright was wrong. On the contrary, he stated:

> As imperfect as he may be, he has been like family to me. He contains within him the contradictions—the good and the bad—of the community that he has served diligently for so many years. I can no more disown him than I can disown the black community.[32]

Obama was not merely accepting or reflecting what the black community as a whole believed. Rather, he was accepting and joining forces with that community's most radical portion. Yet he could have easily denounced Wright without renouncing the black community. It would have been helpful to the black community to have done so and a real liberal should be the first person to renounce Wright as a misleader.

Obama's career was full of roads not taken that illustrate the true nature of his choices. If Obama had not held a radical interpretation of capitalism, America, and race he could have put a priority on being a role model for other young African Americans for how they could succeed through hard work and earned success. Instead, he became—as he sought—a role model of how they could blame and complain and mistrust an unjust system that victimized them. To a large degree, his solution was to offer better terms of dependency on government payoffs and special preferences.

In that persona, Obama might have been a frequent visitor to inner cities, fighting against youth gangs; urging young people to get a substantive education; pointing out the disastrous prevalence of one-parent families; battling against the plague of drugs; and always urging people to take responsibility for their own lives rather than blaming the system. He could have stressed how the door was now open, that institutions were bending over backward to be inclusive, and thus they could take advantage of these opportunities as he had done.

Instead, the first African American president squandered this opportunity. Let's illustrate Obama's own views about blaming whites and the system they ruled with an example of how he interpreted his own life. Obama claimed he didn't make the high school basketball team because the coach was coaching "white" basketball style. Several people interviewed said that Obama didn't make the first team simply because he wasn't good enough. Indeed, they suggested, he was barely adequate to play on the second team.

So here was Obama's message: not one of practicing hard and doing your best but an attribution of failure to deliberate discrimination. Here is the true meaning of Obama's presidential mantra of giving everyone else a "fair chance." If you didn't succeed it was because the system was fixed against you. Perhaps, one might suggest, tongue in cheek, what was needed was a government Fair Play in Basketball program that would have forced the high school, perhaps with a Justice Department lawsuit, to put Obama on the first team.

What better example of both Barack and Michelle Obama's tendency to see events in terms of class and racial conflict, of deliberate injustice, to which they responded with bitterness and resentment. If a high school basketball team cannot be run without endemic racism, what possible hope is there for America?

Consequently, it was no accident that Obama's presidency was marked not with the predicted racial conciliation—an expected "reward" Americans would receive for having elected an African American president—but by an upsurge of friction, black anger, and claims of a victimhood that must take a higher priority than any other factor.

This was the outcome not merely because of Obama's personality but also because of the radical interpretation's dominance. History has certainly known irrational and passionate politics in

America, but this new approach went much further in rationalizing how honest research must not be conducted, open debate allowed, nor common sense followed.

Naturally, such a mechanism was extremely destructive of democratic society and liberal values. To promote a fervent, even hysterical, reaction against criticism, debate, dissent, and the consideration of personalities and issues on their merits violated and broke down the professional ethics of academics, journalists, and experts who are supposed to seek the truth rather than impose a political line or ideology. Of course, the result was to inspire similar behavior on the other side, too, and the public debate descended into a permanent mud-slinging contest.

Yet why, after all, should Obama, if he was no different from, say, Bill Clinton or other liberal politicians, inspire such antagonism? There are two major responses. If Obama is just a normal liberal then the special horror at his policies and views might be attributable to his most outstanding characteristic, his skin color. But if he represents someone far more extreme than his predecessors and his policies are damaging to America, then the strong opposition and criticism then become quite comprehensible and even proper.

At the same time, this is why it is so important for the Third Left and the institutions it controls to discredit any implication that Obama is different in his political substance. Obama's radicalism, like the Third Left's existence or power, must be a forbidden topic. Both Obama and the wider movement simply cannot withstand fair scrutiny; both Obama and the movement have developed techniques to persuade or frighten people away from exploring these matters.

The Wright episode was so important precisely because it amply displayed how Obama managed his own life and formulated his ideas. A usual logical assumption is that when a man chooses a spiritual guide, praises him, renews his allegiance on a weekly basis over many years, and never voices a single criticism, he agrees with what he is hearing. Obama's outspoken respect for Wright, his echoing of the preacher's themes, and his visibly parallel—albeit milder and more subtle—worldview prove it.

Wright's statements amount to a consistent assessment of America and the world. In passion and explicit extremism, they contrast with those of Obama. But in substance there were no real contradictions at all.

First, Wright viewed America's past use of power as systematically selfish and immoral, a stance similar to the Third Left's view of U.S. foreign policy as imperialistic. When Wright said, in regard to the September 11 attacks, that "America's chickens are coming home to roost," he was portraying that event as just punishment for American alleged sins.[33] His argument that America is a terrorist country because of its past treatment of Native Americans, Africans, Grenada, Panama, Libya, Iraq, Japan, the Palestinians, and South Africans was also the same thing Third Left professors were teaching in countless classrooms.[34] What resulted was not a balanced perspective, including an honest recounting of mistakes and tragedies, but rather the insistence that there's something about America itself—capitalism and imperialism—that is immoral and inevitably produces such results. Wright's view basically fit with a president who believed America must repent by using apology as a major theme in its foreign policy, is undeserving of taking global leadership, and must court rather than confront anti-American radicals. Wright praised the Iranian and Venezuelan dictatorships. Obama did everything he could to engage sympathetically with the former and treated the latter better than he did Latin American rulers friendlier to the United States.

Yet on top of his relationships with Davis and Wright, Obama's radical roots went far deeper and broader. They were in plain sight but the mass media and other institutions supporting Obama tried to keep them out of sight. There was, for example, the fully documented revelation, by Stanley Kurtz, that Obama had actually joined a left-wing, anticapitalist party. Minutes of the New Party's Chicago chapter meeting of January 11, 1996, announced that Obama, then a state senate candidate, had spoken there, joined, and signed a pledge to support the party's goals once he gained office. The goals listed included a "peaceful revolution," socialism, and the redistribution of wealth. It viewed the existing Democratic Party as a tool of business. Other party documents confirm this story.[35]

Previously, Obama had participated in activities of the party front group, Progressive Chicago—note the name—and two of his leading handlers were active members of a party front whose task was to identify future candidates, presumably Obama being one of them. The party itself was controlled by ACORN, a radical group that Obama would support and helped get federal funding for, despite widespread accusations of corrupt and unethical practices.

Aside from ignoring these facts, there are three objections to using this material to understand that Obama was a radical, not a liberal, or, to put it another way, that he cooperated with the Third Left in reinterpreting what had been known as liberalism in a way that corresponded with historic left-wing antiliberal movements.

First was to claim the sources were tainted because they came from those critical of Obama. This was necessary, however, because the "nonpolitical" institutions didn't do their job. But the critiques are well documented. The reason one cannot cite historically prestigious mass media or academic scholarly sources on Obama's radicalism—and on the Third Left generally—is that they did not investigate these issues, and even if forced to do so blatantly put the priority on finding a way to clear Obama of any accusations. A key reason why they did not cover such issues is that they have been complicit in concealing them.

Second, many would argue that Obama has changed. But if that were true, he could easily have denounced these ideas and explained in detail what was wrong with them and how he held different ones. That did not happen. Obama did not abandon his earlier radicalism, as from either a preference for a pragmatic philosophy of getting things done more effectively or an opportunistic desire to advance his career by becoming more moderate. There is no evidence at any point, in contrast with others who broke with past leftism, that he ever changed course. Nor did he drastically alter his worldview or the policies he advocated.

Third, there's the claim that his policies in office were not so different from those of previous liberals. Obviously, Obama had to deal with real political considerations, including what might be accepted by Congress, would not create too much opposition among the general public, and, prior to November 2012, would not damage his reelection bid. Yet even given these factors, Obama's rhetoric and efforts (especially administrative regulations) pushed the envelope beyond what any other politician would have done. While his performance in office must be considered separately,[36] the continuing statements of Obama and those closest to him show no break with this radical history.

Michelle Obama also made clear that the usual spectrum of liberal reforms was insufficient and that America needed a revolution, albeit a peaceful, structural, rather than a violent one: "Barack knows," she said, "that we are going to have to make sacrifices; we are going to have to change our conversation; we're going to have to change our traditions, our history; we're going to have to move into a different place as a nation."[37] To "change traditions," "history," and move to "a different place" is not the rhetoric of someone who wishes to continue and slightly deepen the liberal tradition, but rather is about moving to a different track altogether.

This liberal-rejecting radicalism was also reflected in Obama's frequent remarks, after giving minimal lip service to some vague greatness in America's past, that America was unfair, unequal, and denied equal opportunity. He never made clear precisely what had gone wrong or when it had happened. The underlying tone was to suggest he merely wanted a return to a greatness that he subsequently never quite managed to locate in American history.

Typical of the way Obama repeatedly revealed his political philosophy was an October 2008 television interview explaining his worldview at length:

If you look at the victories and failures of the civil rights movement, and its litigation strategy in the court, I think where it succeeded was to vest formal rights in previously dispossessed peoples, so that I would now have the right to vote, I would now be able to sit at a lunch counter and order, and as long as I could pay for it, I'd be OK.

But the Supreme Court never ventured into the issues of redistribution of wealth and sort of more basic issues of political and economic justice in this society. And to that extent, as radical as I think people tried to characterize the Warren Court [referring to the Supreme Court during the years 1953 to 1969 under Chief Justice Earl Warren], it wasn't that radical. It didn't break free from the essential constraints that were placed by the founding fathers in the Constitution, as least as it's been interpreted, and [the] Warren Court interpreted in the same way that, generally, the Constitution is a charter of negative liberties, says what the states can't do to you, says what the federal government can't do to you, but it doesn't say what the federal government or the state government must do on your behalf. And that hasn't shifted.

One of the, I think, the tragedies of the civil rights movement, was because the civil rights movement became so court focused, I think that there was a tendency to lose track of the political and community organizing activities on the ground that are able to put together the actual coalitions of power through which you bring about redistributive change, and in some ways, we still suffer from that.[38]

What Obama said was that one hundred years of liberal changes in America—including the efforts of Teddy Roosevelt, Woodrow Wilson, Franklin Roosevelt, Harry Truman, Lyndon Johnson, and Bill Clinton—had accomplished very little of what he wanted to see. There was no redistributive change, no redefinition of what America is all about, no fair chance for not only the poor but even the middle class. Even the liberal Warren Court, widely regarded as a major paragon of change, was not "radical" enough for Obama, who openly positioned himself on the far left of the American political spectrum. If Obama was a liberal, why did he repeatedly denounce the greatest accomplishments of liberals as insufficient and call for a completely different approach?

Equally enlightening and disturbing was his conception of the Constitution as creating the wrong kind of government and society. To reject the Constitution's priority of individual liberty from government control showed that Obama opposed the fundamental basis of the U.S. system, something liberals had never done. Equally, having a government too weak to be authoritarian was not some mistake, oversight, or eighteenth-century anachronism.

As the founders recognized, and this was a principle on which liberals had agreed, any person or institution granted too much control or special privileges, given immunity from criticism, unelected authority, and the media's subservience, would inevitably abuse their power. Liberals and conservatives disagreed on how strong the government should be but they both recognized the importance of maintaining such limits. One who fails to grasp that point either understands nothing about the United States or is deliberately outside the historic liberal-conservative consensus on how the country should be organized and governed.

Thus Obama was proposing an entirely different approach to

governance. He openly admitted that point, making clear he was opposed not just to conservatism but also to the historic liberal position.[39]

A close analysis of the 2008 statement amply demonstrates this point. Obama was clearly reiterating a Marxist-style, far-leftist political philosophy quite consistent with his prior training and associations. The first paragraph described what a Marxist would call the granting of "bourgeois rights," of formal equality. This is all that one can expect from capitalist democracy. This was a framework liberals accepted as their first principle. Obama was quite correct in stating that from a Marxist-leftist standpoint the Constitution was a bourgeois democratic document.

But for the Marxist or far leftist the bourgeois state and society were merely a launching pad for the next step in human history. It was only by going beyond this point, through a radical transformation into a socialist (or managerial) state, that could there be an escape from the limits of that unjust bourgeois society. In the new order, wealth would be systematically redistributed; the power of the ruling class—which the Third Left would describe as the white male ruling class—would be broken. Only a fully restructured and powerful government could manage that new state, making sure that everything was done properly and ensuring there was no return to the past by counterrevolutionary action.

All previous liberal laws from Congress, liberal presidents, and liberal Supreme Court decisions had only reinforced or somewhat improved America's essential failure to transcend class, race, and gender oppression. As long as the government did not step in and force compliance with all aspects of this alternative program, America would be an unsatisfactory and unfair society. How could Obama possibly have made his antiliberal radicalism clearer?

The liberal president John F. Kennedy, making the usual limited assumption of government, put the relationship between citizen and state in historic, patriotic, and voluntary terms when he said in his 1961 inaugural address, "Ask not what your country should do for you. Ask what you can do for your country." In contrast, Obama's argument was of what the state "must do on your behalf" in a paternalistic sense and with expanding powers to reach into the lives of citizens.

Beyond the superficial rhetoric of assistance, this meant empowering the state's ability to order around individuals and reduce their ability to make decisions about their own lives. While Kennedy was affirming the founders' formula, Obama was saying that the balance of power must be changed. The critical underlying point here was that Obama, unlike every predecessor, reserved the right to edit and rewrite, to fundamentally transform, the American system. This was a radical and not a liberal stance.

There are hundreds of examples of Obama and his colleagues—and far more so his Third Left supporters outside government—revealing their true views. Here's an important symbolic case. Obama decided to misquote the Declaration of Independence on several occasions while making public speeches. We know this was not a mistake because he was reading the proper text from the teleprompter and persisted after the error was pointed out.

Obama left out the words in brackets: "We hold these truths to be self-evident, that all men are created equal, that each of us are endowed [by their Creator] with certain inalienable rights. . . ."

Despite Obama's alleged piety, unlike other presidents he virtually never attended church during his first term. As with all of Obama's actions there are two aspects in this behavior: He didn't choose to attend, and concerns about how the public might react did not change his mind. He was thus signaling that his was a "post-God" presidency. This point was reinforced at the 2012 Democratic National Convention, when, under public pressure, it was proposed to restore references to God in the Democratic platform. The idea was rejected by the majority and even booed. It was only put back in because the session's chair ignored the actual vote.

Belief in God, or pretending such belief, was in no way mandatory for being an American leader. Yet this was, even if maintained hypocritically, an important element in the country's structure. In public as in religious life, the fear of God was considered a bulwark against doing evil. Specifically, as in the Declaration of Independence, citizens' rights were presented as divinely bestowed and thus unalterable. They were neither the gift of government nor at the prerogative of government to take away or to create new ones at will. The Third Left did not accept this notion and neither did Obama.[40] Given his behavior and views, then, there is little evidence that Obama did belong to the liberal tradition, other than that he certainly didn't belong to the conservative one. Those are not, however, the only two choices, even though history has tended to make Americans believe that to be true in their own country.

How can anyone who has studied Marxism and the history of Marxist movements not recognize what Obama was actually saying? That doesn't mean that Obama was a Marxist; he wasn't just as his father was not. But it does mean that he was an heir and advocate of the contemporary leftist worldview that draws on Marxism and revises it. For Obama's father, the goal was to adapt it to Kenyan society; for Obama and the Third Left the goal is to fit it into twenty-first century American society.

All that is left is the ultimate argument: that the idea of the far left taking over liberalism and the Democratic Party, of an American president so outside the mainstream of the historic debate, is unthinkable, too unlikely, too frightening for many to contemplate. But was it really so unthinkable to accept that Obama's background—his youth outside the United States, the leftist influences in his life, the time spent in an ideologically charged academic cocoon, his immersion in a radical church—isolated him from normative American experience? It was no slander but simple truth that Obama was detached from the mainstream liberal-conservative spectrum. What clinched that conclusion were the things he said and did.

How did Obama find his home in a radical perspective, even without being an organic part of any organized movement? Given what is on the public record, despite its neglect, there is no need to posit any conspiracy theory. On one hand, he read the key texts, had a radical left father, mother, personal mentor (Davis), and spiritual mentor (Wright); by his own admission he spent his time in college consorting with radical students and professors whose ideas he has never disputed; he was a community organizer in the context of that being a sort of naturalized left-wing movement activist, and had been close to other radicals (Bill Ayers,[41] Bernardine Dohrn, Valerie Jarrett, a bit with the Harvard racialist, anti-Semitic professor Derrick Bell, and many more); and he had the most left-wing voting record of any senator in 2007.[42]

But that's only half the story. What countervailing intellectual influences did Obama have? He did not engage at all with a more traditional religion, even mainstream African American churches. He has never criticized any leftist movement or Third World leftist dictator. Nowhere in his autobiographies or personal reminiscences does Obama seem to have had a serious conversation with a conservative or mainstream liberal. At no time did he have to engage fully with their arguments, aside from the partisan caricatures he created.

It has been reasonably claimed that we know Obama is a Christian because he embraced that religion, albeit under Wright. But it has never been claimed that Obama embraced the democratic capitalist system by rejecting the radicalism and Marxism of his parents, mentors, professors, etc. He has never critiqued Marxism or Communism to say they didn't work or to discuss their crimes or to contrast his views to theirs.

Essay question for Obama: Communism failed; capitalism succeeded. Discuss.

At a minimum this shows he senses no difference, or no need to make such a distinction.

In any rational discussion the way these facts go together should be inescapable. But it is only escaped by ignoring or demonizing the documentation and the argument about where Obama stands. Again, this does not mean that Obama is a Marxist or a Communist. It does mean that he was a contemporary American leftist who in most ways that mattered had more in common with today's Bill Ayers than with Bill Clinton.

It is an ironic disproof of the sour vision of America held by the Third Left and both of the Obamas that the country was extraordinarily generous in its interpretation of Barack Obama. After all, the American people elected twice as president a man who was more potentially vulnerable to the hatreds of bigotry than any other presidential candidate in history. He was a person of mixed race, African American, born to a bigamous and thus illegal marriage. He was the son of a Muslim father and as a child had himself been registered as a Muslim in school. He was born not only to a foreigner but a leftist politician unfriendly to the United States. Obama associated with shady characters (Tony Rezko) and was involved in behavior of questionable morality (leaks and slander that seemed to dispose very neatly of his political opponents). Compared with the nonsensical birth certificate debate, all of the above were easily demonstrable points on the public record.

Yet nobody used these incredible potential handicaps against him, and if anyone had tried to do so the accuser would have been the one whose career quickly ended in disgrace. America not only rewarded Obama with a shower of privileges but bent over backward to give him the benefit of the doubt. Ironically, then, few things prove better than Obama's own life—his real life, not his semifictional version—that America does give people a fair chance, of how minimal the effect of racism has become, of how open and tolerant a society the United States is at present.

Ironically, America was so busy giving Obama a fair shot that it forgot to examine his political ideology and program.

Given that treatment and the course of his life, Obama might be expected to have emerged with profound gratitude to America. That might have happened if he had not already been committed to a different worldview. Such an Obama would have been a liberal patriot, defender of the American system while seeking reasonable ways to make it even better while also preserving it. His speeches would be inspiring odes to the benefits of education, hard work, pride in America's history, and love for the country. By the same token, Obama would be an enemy of totalitarianism abroad and radicalism at home, seeing through the pretenses of those who claimed to be for fairness, equality, and "positive liberties" through more government control.

Because of his ideas and ideology, however, this was not the Obama that America got. And institutions largely under the sway of Third Left ideology persuaded many Americans to accept the same ideas that Obama held while suppressing facts to the contrary about America or Obama.

In his memoir *Dreams from My Father*, Obama said this of his time at Occidental College:

> To avoid being mistaken for a sellout, I chose my friends carefully: the more politically active black students; the foreign students; the Chicanos; the Marxist professors[43] and structural feminists and punk-rock performance poets. . . . At night, in the dorms, we discussed neocolonialism, Franz [*sic*] Fanon, Eurocentrism, and patriarchy. When we ground out our cigarettes in the hallway carpet or set our stereos so loud that the walls began to shake, we were resisting bourgeois society's stifling constraints.[44]

The most significant aspect of this statement was not the existence of his youthful radicalism but the lack of any "second act," as in a renunciation of this orientation and an explanation as to why it was wrong. Since Obama never came close to such a reassessment, why should anyone believe that he ever rejected this view?

For someone who aspired to high political office, to assure the public of his moderation or mainstream liberalism would seem to be of the highest importance. Even if Obama would have been lying, he had every reason to claim that his views had changed. But he never did and the mainstream media and other institutions never pressed him to do so.

While not showing much continuing interest in punk poets, Obama still regards the other five groups with importance. Speaking of "politically active" black students, Obama was using a euphemism for radicals who viewed America as intrinsically racist. He records no contacts with those of milder views. Obama never had an experience or engaged with any person who might have given him the idea that the Weathermen were wrong, that African Americans were not restricted to being either militants or sellouts.

Regarding "foreign students," he was referencing an alienation from America that was reinforced by his interactions with other "outsiders," who, from what we know about his non-American friends in college, were unfriendly to the United States. They didn't see America as well intended but sometimes tragically mistaken; they saw it as imperialistic.

In his reference to feminists, the word *structural* was highly significant since it indicated not just women's rights activists but those who thought American society was innately and irretrievably sexist and thus required fundamental transformation. It was not just a matter of raising consciousness but of permanent judicial and governmental intervention to hold back the inevitable tide of patriarchal domination.

As for the Chicanos, again, Obama's implication is that these individuals were militants. Even as president, Obama continued his association with La Raza, the most radical of the Hispanic groups,

an organization that opposed all attempts to control or stop illegal immigration. They identified themselves as an internal Third
World presence in America, with separate interests at conflict with
the overall society.

And all these blocs of angry, alienated people hostile to the
existing American system—none of whom would have described
themselves as liberals—were tied together by the Marxist professors, the people teaching Obama how to think about America and
the world, recommending books for him to read, and serving as
role models for the proper attitudes one should have.

What Obama was testifying to in that passage is not merely
that he—like tens of thousands of other college students—was the
target for radical indoctrination, but that he fully accepted these
ideas. Indeed, Obama was more prepared to be fertile soil for their
ideological seeds than virtually any other student in American
universities. Unlike many of his naive classmates, after all, Obama
had already been shaped from a radical father, radical mother, and
radical mentor.

Thus Obama became a successful example of the program-
ming at the heart of the Third Left's campaign to seize and use the
idea- and attitude-shaping industries of education, entertainment,
and mass media to create a new, radical-oriented elite. And that is
another reason why Obama never essentially wavered from these
beliefs, not to mention the fact that he was isolated from contrary,
real-life experience by the shelter of law school, community organizing, and part-time university teaching, as well as a wife and
minister of similar views. And, as Stanley Kurtz shows in detail,
community organizing was not a profession—based on those who
were defining the job and training those who performed it, it was a
euphemism for being a full-time left-wing activist.[45]

What and who did Obama encounter that might have contradicted his ideology? What are the names of the liberals who could
have challenged his assertions by explaining to him how they be-

lieved in moderated capitalism, opposed radicalism, and exalted America as a great, free society where there was plenty of opportunity?

Where are the liberal equivalents of Davis, Wright, and all the rest on his long list of radical mentors? For that matter, where were the conservatives from whom he might learn at least how they saw things and who critiqued the notions that he took for granted? Not one such person can be named by Obama, and he didn't even feel the need to make a pretense about hearing both sides of the story.

What is impressive, then, is how much evidence there is for arguing that Obama held[46]—and holds—radical views and how little there is to the claim that he had liberal ones. For instance, in his autobiography, Obama made clear that he viewed America and other Western countries as imperialist not only in Kenya, Indonesia, and other places but also in his own Hawaii, which he said white settlers and big corporations had dominated and exploited.[47] When Obama said that Hawaii was part of Asia, in a November 2011 speech at an Asian summit, perhaps that statement was less of a slip than an indication of his view that the United States had stolen it.[48]

While one could justify some of Obama's analysis of Hawaiian history—as with all of the Third Left critique of America's past—his profound bitterness and one-sidedly hostile view of American society came through clearly. And the key to seeing this attitude was not just secondhand family tales he received about Kenya and the British from his father's family, or about Indonesia and the Dutch from his stepfather, but rather the ideas he himself formulated about Hawaii, his own "hometown," and the Americans.

In discussing Hawaii, Obama's reference to "ugly conquest . . . through aborted treaties and crippling disease brought by the missionaries" makes it sound like the American annexation of Hawaii was a war crime and an act of genocide rolled up into one. Indeed, the way it is written would make a reader conclude that the well-intentioned missionaries deliberately infected the Hawaiians the way that Reverend Wright claimed whites deliberately spread AIDS in the African American community.

Obama continued that American companies and "white settlers" seized the land and indentured workers from "sunup to sunset" while interning Japanese Americans during World War II. The mainland's "rigid caste system" had not spread there, because there were so few blacks "that the most ardent segregationist" could enjoy a vacation there.[49] The point here is not to engage in a detailed dispute on Hawaiian history but rather to note that Obama couldn't find a good thing to say about America, its history, or its system.

And he applied the same criteria to the mainland. Consequently, he clearly concluded that the United States was based on a racist, oppressive, imperialist capitalist system that had never worked and must be fundamentally transformed. This was precisely the stance, albeit cleaned up somewhat in terms of language and with sporadic patriotic camouflage thrown in, that he continued in the presidency.

Again, that doesn't mean a liberal or a conservative for that matter couldn't find lots of things in American history to criticize. But the difference is that they would also find a large or larger amount of positive behavior. The key concept for Obama and the Third Left was that these historical developments were not mistakes, accidents, or shortcomings but in fact the inevitable outcome of an unjust imperialist system. That was where the line was drawn between liberal and radical. And Obama was on the latter side of that boundary.

Obama notes the books he read and lectures he heard that taught him about neocolonialism, Frantz Fanon, and Eurocentrism, concepts that also fit into his Third World radical persona. Neocolonialism meant that even after European countries gave independence to their colonies, they continued to hold them in bondage.

The failure of most Third World countries to develop was not due to objective problems or to radical ideologies and policies pursued by dictatorial regimes, but to victimization by the West.

Fanon advocated militancy—not moderation and democracy—as the way to overcome that oppression. He even maintained that killing people from the imperialist countries was therapeutic for the colonialized oppressed. Obama does not say anything about disagreeing with him. Fanon's twenty-first-century embodiments could be found in people like Hugo Chavez, the late Venezuelan dictator, and—though their basic ideology was nominally quite different—the revolutionary Islamists. Eurocentrism argued that the West—including the United States—had too much power. Obama did not really critique this analysis of America, either, except to insist that the United States really did like Muslims.

Equally, the Third World radicals viewed Western development as being largely due to the exploitation of the Third World, rather than attributing it to capitalism's successful qualities. Thus, to apply Obama's phrase, they concluded that the Western system never really worked. Class struggle had merely become international, with the Western proletariat benefiting from its national and racial privilege. Obama did not critique this theory, either. The Third Left in fact agreed with it.

These ideas had basically reached the leftist canon from Lenin's writings but had gone through many permutations over the decades. It was developed and transformed by a variety of people, including Third World Marxists such as Fanon and others whose ideas were taught to Obama and hundreds of thousands of other American students by leftist professors from the 1960s onward. When the Venezuelan dictator Chavez handed President Obama a copy of Eduardo Galeano's book *Open Veins of Latin America*, a classic of this genre, he was sending this message.

One implication of this worldview was that the living standards of Americans, including workers, would have to decline in order for justice to prevail and a better world to be created. This was obviously not going to be a popular theme with the intended victims if it was made too explicit. It needed to be dressed up under slogans about saving the earth from environmental disaster and man-made global warming, among other things.

The Third Left's revised concept of imperialism portrayed the American working class as among the exploiters. Who, then, was the revolutionary vanguard? It was the Third World's struggling masses and, in the West, nonwhites, structural-feminist women, and gays, all of whose oppression allegedly inoculated them against the temptations of "white skin privilege," assimilation, consumerism, and patriotism.

The ideas Obama took in were in sharp contrast to liberal concepts of international affairs and economic development. He recorded no counterarguments by others or by himself on these points. These liberal views rejected the idea that after independence, Third World countries could not make progress because they were held back by continuing imperialist exploitation. Similarly, liberals emphasized that the keys to success had to come from within these countries through urbanization, education, democracy, and a relatively free economy.

In other words, liberals emphasized domestic changes while the radicals—like Obama—insisted the problem had been external. For liberals, the West could help; for radicals, the West was the problem. Thus Obama ultimately concluded that as authentic militants, revolutionary Islamists would make a breakthrough precisely because they were not American clients.

On an international level, injustice could be overcome and international benefit achieved only by a systematic weakening of American and Western power through empowering the Third World, supporting "legitimate" (radical rather than truly democratic and free-enterprise-oriented) regimes, and systematic wealth transfers. This, too, was quite different from the liberal concepts that had produced such success stories as Japan, South Korea, Singapore, and even China.

Instead, as Obama's father posited, since the Western model was unjust and alien, a different model was needed that might be statist socialism or even Islamism. The problem was that these radical approaches actually ensured stagnation for those Third World countries where they prevailed and brought on war, dictatorship, and suffering. Western radicals romanticized these failures as more "authentic," just, and egalitarian.

The thoroughness of the leftist, rather than liberal, worldview in the Obama family could also be seen in the expressions of Michelle Obama. Given the couple's radical rejection of America's history and structure, no wonder she could repeatedly say that only at age forty-four in 2008 "for the first time in my adult life I am proud of my country."[50] She saw America as "just downright mean" and "guided by fear."[51]

Those were not accidental phrases but reflections of the Obamas' view that nothing in previous American history deserves praise. And even now, she explained, things were getting better only because the American "people are hungry for change,"[52] that is, they wanted to implement the radical program and elect Barack Obama.

Michelle Obama's senior-year thesis at Princeton University expressed her fundamental alienation from the institution and from America, too:

I have found that at Princeton, no matter how liberal and open-minded some of my white professors and classmates try to be toward me, I sometimes feel like a visitor on campus; as if I really don't belong. Regardless of the circumstances under which I interact with whites at Princeton, it often seems as if, to them, I will always be black first and a student second.[53]

Think about that passage's meaning. First, she is saying that no white's behavior can be acceptable and that American society is closed, unfair, and racist. Even if whites honestly tried they could not overcome this problem. Liberalism is insufficient. She will remain profoundly alienated unless the post–civil rights, post-integration society would be completely revised to her specifications.

Second, though, she draws the wrong conclusion about her fellow classmates' behavior. Why do the liberal professors and students view her as "black first"? The answer is that this view reflects the radical conceptualization of race as the central category in American society. It rejects integration and pluralism, sets aside the views of Martin Luther King Jr. and the traditional—albeit only practiced in recent times—American ideal. After all, Michelle Obama says she feels "black first and a student second." So why should those who see that fact treat her as if she did belong? After all, she openly declared that she wants to be separate.

In contrast to the liberal integrationist approach, in which everyone should be treated as equal, the radicals' multiculturalism set off race as the focus of principal loyalty, as organic units each with its own interests. Even religious groupings (Muslims) and various nationalities of Third World national origins were reclassified as "racial." Instead of the equal treatment of individuals, this meant the corporate empowerment of such groups with special privileges and characteristics. Indeed, her husband's whole autobiography was built around that point. If those Princeton white liberals had read Barack's books, wouldn't they inevitably think the way Michelle recounts and complains about?

And isn't this also precisely what Davis had told the young Barack Obama—and Obama seemed to believe—that the university sought to keep blacks in their place? It sought to bribe them into "[l]eaving your race at the door. Leaving your people behind. . . . You're not going to college to get educated. You're going there to get trained."[54]

By the time Barack and Michelle arrived at a university, however, the people who thought like Davis had largely taken over. Now they would stress race consciousness and rebellion. The training that would go on in the university was not designed to tame militancy, as Davis complained, but to indoctrinate that militancy into the students as an official task of the institution!

So if someone like, say, Bill Ayers and tens of thousands of radical professors and teachers were doing the educating, along with thousands of radical journalists and other "intellectual workers" doing the opinion-forming, they would shape the "men who change circumstances." And one such man who went through that process was named Barack Obama.

Marxists called the process of trying to seize cultural-intellectual and other institutions "entryism." American Communists had used it extensively, especially at their high point in the 1930s and 1940s. Obama's mentor Davis was an expert at this tactic. But they were usually too clumsily obvious since the captured "front" organization exposed the hidden agenda and alienated non-Communist members by always precisely following the changing party line. The Communists also didn't have enough cadres to take over major institutions and faced strong, organized, and even united opposition from social democrats, liberals, and conservatives.

The goal of the whole process was to make white students feel guilty and inferior. They were to suppress their own tainted views of the world as wrong and instead to follow, as the Weathermen had demanded, black leadership wherever that led. In other words, those white liberal students had been shaped by the black militant movement, the New Left, and the Third Left. No doubt most of them later voted for Barack Obama.

They had accepted much of the basic thinking of Davis and Wright. They were not racist but highly sympathetic, believing that of course you should give your first loyalty to your black community; you have been and are being so oppressed that you should see yourself as at odds with American society. We assume that as a member of a separate group with a righteous grudge against American society you don't want to talk to us, given our white guilt as oppressors. We are afraid to interact with you because, on one hand, we might say or do something that would be deemed racist and, on the other hand, you are a separate group that naturally wants to hang out at the Third World student building.

The problems Michelle was describing, then, were merely the outcome of her side's victory. What she describes as victimhood was really the barely disguised fruit of having received special privileges. And it was the outcome of this process that Michelle was blaming as the foundation for her alienation and as her motive for taking a radical stance.

While it can be argued that Barack and Michelle were merely receiving the kind of special treatment as African Americans that had formerly been reserved for those who were rich and white, nevertheless a considerable sector of nonwhites were beneficiaries of an American attempt to make up for past racism. Didn't this disprove that America was innocent of current racism?

Nor did Michelle's special privileges end with the university. In 2002 she was given a job as executive director of community and external affairs at the University of Chicago Medical Center, the very type of high-prestige, high-pay, and productively useless—or even counterproductive—job so typical of the Third Left. By 2005, Barack made $162,000 as a senator and Michelle received $317,000 from the hospital, though her heavy involvement in the campaign made her later go to a part-time schedule. Still, this is the kind of situation that helps explain spiraling medical costs.[55]

The doubtful nature of her job was shown by the fact that the position was created for her and then eliminated after she left it.[56] In other words, Michelle was making seven times the average American salary for doing nothing. And as a U.S. senator, while his wife was still working at the hospital, Barack Obama tried to pay it back by requesting a $1 million government grant for building a new wing. This did not get through the U.S. Senate. The job then was simply tailored to do a favor for her husband so he would get the hospital taxpayer money.

The Obamas were not only swathed in special privilege but the agencies for providing those benefits was the state and interventionist laws. No wonder, then, that they believed in statism and differential treatment of racial groups. Still, that caste interest did not justify the antagonism and ingratitude to the system that gave them what they wanted.[57]

Whatever the case, how ironic it was for Michelle Obama to tell others that they couldn't achieve success because the American system didn't work. Barack Obama would purport that nobody "makes it on their own" without governmental help, because that's what happened to him and his wife. Yet all the time they were making such claims they were insisting on their own structural alienation from the American system. She wrote in her thesis:

> These experiences have made it apparent to me that the path I have chosen to follow by attending Princeton will likely lead to my further integration and/or assimilation into a White cultural and social structure that will only allow me to remain on the periphery of society; never becoming a full participant.[58]

This is the woman who cried discrimination and just a few years later became First Lady! Yet this had no effect on her conviction that the system would always be unfair to African Americans. This view did not come from life experience—which proved the opposite—but from ideology, just as Davis told the young Barack that the university will pull "on your chain and let you know that you may be a well-trained, well-paid n——, but you're a n—— just the same."[59]

In short, America needed to be fundamentally transformed. Nothing Obama said or did as president contradicted all of these principles. This radical worldview continued through the long series of Obama's associations. When he became president this stance was continued with such like-minded people as Valerie Jarrett, David Axelrod, and scores of other Obama appointees— though obviously not all of them—as well as policies. In the Justice Department, for example, every single new hire in the Civil Rights Division had a leftist background.[60]

If Obama had ever seen the radical approach's faults and failings, he would have to be able to refute them in detail and explain why there were better, liberal alternatives. Since he never took that route there is no reason or evidence to believe he no longer thought this way.

And the fact that Obama accepted this whole framework of thinking is the key to understanding why as president he treated America's friends as enemies and its enemies as friends. After all, the enemies—Iran, Syria, Chavez's regime, and others—were on the right side of history. Obama felt himself to be on the same side as well. It was not Obama's fault that some of the Third World radicals—notably in Tehran and Damascus, as well as the Palestinian leadership—refused to go along with his open-handed offer of friendship and cooperation.

If Obama was merely an opportunist or a careerist politician, with little ideology and only a concern to advance himself, then why did he not do the pragmatically advantageous thing and distance himself from these ideas and associations? Ultimately, we know Obama was a radical and not a liberal because he repeatedly told and showed us so. No matter how many times his supporters and apologists denied this point, Obama himself never did in any substantive way.

Obama needed to adjust to political reality to some degree in a way that the radical professors never had to do. Still, he never betrayed his principles. In his autobiography he wrote that he would not want to be "mistaken for a sellout." Faithfulness to his radical viewpoint was a major reason why his administration failed so disastrously, though its concealment let him succeed politically. If Obama had been a closet pragmatist or opportunist he would have been a better president. Instead he chose to remain an ideologue, propounding an antiliberal ideology that seemed self-evidently correct to so many who had also been trained by Third Left ideas, but that simply did not solve America's problems or really benefit most of its people.

It is clear Obama was a radical socialist, and if the biased media and academia had not protected him, there would have been a boatload of evidence to that effect. American institutions and democracy were betrayed.

CHAPTER 8

Obama at Osawatomie

We have seen Obama's ideological formation, which was parallel to millions of other people of his generation. But how was this expressed in argumentation and rhetoric, as well as implemented in the course of his policies?

Certainly, the Third Left was ambiguous in presenting its basic view of America. When more candid, the Third Left's cadre said that it had "never worked," that the system was fundamentally flawed, was designed and controlled by a tiny rich, racist, sexist, white male minority. Capitalism, unless systematically restructured, could not give the overwhelming majority, and especially minority groups, a fair chance.

In every way, Obama's approach contrasted with this traditional liberal approach. And nothing laid out his worldview as president more systematically than his December 2011 speech at Osawatomie, Kansas. A close analysis of this presentation should put to rest any notion that the dominant ideas of the day were those of traditional liberalism.

A recession that could have been dealt with far more easily

with traditional remedies was presented as a collapse of the middle class. The proposed remedies, however, greatly deepened the crisis because the proposals were based on an ideology that opposed capitalism, the due process of law, American exceptionalism, and U.S. international leadership.

To justify this position, especially in the context of historical liberalism, the Third Left hinted that at one time the United States was a great place, but then something went wrong. What that was and when it happened were deliberately left vague. Why were institutions functioning effectively until a certain moment at which they suddenly became ineffective? What had changed to require a completely different role for government and its subordination of the private sector to an unprecedented extent?

Obviously, the immediate problem was the economic downturn begun in George W. Bush's last year in office. Obama was helpless to fix this mess and seemed to make it worse. If Obama had the right answers, why was he so unable to cope with the economic crisis? Perhaps that had something to do with policy choices that put restructuring the American system as a higher priority than addressing the immediate effects of the depression.

Temporary recessions have been a feature of American life since the early nineteenth century and the country bounced back stronger in each case. If Obama was a normal liberal president, he simply needed to apply methods used by predecessors in such circumstances to get the economy going again. A pragmatic liberal politician like Bill Clinton would not have hesitated to pursue that kind of policy, if for no other reason than that he knew it would be necessary to succeed. Obama either did not understand this necessity or put ideology over both personal and national interest.

These steps would have included tax cuts; eased regulations; creating a business-friendly environment so people felt secure in investing, hiring, and starting small businesses; helping the existing energy industry expand; and so on. Under these circumstances, such a president could have secured concessions from Republicans for things he wanted. The result would have been relatively quick recovery, universal approval, and easy reelection.

Explicitly, Osawatomie was chosen for this key policy speech on the one hundredth anniversary of a major address given there by President Theodore Roosevelt. Obama wished to associate himself with Roosevelt's version of Progressivism, so sharply at odds with that word's usage in the Obama era. There was a big difference between Roosevelt's attempt to balance out a capitalism then characterized by near monopolies and virtually no government power and that of the Third Left, which sought to break a long-tamed capitalism altogether and give government a near monopoly on power.

Obama began his speech by laying out, in vague terms, the America he would like to see:

> Millions of Americans who work hard and play by the rules every day deserve a government and a financial system that do the same. It's time to apply the same rules from top to bottom. No bailouts, no handouts, and no cop-outs. An America built to last insists on responsibility from everybody.[1]

Had such a system existed before? Didn't government previously play by the rules and apply the same laws to all? Despite past discrimination, hadn't the American system reached such a situation as much as any government in history?

And wasn't it Obama himself who had violated every condition of his supposed ideal society? Nobody had created more "bailouts" than Obama himself; "handouts" went to crony capitalist enterprises while entitlements reached all-time highs. Never before, too, had unequal rules been so systematically and explicitly justified, whether for the creation of virtual social castes or in the exemptions to favored groups given in the Obamacare program. And never before had a philosophy of dependency replaced the traditional American emphasis on personal "responsibility."

So the first step in the Third Left's case was to accuse America of being guilty of political crimes that didn't really exist, then to propose remedies that actually embodied such characteristics. Bailouts, handouts, different rules, giveaways, and dependency, rather than "responsibility from everybody," were justified in the name of fairness, equality, compensation for past wrongs, and social justice.

This required a dramatic change in the American worldview and a serious distortion of history. Consider the question of bailouts. There were two alternatives, not involving massive government intervention and financing, that have been used throughout American history.

The law provided for bankruptcy to manage the inevitable problem that some businesses fail. When a company declared that it cannot cope with debts and losses, it asked a court to appoint an outside manager to set priorities, distribute resources, pay debts as much as possible, and implement a reorganization plan. The Third Left media and Obama administration misled people to think that "bankruptcy" meant the company would go out of business completely and every job would be lost.

Thus, after Mitt Romney wrote an op-ed in the *New York Times* suggesting automakers go through bankruptcy—suggesting ways to cushion the process—the Obama campaign and others made it sound like he uncaringly sought to destroy those companies altogether.[2] Yet in fact, even in the context of the Obama bailout, many plants were closed, jobs lost, and dealerships abandoned.

A second method for dealing with the problem was for venture capitalist companies like Mitt Romney's Bain Capital to spot enterprises they thought could be better managed, buy and restructure them, and then sell them for a profit if they succeeded. If they failed, bankruptcy or the selling off of assets, and thus preserving them, were still options.

If the reorganization worked out either through new management or bankruptcy, the company could return leaner and stronger. Jobs were saved if they could contribute to the company's productivity. And if they couldn't, "saving" them was illusory since more money would be thrown away and the jobs would be lost anyway.

Ironically, while the Obama administration made use of bailouts and the Third Left supported them, this procedure was made to seem like some ultimate capitalist strategy, an example of unfairness in that public assets were used to secure the private property of selected, already wealthy people. Yet the bailout strategy was a left-wing, not a capitalist, stratagem. Government officials chose the businesses to be saved, used taxpayer money to gain leverage over the companies for themselves, and often made the deal—as notably was done in the automakers' case—to benefit Third Left client trade unions.

To take a step back, one could then ask why the auto industry had so many problems. While this was due to certain long-term structural trends and wrong decisions by management, a key factor was the regulatory pressure of government on gas mileage, environmental, and safety standards. The companies also found it harder to compete with foreign manufacturers. In other words, much of the problem originated not in the functioning of capitalism but in the way that the system was being managed politically.

No company should be too big to fail. The founders of America and of American capitalism understood that it was better to let companies fail and to clear the ground for something better. How many brand names have gone out of existence? How many absorbed by competitors? None were ever bailed out yet their industries prospered. Workers found different jobs. Bailouts were thus not a failure of the American or capitalist system but of misplaced social engineering impulses.

Finally, when we speak of bailouts or handouts, the biggest, most consistent bailouts have been the subsidies to failing government enterprises: the postal service, Amtrak, institutions that have spent far more on payrolls and pensions and other benefits than they could ever take in. There were scores of programs and institutions that failed, drained money, but were never terminated. Perhaps they could be called too "well intentioned" to fail? These were the most destructive bailouts. They never end, but indeed continuously expand and return little or nothing in value.

The second leg in the Obama critique of how America functioned was the "same rules" mantra. But what rules are these? Why did the rules work up until a certain point and suddenly cease functioning? At one time, there were different rules based on race. That was called "segregation" and long ago declared illegal. There were also more unofficial but widely practiced rules that discriminated on the basis of gender. They were long since abolished. The principle of America's founding—though it was not always practiced—had at last been vindicated. Everyone operated under the same rules regardless of race, religion, gender, and other categories. Yet the very basis of the Third Left has been to oppose the principle that the same rules apply to everyone.

At times, rules were laid down with a specific end in mind, sometimes to favor special interests but often to promote the economy's successful functioning. For example, the law was deliberately written to distinguish between far higher income taxes for the wealthy combined with much lower capital gains taxes. People pay income taxes when money first comes into their possession, but when they invest that money—on which they have already paid income taxes—they pay a lower rate on the profits.

Is that unfairness? No, it has been carefully formulated—and it works—to encourage people to invest. It was based on the principle that profit was a good thing that helped create jobs and wealth. For those who view profit as a bad thing, as inevitably exploitative, this structure is unfair. Those people can be called anticapitalist. Unfortunately, if they continue to get their way they will wreck the American economy.

Obama and his supporters misstated this point for ideological reasons. Here is Obama at Osawatomie:

> That is the height of unfairness. . . . It's wrong that in the United States of America, a teacher or a nurse or a construction worker, maybe earns $50,000 a year, should pay a higher tax rate than somebody raking in $50 million. It's wrong for Warren Buffett's secretary to pay a higher tax rate than Warren Buffett.[3]

Obama applies ideology disguised as morality to economic issues. He speaks about "the right thing to do" or the "wrong thing to do" or as "fair" or "unfair." The proper question is the effect of a given choice, not his irrelevant judgment of what is the "right" amount for Warren Buffett or his secretary to pay.

Leaving aside that the basic numerical facts of this claim might be untrue—Warren Buffett's secretary was well paid and filed a joint return with a wealthy husband that put her in a higher bracket—such a policy was not wrong at all. The tax system's goal was not to be fair in some abstract sense—no doubt, the North Korean system is "fair" in a statistical sense—but to promote prosperity. At whatever rate Buffett is paying, he is still paying many times more than his secretary in terms of the total amount of money.

Was the broader argument true? The answer is no. In 2007, according to the Congressional Budget Office, the top 20 percent of income earners paid 70 percent of federal taxes.[4] Other studies show parallel figures: The rich paid a very high proportion of taxes.

Yet the goal of a tax system was also not an exercise in envy, resentment, or revenge. American society wanted Buffett to invest money and gave him an incentive to do so in order to create jobs and wealth. The problem with Buffett personally was not that he was paying the proper rate of capital gains tax, which amounts in total to a huge amount of money, but that he was paying lawyers massive piles of cash to avoid paying what he legally did owe.

This was a point Obama never mentioned, because he wanted to use Buffett as the example of an honest man who yearned to pay more taxes if only invited to do so by the federal government's raising rates on anyone who made above a certain amount of money.

Thus, not only was Obama ignoring the fact that he was comparing different rules—apples and oranges—and praising a man whom the Internal Revenue Service in effect was accusing of criminal behavior, but he, too, selectively applied rules. After all, Obama's crony capitalists at General Electric had an even worse tax record.

Like Buffett, another White House favorite who advocated increasing taxes on "the rich" while failing to pay his own taxes was the radical African American leader Al Sharpton. As of 2010 he personally owed $2.6 million in income tax and about $900,000 in state tax. His National Action Network, whose annual meeting was attended by more cabinet members than that of any other organization, owed over $880,000 in unpaid federal taxes. This kind of behavior was habitual with him. In 1993 he pled guilty to a tax crime to avoid indictment on two more serious charges. As for being a member of the much-disdained economic elite, Sharpton received $240,000 annually just from his own organization, not to mention his television show and other income.[5]

On the surface, the political views expressed by people as diverse as Buffett and Sharpton seemed to conflict with their interests. But that was in fact untrue. By taking the side of those advocating class warfare, they gained immunity from government pressure. They improved their image in the mass media, which tended to portray them as heroic. And they also pursued material interests by gaining government patronage, contracts, policies that subsidized their work, and the backing of the powerful Third Left institutions.

Facts, however, were irrelevant. The Third Left succeeded in selling the idea that the rich did not pay their fair share of taxes; it did so partly through endless and systematic media repetition but also, of course, because suspicion of the rich is a real, and in some ways healthy, American characteristic. Remember that historically, no matter how much this factor eroded over time, European societies were built on respect for tradition and authority. Americans were proud individualists who thought themselves as good as everyone else.

This had been a key to America's success: teaching people not to be passive but to work hard, innovate, believe in themselves, and compete with others. Unfortunately, the Third Left ideology undermines all of those virtues.

Yet what's more important was the highly manipulative nature of this argument about the rich not paying their fair share. Consider the following points:

The goal was to get people to hate the rich, including many small- and medium-business owners. Their total incomes made them a target of punitive tax and regulation actions that stripped them of potential investment capital that otherwise could be used to create jobs, and instead gave that investment capital to the government to pay crony capitalists, public employees, and institutions supporting an ideological movement. And the way for rich people to buy immunity from these attacks was to support the Third Left's programs through political contributions or support for specific proposals. The Third Left had learned something no previous leftist movement ever figured out: a systematic way to get rich people and capitalists to support its views and donate to its causes.

There is nothing particularly conservative about the above argument. The liberal view has been that a certain level of funding was needed for government activities and programs. Money could only be raised from an economy capable of producing the needed amount, since squeezing the economy too hard and draining too many resources would reduce the overall size of the pie. The goal should not be based on revenge or making people feeling good, or inciting class warfare. Deficits were often necessary for specific reasons—war-fighting, emergencies—but should be kept within bounds and reduced as soon as possible. And if there wasn't enough money to pay for everything, then spending must be reduced. Conservatives and liberals might well have disagreed on every detail but they were in the same ballpark on all of these basic principles. Radicals are outside this consensus.

The same point applies to another Third Left–Obama theme: that the American people "deserve" a system in which the government makes everyone play by the same rules. By constantly multiplying rules and regulations, an ever-bigger government makes it expensive and even impossible for well-meaning people to comply with them. Some are contradictory; others ambiguous. Business, the public, and localities must spend more time and effort on rule compliance instead of on wealth creation, and that weakens the economy.[6]

Over time, rules deal with tinier and tinier details to the point where they do no one any good. Regulatory agencies in effect make laws without reference to elected representatives. By piling on more and more rules, selective enforcement is inevitable, and in this complex regulatory environment the government can thus treat every firm differently, depending on whether its management is politically palatable (crony capitalism) or whether the administration wants to pick its enterprise or product as a winner or loser. Rather than arrogant companies doing as they please, they tremble at the harassment or persecution by government agencies.

Then there is the Obama administration's remarkable innovation of exemptions in which the government can arbitrarily permit some group or institution not to obey a law. Hundreds of such special privileges were given over provisions of Obamacare. This ability, of course, is perfect for blackmail or soliciting campaign contributions, since it is possible to buy government protection. The Internal Revenue Service and electronic surveillance of journalists in 2013 showed how discriminatory patronage worked in rewarding supporters and punishing critics. In a world populated by real people, rules will never be applied with absolute fairness; they tempt governments to use them as blackmail to gain support and campaign contributions.

Let's suppose that the owner of a chicken sandwich shop gives some of his money to favor groups supporting the definition of marriage being between a man and a woman—something hardly a hanging offense a few years earlier. It is one thing if gay activists want to complain or protest—their right under freedom of speech—but quite another if mayors of major cities discriminate by denying business permits to Chick-fil-A stores—a violation of freedom of speech.[7] And what if a store is disliked for being too successful and is banned by cities for that reason, as happened with Walmart, even though the same governments have been complaining about the lack of low-priced stores for poor people?[8]

So, yes, rules are always going to be applied unequally, especially by ideological politicians who assert they have a right to tell others how to live, allegedly for their own good.

This brings us to *handouts*. The implication of a handout is of money given to someone who doesn't deserve it. Yet Obama has fabricated nonexistent handouts, for example claiming that oil companies receive handouts repealed decades ago. What of handouts to "green energy" companies that end up being stolen and producing nothing of value? And aren't "entitlements" just a fancy way of assuming that someone has a right to a handout?

Then there are the ever-bigger salaries, pensions, and fringe benefits paid to bureaucrats who write the rules, hold endless meetings, produce endless memos, pen endless reports, and harass people with easily manipulated rules.

Finally, we end the litany with *cop-outs*. A cop-out is when a president or high official lies, does wrong, and escapes the consequences. Usually, cop-outs are limited in a democratic society by institutions meant as watchdogs, such as media, nongovernmental organizations, and academia. Yet no president in history has come anywhere near being permitted to engage in cop-outs as often as Obama, because Third Left–dominated institutions shield him from having such contradictions pointed out.

Aside from his complaints about America, at times Obama was quite capable of speaking about the glories of America in terms like that of any other president. Yet such praise was usually a setup to claiming how far America has fallen:

> My grandparents believed in an America where hard work paid off, and responsibility was rewarded, and anyone could make it if they tried—no matter who you were, no matter where you came from, no matter how you started out.
>
> And these values gave rise to the largest middle class and the strongest economy that the world has ever known. It was here in America that the most productive workers, the most innovative companies turned out the best products on Earth. And you know what? Every American shared in that pride and in that success—from those in the executive suites to those in middle management to those on the factory floor. So you could have some confidence that if you gave it your all, you'd take enough home to raise your family and send your kids to school and have your health care covered, put a little away for retirement.[9]

Note something interesting here. If any other president or even politician made such a statement, the response would be—

certainly from a Third Left cadre—that this is all a whitewash! What about racism and sexism? How dare you paint such an idealized portrait of America! Yet it is, of course, far more accurate than the one portrayed in the left's history books.

So what did happen? What is notable is how Obama highlights frivolous issues and leaves aside important ones that would undermine his analysis and policy prescriptions.

When did things go wrong and tyranny reign? Eisenhower's America was an era of prosperity and the beginning of the civil rights movement. That was followed by the Kennedy and Johnson administrations, progress toward racial equality and equality for women, a time so prosperous that Johnson dared try to storm heaven to wipe out poverty altogether. He failed miserably, maybe made things worse, but that showed how hard Americans tried to do right, not that America didn't work.

The system overreached in its hubris, not a sign of systemic failure but overreaching ambition. True, there was Vietnam and riots, but the middle class still flourished. Then environmentalism arose and was accepted with remarkable speed to clean up rivers and the air. Was that not glorious? Did not that prove the system worked? Capitalist greed did not prevent or even significantly slow down a dramatic turnaround.

There was Carter and malaise and Iran but again, no collapse of the middle class, no failure of the system. The Reagan years were again ones of prosperity, as it was morning in America again. The country also did well under Clinton. So, by 1990, all the good things Obama said about the earlier American system still applied, right? Women advanced and African Americans moved toward equality faster than anyone would ever have believed. What a great performance by a society, one that should have been a cause for pride and celebration.

America was still a big success.

When, then, was the crisis, where the need for fundamental

transformation? When was the great leap backward? When were the poor newly oppressed, minorities and females freshly aggrieved, or big corporations ravaging America like so many tyrannosaurs? No, it was still what Obama called "that American system that allows you to thrive."

There were, then, three possible causes of the contemporary malaise that Obama claimed to have crashed down and put America on the very brink of middle-class Götterdämmerung.

The first, which Obama and the Third Left and their captive institutions never admitted as the cause of the trouble, was a course toward more statism, regulation, taxation, and big government. Things had gotten out of balance; the allocation of more and more resources toward bureaucracy, unnecessary institutions, environmentalist handicaps, parasitical employees, and added costs made America less competitive, inhibited innovation, and undercut flexibility. In other words, the Third Left's prescription was the exact opposite of what was needed.

The second possibility was that the problems were a result of the Bush-Obama recession. What makes this unlikely is that such a dislocation could have been managed without fundamental transformation. What made this issue go on for more years was Obama's failure to deal with the recession—he pursued even more problems that tied capitalism's hands, poured money down rat holes, instituted bad tax policies, and sabotaged energy production. Such were the problem's cause.

Finally, there was the point that things had been going pretty well—that the system was rotten and that only fundamental transformation could save America. For example, coal and oil must be abandoned, to be replaced by "green energy." Whole industries must be closed down, with massive employment losses, because they are not environmentally satisfactory.

This was, of course, the Third Left's real agenda, that the Weatherman program had been right four decades earlier: America was horrible, evil, and should be shut down. In this case, as Obama's top advisor Rahm Emanuel had said, the "good crisis" of the economic recession should not be allowed to "go to waste" but should be used as an excuse for changing a highly successful, free society into one far less so.[10]

That might be called Obama's 1912 option. It is a century ago. Lenin is agitating in Russia, red flags are flying, robber barons are growling, brave unionists are fighting the bosses, and Socialism is the only way out. It is the golden age of leftism. Middle classes of the world unite! You have nothing to lose but your chains. You have a world to win!

Of course, it isn't exactly like that, but it is. Capitalism is a failure, and fundamental transformation of the world is needed. It isn't just a chance to stop starvation but an opportunity to build utopia. Nothing has changed except you are there.

It is the fantasy America, that of the 1877–1912 or so period of primitive capitalist accumulation. Segregation and the rollback of Reconstruction; women without the vote; reactionary conservatives; no or only pitifully weak unions; monopolies that did what they pleased; hardly any regulation; a middle class outraged at corporations and greed and fearful of falling into the pit of poverty.

This, of course, has nothing to do with a century later. And even that laissez-faire era was laying the foundation for American success and prosperity, which, due both to its own development and to the successes of liberal reform, became even better. But can people be fooled into thinking differently by charisma, fearmongering, censorship, indoctrination, manipulation, demonization, and pitting one group against another? Perhaps.

And all this is supposedly necessary not because there is still child labor and sharecroppers living in tar shacks but because Obama has mishandled a recession that could have been solved years ago. And that's the great excuse for redoing all of American society and destroying free enterprise, turning the negative liberty

of individual liberty into the positive liberty of government patri-
archalism? Apparently so.

So here is Obama's case.

Today, we're still home to the world's most productive workers. We're still home to the world's most innovative companies. But for most Americans, the basic bargain that made
this country great has eroded. Long before the recession hit,
hard work stopped paying off for too many people. Fewer
and fewer of the folks who contributed to the success of
our economy actually benefited from that success. Those at
the very top grew wealthier from their incomes and their
investments—wealthier than ever before. But everybody
else struggled with costs that were growing and paychecks
that weren't—and too many families found themselves rack-
ing up more and more debt just to keep up.

Now, for many years, credit cards and home equity loans
papered over this harsh reality. But in 2008, the house of
cards collapsed. We all know the story by now: Mortgages
sold to people who couldn't afford them, or even sometimes
understand them. Banks and investors allowed to keep
packaging the risk and selling it off. Huge bets—and huge
bonuses—made with other people's money on the line. Regulators who were supposed to warn us about the dangers of
all this, but looked the other way or didn't have the authority to look at all.

It was wrong. It combined the breathtaking greed of a
few with irresponsibility all across the system. And it plunged
our economy and the world into a crisis from which we're
still fighting to recover. It claimed the jobs and the homes
and the basic security of millions of people—innocent,
hardworking Americans who had met their responsibilities
but were still left holding the bag.[11]

So that's the great failure of a century of governmental controls, safeguards, and American capitalism? The central exhibit in Obama's case—the housing market's collapse—was in fact mainly caused not by banks' preferred practices but by political and legal pressure, mainly by Democrats in Congress, including Obama himself, to lend money to people who couldn't pay it back. This was an artificial policy pressed by the Third Left against all proper capitalist practice on the grounds that not to do so was racist. Yet, according to Obama at Osawatomie, these were "[t]he same policies that stacked the deck against middle-class Americans for way too many years."

Yet this was simply untrue. Rather, the Third Left and its allies caused a crisis and then used it as alleged proof that capitalism was failing. Obama's argument that there is a profound structural crisis was without merit.

This was truly bizarre. Under the basic rules of capitalism that America has used for so many decades, the deck was stacked against the middle class? How? And was that system one of pure anarchy and no rules? Or can rules only be imposed by total government control? Obama presents us with an unrecognizable America, one that has nothing to do with what actually existed. As if no massive federal bureaucracy was in place: the Interstate Commerce Commission, the Securities and Exchange Commission, the Federal Communications Commission, the Federal Aviation Administration, the National Labor Relations Board, the Environmental Protection Agency, the Federal Reserve Board, the Food and Drug Administration, and on and on and on, as the red tape reaches up and into and through the clouds. This is a situation in which those who opposed Obama wanted people to "fend for themselves," while the affluent sought to "play by their own rules"?

What Obama tried to do was to compare the 2012 crisis with that of 1912—which Teddy Roosevelt sought to cope with in his

Osawatomie speech. It was as if all of that intervening history had never happened:

> Now, for this, Roosevelt was called a radical. He was called a socialist [*laughter*], even a communist. But today, we are a richer nation and a stronger democracy because of what he fought for . . . an eight-hour work day and a minimum wage for women—insurance for the unemployed and for the elderly, and those with disabilities; political reform and a progressive income tax.

Yes, it is true that some called Roosevelt a radical. But it was also true that the majority of conservative Republicans voted for him, which is why the conservative, Republican candidate, William Howard Taft, finished in a distant third place in the 1912 election. And every radical, Socialist, and Communist viewed Roosevelt as a reactionary rich guy trying to save capitalism, in the same way that Obama portrayed his own rival in the 2012 election, Mitt Romney.

Moreover, all of those reforms were adopted and changed America into a place where there had been some real anarchy to a highly rule-regulated society. Over the coming decades the rules were added to steadily. Hundreds of thousands of pages of laws were passed by Congress; hundreds of thousands of pages of regulations were arbitrarily created by government employees without legislation. Obama never mentions any of this.

Both the problems Teddy Roosevelt faced and the solutions he implemented were the precise opposite of Obama's. Roosevelt's formula, and that of the victorious third candidate, Woodrow Wilson, in 1912, was minimal governmental intervention to preserve fair play among the teams. Obama's solution is to have the referees take over the game and order around the players and coaches, call the plays, and change the rules at will.

Roosevelt had to break up monopolies; Obama created, in effect, new advantaged monopolies by picking winners (coal bad, green energy good). Roosevelt wanted to set minimal rules so the system could continue; Obama to set straitjacket rules to fundamentally transform the game. Roosevelt fought to continue high productivity in the context of an eight-hour workday; Obama to provide money for unproductive employment and for no employment at all.

The specific problem Obama highlighted was the flight of companies. And companies were fleeing due to government regulations and union power. Faced with these restrictions auto companies couldn't compete. Traditional incandescent lights were made illegal. Coal mines were made harder to run; coal-fired power plants were made impossible to build and many closed, lowering overall electricity-generating production; oil drilling was barred on almost all public property; drilling rigs went abroad where they could work, create jobs, and create wealth.

Pressure was applied to stop the new technology of fracturing. Energy companies saw research money drained into unworkable green energy schemes (run by an open Marxist, no less) that lined the pockets of big presidential contributors. More and more resources were demanded for government budgets, including billions to provide services to illegal immigrants.

The question Obama and the Third Left must answer, and never have, is how the government could make it more attractive to do business in America. Their answer was to propose ways to make it less attractive to do business in America. Rather than get out of the way, they proposed more regulation and restrictions, more "fairness" and doing "right" that made no sense in economic terms.

It sounds good, for example, to speak of rules that everyone must obey equally, but that was a fiction. Here is an example. Al Almendariz was a left-wing environmental activist whose career consisted of academic work and getting grants. He hated energy companies. In this background and opinions he was typical of many Obama administration officials and Third Left cadre in all areas of expertise.

He was forced to resign as chief of EPA's Region VI after some of his remarks at a closed EPA meeting came to light about how he would enforce regulations—not laws, mind you—trying to limit the use of hydraulic fracturing in oil and gas extraction, one of the most important new technologies for producing domestic, lower-cost energy:

> It is kind of like how the Romans used to conquer villages in the Mediterranean—they'd go into a little Turkish town somewhere and they'd find the first five guys they saw and they'd crucify them. Then that little town was really easy to manage for the next few years.
>
> And so, you make examples out of people who are, in this case, not complying with the law. You find people who are not complying with the law and you hit them as hard as you can and you make examples out of them. There's a deterrent effect there.[12]

Yet in the cases Almendariz conducted, he always lost. The companies had not broken any laws and it was far from clear that their techniques did any damage at all. This is what companies could expect at the mercy of the regime that promised to impose the same rules on everyone. And this is precisely why America's founders distrusted and wanted to limit the power of government.

Under Almendariz's control, America's energy production, and hence, its economy, would be crippled. He got caught; others didn't. And there were thousands of Almendarizes everywhere, not only in government but among lawyers and "experts" ready to harass companies to block the very technology that promised to set off a massive wealth-creating, independence-enhancing, job-creating energy boom in America.[13]

If businesspeople were demonized, if small business were handicapped, if there were threats of even more restrictions, and if calls for transferring wealth abounded, why should they keep their funds and take their risks in America? The easily available statistics on tax payments were constantly misrepresented to make villains out of those who backed innovations, took risks, and created jobs.

WHO PAYS INCOME TAXES AND HOW MUCH?		
Tax Year 2009		
Percentiles Ranked by AGI	AGI Threshold on Percentiles	Percentage of Federal Personal Income Tax Paid
Top 1%	$343,927	36.73
Top 5%	$154,643	58.66
Top 10%	$112,124	70.47
Top 25%	$66,193	87.30
Top 50%	$32,396	97.75
Bottom 50%	<$32,396	2.25
Note: AGI is Adjusted Gross Income Source: Internal Revenue Service		

The wealthiest do pay their fair share of income taxes. The lowest one-half of income-earners pay almost nothing. It was understandable that those less able to pay also do pay less. But the fact that they do so creates a problem. They no longer have a vested interest in how high taxes, debts, and deficits grow. On the contrary, the more money pours out of the Treasury in welfare, entitlements, and other payments, the more they profit. In other words, a virtual majority actually benefits from a badly run economy. And that is one of the reasons why elected officials do run the economy badly.

Yet there is also another factor of tremendous importance. And that is the issue of where investment in the economy comes from. In the view of liberals and conservatives, the bulk of investment in the economy should come from private and individual sources. For the radical left, investment should come from government. And that is the central plank in its platform.

Historically, liberals and conservatives favored the idea that everyone should have individual equality of opportunity, though the results would differ. Contemporary radicals, whatever they pretended to be, direct liberalism and the American system in a drastically different direction, departing from the historic liberal-conservative spectrum to become something else entirely:

The state, as representative of society, would give special advantages over others to certain groups defined by race, religion, and gender. If equality of result was not achieved, the state identified this as discriminatory and took measures to remedy the problem. For example, if too many whites did better on the examination for some kind of civil service position the test could be altered to make it "fair."

The state would determine proper behavior of people to a previously undreamed-of extent, the food and drink they consumed; their ability to engage in any enterprise; their consumer choices; and any other aspect of life in which it chose to intervene.

Rather than a limited state having to prove a serious social need to expand its power, the burden of proof was put on those who would limit the state's power. Instead of property being held by citizens, and the state having the right to interfere only due to extraordinary circumstances, the state could interfere if it decided that would improve "the common good."

The claim to superior wisdom will always find rationalization and it will always prove self-interested and in large part wrong, ultimately inferior to the individual decisions of a free people. There could be no more obvious lesson to be drawn from the American experience of successful growth, improvement, reform, and relative prosperity.

Obama simply did not comprehend why Americans were suspicious of government. Yet that suspicion was rooted in many years and examples of bureaucratic surfeit. He sneered:

> We have to admit, it's one that speaks to our rugged individualism and our healthy skepticism of too much government. That's in America's DNA. And that theory fits well on a bumper sticker. [*Laughter*] But here's the problem: It doesn't work. It has never worked. It didn't work when it was tried in the decade before the Great Depression. It's not what led to the incredible postwar booms of the 1950s and 1960s. And it didn't work when we tried it during the last decade. I mean, understand, it's not as if we haven't tried this theory.

Yet, of course, it had worked and worked more effectively after adjustments. The fact that Obama did not comprehend the basis of American success was very disturbing. In fact, it was the opposite system, the one Obama advocated, that had never worked. Look at every failed state, at the suffering Third World, at the oppressed and repressed, and "skepticism of too much government" was not some bumper sticker slogan to snicker at. It is the very essence of political wisdom. There was a time, not so long ago, when every liberal understood that, too.

But, Obama said in a speech at Pueblo, Colorado, on August 9, 2012, "I believe in this American industry, and now the American auto industry has come roaring back and General Motors is number one again. So now I want to do the same thing with manufacturing jobs not just in the auto industry, but in every industry."[14]

Actually this was inaccurate. General Motors was only briefly number one because its main Japanese competitor was temporarily damaged by a storm. Aside from this point, however, Obama preferred an economy in which the government would control investments, subsidies, and the direction or distribution of research and development. General Motors was now the ideal; the bailout the baptism of this brave new world in which the state would direct the means of production.

Notice that while Obama believed in workers and industry, he did not believe in the corporations or the industrialists. Without such people, there would not be the "one percent" or "inequality." And so had come the moment the radical left had been awaiting since its origin, a moment that could not have seemed further away when the handful of a handful of Weatherman crackpots put forward their manifesto and in their magazine called, by ironic coincidence, *Osawatomie*, after the massacre carried out by the abolitionist John Brown in that Kansas town 150 years earlier.

Now there is no limit to what might be said from the lips of a president of the United States regarding class struggle:

> Inequality also distorts our democracy. It gives an outsized voice to the few who can afford high-priced lobbyists and unlimited campaign contributions, and it runs the risk of selling out our democracy to the highest bidder. It leaves everyone else rightly suspicious that the system in Washington is rigged against them, that our elected representatives aren't looking out for the interests of most Americans.

This rang most ironic at a time when the far left, now cast in the old conservative role, had created a new form of inequality in terms far different than those existing in 1912. The privileged lobbyists were there, all right, but they came from unions; entitlement collectors; radical activists from privileged factions of minority groups; ideological cadre from nongovernmental organization front groups; and crony capitalists, to all of whom democracy was sold out to the highest bidder, in terms of votes as well as donations that often came originally from the taxpayers being looted.

Equally remarkable was Obama's unself-consciously ironic discussion of education as a central part of his program for reviving what he presents as a failing American system. Everyone understands that education plays an important role in letting countries compete in an increasingly more sophisticated, knowledge-based international economy. Obama, however, explained that the U.S. economy could not without government direction compete in the new technical and innovation-based economy.

The problem, he said, was that education must be in a real sense nationalized and that this required more teachers and lower university tuition rates. Yet, as in other areas, his answer was that more government intervention was needed. But on the contrary the draining of investment capital out of the private sector sabotaged innovation, while growing regulation makes it far harder for entrepreneurs to be more driven or daring. It is precisely those things "that have always been our strengths" that were being squandered.

And in a rapidly changing environment, the slow pace and delayed flexibility of government would make the situation worse, as indeed had happened for decades. The growing indoctrination and other changes in education wrought by Ayers, Klonsky, and other Third Left educational theorists had presided over poorer content and more administratively top-heavy systems. For example, the powerful teachers' unions made it impossible to get rid of the worst among them.

At times, Obama's ideas seem like satire, more appropriate for the Kenya of his father's day than for twenty-first-century America. Who should not be shocked at this statement:

In today's innovation economy, we also need a world-class commitment to science and research, the next generation of high-tech manufacturing. Our factories and our workers shouldn't be idle. We should be giving people the chance to get new skills and training at community colleges so they can learn how to make wind turbines and semiconductors and high-powered batteries.

And so this is the image of America's brave new competitive economy: kids sitting on community college classes learning how to make wind turbines while America's coal, oil, and natural gas production is sabotaged by regulations and while China is so far advanced and unfettered that no serious competition is likely.

Yet even more startling was a vision of America in which everyone was sitting around waiting for the government to take the lead on developing science, high-tech, getting factories going, and training people. Couldn't the needed individuals and institutions figure this out for themselves? Hadn't that always happened before?

The bottom line: Either the American economic system or the American governmental system was the problem. What was needed was either some form of reasonably regulated capitalism— and it already existed—or some form of state-directed noncapitalism that might be called state-managed capitalism or socialism.

Another difficulty was that Third Left ideology put economic efficiency behind a politics-in-command standpoint as well as a view that prosperity itself was immoral. Consequently, it must take a backseat to "fairness, "equal rules," preferable treatment for certain groups, a high burden of entitlements, and a whole long list of other items that taken together made a prosperous economy impossible.

After all, such an economy must be conducted within the binds of tight government regulation and a tax system to make sure someone doesn't make "excessive" income to the extent that risk becomes not worth taking and entrepreneurship becomes not worth doing. The question becomes what is preferable: an auto business going bankrupt by producing electric cars that no one wants or more popular, practical vehicles? To have massive amounts of relatively low-cost coal and other fossil fuels obtained by fracturing, or far smaller amounts of high-cost, inefficient green fuels?

No government or leadership in history, liberal or conservative, Democratic or Republican, would have conceivably answered any of these questions in the same way as did the Third Left elite. Nor was this merely a matter of ignorance. The interest groups that made up the first truly broad-based left-wing coalition in history benefited from what historically and pragmatically was viewed as an economic, political, and social disaster.

It is vital to understand that the Third Left ideologically does not believe capitalism can function outside the laws of the jungle or that the market cannot manage itself. Here is Obama explaining the requirement for still another consumer protection institution to come into existence:

> Every day we go without a consumer watchdog is another day when a student, or a senior citizen, or a member of our Armed Forces—because they are very vulnerable to some of this stuff—could be tricked into a loan that they can't afford—something that happens all the time. And the fact is that financial institutions have plenty of lobbyists looking out for their interests. Consumers deserve to have someone whose job it is to look out for them. And I intend to make sure they do.

And how many tens of millions were not tricked into loans because they exercised reasonable judgment, or in some cases had a devious purpose for obtaining a loan they should not have received? For Obama, a capitalist was little better than a criminal who has not yet been caught, except, ironically, crony capitalists, who often more closely meet those criteria than others.

Most important of all, the Third Left has devised a new economic theory that solves the problem of justifying statism in a way never done before and quite contrary to Marxism. Many people believe that this view is normative liberalism. It can be called the Social Theory of Value.

Marx and Marxists advocated the labor theory of value, which claimed workers created all wealth by the work of their hands and the sweat of their brows, and thus it pretty much all belonged to them. In reality, capitalists had earned nothing and there was no need for them.

The lazy, the shirker, the lumpenproletariat had no more claim to that wealth than did the capitalist. The material goods of this world were earned. And only if everyone was made into a proletarian or an agricultural worker would they have a right to their "fair share." In Lenin's phrase, he who does not work does not eat, and the word "work" was defined narrowly.

This approach, however, was obsolete because it was so clearly untrue. In modern capitalism, methods of organization, innovation, and technology have clearly been the main factor increasing overall wealth. Scientists, engineers, and other highly educated, well-paid, skilled professions play a huge role while assembly-line workers are proportionally far less important than a century ago. The high-technology revolution is a prime example of this reality.

But this has nothing to do with the Third Left approach based on the Social Theory of Value. Merely being alive, and hence part of the society, gave everyone an equal- or near-equal right to wealth, an approach much closer to the utopian socialism that Marx condemned. The first politician to advocate the Social Theory of Value was Elizabeth Warren, a Harvard Law School professor, former chair of the Congressional Oversight Panel, and special advisor for the U.S. Consumer Financial Protection Bureau. Note the words *oversight* and *protection* in those job titles. The government, as the people's representative, would supervise and manage.

And yet this view does make some sense to the Third Left coalition. If your wealth comes from government or institutions that generally don't directly produce wealth (such as universities, the contemporary mass media, or nonprofit groups) and much of whose wealth comes from government, then government to you does seem to be the source of all wealth. Consequently, to tax and spend works in building a successful economy.

As for the invest-risk-work-profit system, the new Third Left elite had no experience of such things. Their high incomes appear as if by magic, just as milk appears on supermarket shelves or cars appear in showrooms. Since this system is magical, you can place any burden on it—say, increasingly restrictive environmental standards, higher pay, higher taxes, endless paperwork—and things will still work just fine.

And of all extremist concepts, this Social Theory of Value was quickly taken up by Obama. In sum, if you are a success, if you have property you are the beneficiary of society.

Yet that does not mean, as it would to a seventeenth- or eighteenth-century philosopher, the community of all human beings, but rather the organization of that community as embodied in the state. The emphasis is not on family or religion, charity or acts of loving kindness, but on the doings of government. To Obama, for the wealthy to "give something back" means to pay more taxes—so he can put the money to his own wiser uses—and not the tax-deductible charity deduction to make their own selections. And if it means anything the Social Theory of Value maintains that the state has first claim on all property.

All of this talk is related to the fact that these are clear state contributions to the economy. Yet the way the Third Left applies them is misleading. Every society in world history, back to the pharaohs, has produced public works' projects. The hidden factor here is that Warren is providing an alternative vision based on the Third Left antiprosperity coalition. For her conclusion does reflect her personal experience and that of her colleagues.

There is nobody in this country who got rich on his own. Nobody. You built a factory out there—good for you.

But I want to be clear. You moved your goods to market on the roads the rest of us paid for. You hired workers the rest of us paid to educate. You were safe in your factory because of police forces and fire forces that the rest of us paid for. You didn't have to worry that marauding bands would and seize everything at your factory. . . .

Now look. You built a factory and it turned into something terrific or a great idea—God bless! Keep a big hunk of it! But part of the underlying social contract is that you take a hunk of that and pay forward for the next kid that comes along![15]

Despite the blandness of some of these formulations, this was shocking, and it was one of the few concepts that Obama directly plagiarized.

No American leader has ever so thoroughly detached virtue from success:

If you've been successful, you didn't get there on your own. . . . I'm always struck by people who think, well, it must be because I was just so smart. There are a lot of smart people out there. It must be because I worked harder than everybody else. Let me tell you something—there are a whole bunch of hardworking people out there.

This approach is inconceivable in the framework of normative liberalism or Marxism. A Marxist would say that no one got rich on his own because of the workers created value; the liberal that all profitably employed people did so.

Under conservatism the owner exercises control and decision-making power with a lower degree of regulation; under liberalism the level of regulation is higher. In Marxism, the workers supposedly take over the factory. In the first three cases, the goal is to make money. Wealth must be created to pay for everything. As for the Third Left, the government takes over the factory in practice because of a very high degree of managerial power, regulation, and taxation. Profit and increasing the store of wealth is no longer relevant. All the matters is the proper form of regulation. But the Third Left does not agree, despite the real exchange of earned wealth, because the process of creating or earning has nothing to do with the idea of sharing. The Social Theory of Value is purely passive. No one had to do anything to earn it but merely to be a citizen, thus all citizens have the same claim, and all citizens are represented by the state.

The autoworker has no more claim on the auto factory than does anyone else. And even if the auto factory loses money—and thus the capitalist does, too—the autoworker is entitled to the same amount. No one loses a right to a relatively equal share even if they don't pay taxes and thus don't even contribute to the store of funds that the government passes out. Wealth will come from the "rich" or from somewhere. The economy simply must work. It is understandable that this approach maintains a depression, with high taxation, low employment, reduced investment, and the massive printing of money and debt.

Warren's own career proved why the Social Theory of Value was so appealing and how the new Third Left elite was formulated. A large part of her success was based on her pretending to be a Cherokee Indian, an ethnic identity that helped her obtain a law professorship at Harvard and other benefits.

There are many ramifications to this scam. First, her claimed heritage was not only untrue; she was never asked to offer any documentation. Second, even if her claim had been true, the possession of about 1/32nd Cherokee genes had not exactly made her heir to massive suffering and dislocation due to events of more than 150 years earlier. Third, why should there be discrimination at all on behalf of such extraneous factors? If there was a better candidate for the job based on merit, that person should have received it.

And finally, Warren was blatantly unapologetic. She seemed to believe she merited special treatment not only based on the alleged historical suffering of people she had never met or knew; she seemed to believe that she merited special treatment even if the whole thing was a lie. Harvard was equally unrepentant. It showed no shame for hiring someone mainly or especially because of "racial" preference (despite the sad story of such things in U.S. history) but saw no need to act when the whole thing was exposed as a fraud.

Merit, then, became irrelevant, as did integrity and willingness to repent—three things one might expect to find most of all in a law professor. Warren was entitled to big honors and a big salary by the nature of her social category. Then she used that platform based on special privilege and the promise of that to others to be elected to the U.S. Senate. How could one conceive of a better embodiment of Third Left ideology and the rewards for holding it?

Yet, again, the Social Theory of Value does make sense for the "new ruling class" and those who benefit from its policies on which the Third Left has mobilized as a base. These people are indeed dependent on government. They did not get rich "on their own" or take any risks or have responsibility for creating wealth, meeting a payroll, or complying with thousands of pages of regulations. On the contrary, they received money directly or indirectly from government or—irony of ironies—worked for tax-free institutions. Already wealthy Harvard, for example, gets the benefit of public police, fire departments, roads, bridges, and other facilities while paying nothing.

And so in the best Marxist sense, ideology reflects class interest. The same applies for community organizer–state legislator-senator-president Obama and so many other career politicians, bureaucrats, parasites on government, and crony capitalists.

One might ask such people: How can you misunderstand, slander, and demean a system that has done so well for you? The answer is simple: They have done so well by a different system, one they now wished to extend further. It would be a system in which companies succeeded not because they had a good product, daring innovation, hardworking leaders, and a well-thought-out business plan but precisely because they contribute money to the government and get big subsidies as favored clients. It doesn't matter if they throw the money away or, more accurately, steal it. This is how the economy works in Third World dictatorships and that's why it doesn't work very well.

The same points apply to the political level. In the context of the Social Theory of Value, Obama and the Third Left act as if the government is doing citizens a favor by providing them services. Yet it is the citizens who paid for all these services, with the richer and the economically productive middle class paying proportionately the most. Even if, for example, a wealthy person—and many middle-class people now do so—sends their children to private schools, they pay for public schools. And much of their income goes to help the less fortunate. That is as it should be, but this social reality—which has not been resisted but even supported by most Republicans—should be a matter of praise, not anger and bitterness about a supposedly bad system.

Imagine Warren as a medieval duchess explaining to the merchants and peasants that they didn't do anything on their own because all they possessed was due to the protection of her feudal soldiers—whose salaries they paid for. Yet through her grace they would be allowed to keep a "big hunk" of their money, though she would determine how much.

If the concept of modern democratic liberal capitalism is replaced by randomness, then how can the values taught America's children and adults still produce social stability and prosperity? People who worked harder and were smarter or perhaps luckier—or at least wiser or smarter in socially productive ways—and paid attention to their teachers did tend to do better. Those with good moral values learned from religion, at home, or school, or from good influences were likely to fare better in life. Isn't that the lesson of thousands of years of human society?

Then there is the whole other side of the coin: failure. For if no one can claim responsibility for their own success, then no one is responsible for their failures, either. They can blame them on bad teachers, or roads, or bridges. America has often seen underprivileged people, individuals disadvantaged by personal backgrounds or difficult family lives or personal tragedies, rise to the highest successes of the human spirit.

So Obama merely begs the question: Why do parallel conditions in many respects—certainly in regard to access to governmental infrastructure—produce such different results among different human beings? A participation trophy does not cut it in building a prosperous economy.

And it is this point that is at the very core of the American system. Everyone has the right to life, liberty, and the pursuit of happiness. But they don't have a right to equality of result. Only if personal character and behavior matters then will people compete. And only if they compete can they strive to achieve better. The desire to emulate and succeed, too, produces results; resentment and the belief that your wallet is my playground do not. It is on that rock that America's success stands.

Another perfect example of the Third Left–Obama economic miscalculation about the freedom and prosperity that government-centrism and supervision provide is the Third Left's use of the Internet as a case study. Obama opined: "The Internet didn't get invented on its own. Government research created the Internet so that all the companies could make money off the Internet." This story is not, however, true.[16]

What would become email—and not the Internet, which is

not the same thing—was an army research program to maintain communications in case of nuclear war. No commercial application was ever considered. Private entrepreneurs saw the potential and without government subsidies and with a minimum of government supervision developed it.

Obviously, there are certain public services that government can and must carry out, and these are distributed among federal, state, and local government. These include public highways, the postal service, national defense, police, fire, and public schools among them.

But far from being areas for high potential profit, these are sectors that must be done by government precisely because they do not yield an immediate material return, no matter how vital they might be. In other words, government is a specialist—and ought to be so—in projects that lose money directly despite their potential long-term social value. America must be defended but the government never makes money buying a fighter plane or building a highway.[17] Thus, government is the exact opposite of the institution needed to run a strong economy, and the higher the level of government the relatively higher the cost.

And of course Obama leaves out entirely—and this is a remarkably revealing shortcoming in his thinking and that of the Third Left—the third great factor in American life. For aside from government and the private economic sector, there is also the independent community. In this last sector, Obama is only interested in agenda-driven groups, organized ethnic-racial blocs, and trade unions.

Yet if America has been great it has been in large part because of family, religious groups (and often semiautonomous or locally organized ones), neighbors coming together in a nongovernmental setting, charities, voluntary organizations including everything from the Lions Club or Rotary to groups created to help the blind or to promote hobbies and skills, and on and on. In no other country in the world is there anything like this large, independent, grassroots type of structure.

In America, the people do what in other countries is done by dictatorships. And in America—and this is dead-on accurate—the people have done very much of what the government does in other democratic countries. Aside from America's historic new start, natural resources, geographic defenses, and enormous size, it has been this activism of the free citizen and voluntarily created (and locally controlled, not top-down) community that has been the great secret of success. Indeed, it is the human element of success.

And while conservatives in recent years have put far more emphasis on community, as many or most liberals have become enthralled with the let-government-do-everything approach (which has led to such marvels as the collapse of many American cities), that community philosophy doesn't have to be a conservative monopoly historically. Liberals often pioneered, especially in the more highly populated areas, the building of independent, citizen-based communities. It is a flexible system, far less costly, compatible with liberty, and usually (of course, not always) more effective.

Why abandon one of the greatest of all American social inventions for the cold embrace of the state? And how incredibly revealing is the left's cynical combination of dismissing this third element or using old Communist and Alinsky tactics of taking over, creating, or giving extraordinary privileges to front groups where they pull the puppet strings.

Even when Obama spoke about the proper function of government, he got it wrong, with an approach totally outside the traditional liberal consensus. His stimulus package and other programs were not about carrying out better the traditional mandated government functions. Instead, Obama favored unproductive and even counterproductive spending priorities. And one proof of this was how after spending so much money, it was Obama who spoke of infrastructural decline, precisely the responsibility that had been his—heralding the failure of his own policy and the wrongness of his own strategy.

The problem is not the transfer of wealth from the "middle class," a term increasingly devoid of meaning, to the very rich but from one sector of the middle class—which tends to be the more productive one—to another that creates either nonproductive products (studies, increasingly low-quality education that produces more highly trained nonproductive people; wasteful or counterproductive government services; not useful and high-cost energy; growing layers of bureaucracy, etc.) or nothing at all.

The same goes for the working class, which increasingly gives up assets to the nonworking class and lumpenproletariat. It sees less of its work benefiting itself.

What is produced, then, is alienation, as Marx would put it, but not alienation prompted by the capitalist theft of labor value; rather, this is created by the governmental-entitlement-crony-capitalist complex. Moreover, government policies lead to the export or loss of jobs due to companies closing or entrepreneurship being killed in advance.

Thus the Third Left is not liberal, because the movement and ideology's goals were not to do the historic job of government better but to build its own political base, seize control of economic investment, tame the private sector, and strengthen its control over social life in order to tell people how it wants them to live.

A liberal says that society, which sometimes but not always means government, has its legitimate claims. A Third Left, "Progressive" radical says that "society," by which they always mean government, has the prior claim. This is the opposite of the concept under which America was founded, has lived, and has flourished.

Inasmuch as it is indeed true that no one can take sole credit for his or her achievements, most of the rest of that credit goes to the rest of the individual citizens—family; the people you live among;

individuals who helped you; personal friends; charities and helping organizations; those whom you worshiped with; those who co-
operate based on their common background; groups formed by
Americans using their freedom; banks and investors; those you
worked with as partners, employers, or employees—and not to
government.

As for the Third Left and Obama's Social Theory of Value, it is
an idea that a Marxist would view as the reactionary notion of the
lazy, the looters, and a predatory medieval aristocracy. After all,
the axe swings both ways. For according to this view the proletariat
has no special, basic claim, either. The worker, too, didn't do it by
himself. He owes the state and the capitalist. A century ago, the
Social Theory of Value would be used by reactionaries to explain
why workers had no right to form trade unions.

Indeed, the Third Left–Obama ideology might be called the
Grasshopper Principle, after the story of the ant and the grasshopper. For has not nature given all insects an equal basis for
success—the sun, the rain, the plants? If the ant thrives because it
works hard and the grasshopper dies because it doesn't store food,
is that just? For doesn't the ant owe its success to the government
of nature?

Of course, it is easy to reduce this philosophy to nonsense. But
that's the point. There is nothing liberal about the Social Theory
of Value. It is a profoundly antiliberal philosophy that, if it had
prevailed over liberalism, would have kept the world living in the
eighteenth century.

What then is the basis for its contemporary appeal? In part, of
course, the Third Left wants to conceal its real aims. The government and the apparatus of institutions it controls will gain power
as the representatives of all the efforts of all the people. It also has a
populist appeal: Those who have succeeded or become rich are no
better than you, because they owe everything to you. There is even
something essentially American—a profound sense of personal

egalitarianism—in it, but which is turned from the heady wine of individualistic pride to the sour vinegar of envy.

It also a key element, for if everyone had all this huge help then your failure is all the more inexcusable. Equally, it never mentions that if someone failed perhaps it was because of governmental incompetence, like bad schools and bad policies, policies like those of Obama that hold the country back.

And finally, it tells everyone loudly that "you are the rightful owners of all that the rich have." Much more quietly, it whispers, "We, the government, are the rightful owners of all that you have, too."

Here one must turn to one of the most effective refutations of the whole Third Left, Osawatomie Obama philosophy ever produced, written not by some privileged graduate of expensive private schools and coddled by a life of magical money paid out in large quantities for just showing up. He is an average American with real-world experience.

John Kass was born in 1956 into a poor Greek American family in Chicago. He was a sailor, day laborer, and waiter before attending a local college and discovering his talent as a journalist. His columns in the *Chicago Tribune* are usually light and funny. But then something broke wide open inside him and he wrote about his own experience in the same city where Obama became a master of the universe consorting with the rich, powerful, and corrupt while posing as people's tribune.

And thus Kass wrote on July 12, 2012, about the real America:

There was no federal bailout money for us. No Republican corporate welfare. No Democratic handouts. No bipartisan lobbyists working the angles. No Tony Rezkos. No offshore accounts. No Obama bucks.

And for their troubles [his family's grocery business was] muscled by the politicos, by the city inspectors and the chiselers and the weasels, all those smiling extortionists who held the government hammer over all of our heads.

"You didn't get there on your own," Obama said. . . . If you've got a business, you didn't build that? Somebody else made that happen?

Somebody else, Mr. President? Who, exactly? Government?

One of my earliest memories as a boy at the store was that of the government men coming from City Hall. One was tall and beefy. The other was wiry. They wanted steaks.

"We didn't eat red steaks at home or yellow bananas. We took home the brown bananas and the brown steaks because we couldn't sell them. But the government men liked the big, red steaks, the fat rib-eyes two to a shrink-wrapped package. You could put 20 or so in a shopping bag.

"Thanks, Greek," they'd say.

That was government.

We didn't go to movies or out to restaurants. Everything went into the business. Uncle George and dad never bought what they could not afford. The store employed people, and the workers fed their families and educated their children and put them through college. They were good people, all of them. We worked together and worked hard, but none worked harder than the bosses.

It's the same story with so many other businesses in America, immigrants and native-born. The entrepreneurs risk everything, their homes, their children's college funds, and their hearts, all for a chance at the dream: independence, and a small business of their own.

Most often, they fail and fall to the ground without a government parachute. But some get up and start again.

When I was grown and gone from home, my parents finally managed to save a little money. After all those years of

hard work and denying themselves things, they had enough
to buy a place in Florida and a fishing boat in retirement.
Dad died only a few years later. You wouldn't call them rich.
But Obama might.[18]

Whatever Kass's personal political view, he writes as the kind
of person who historically would have voted Democratic. And thus
his hatred for Third Left ideology comes precisely from the traditional liberal approach. No country club conservative, no cigar-
chomping exploiter of labor, but a guy who knows how America
has worked and become great by simultaneously battling such
people and government power.

Kass concludes:

Gone is that young knight drawing the sword from the
stone, selling Hopium to the adoring media, preaching an
end to the broken politics of the past. These days, he wears
a new . . . persona: the multimillionaire with the Chicago
clout, playing the class warrior. . . .

But Kass doesn't think Obama is the class warrior for the real
little people; he's for a new coalition of the privileged.

What America needs is not the destruction of the traditional
liberal-conservative framework, but the formula for success that—
yes, indeed—has worked over and over again, and only whose
abandonment has led into a dead end. No, America needs legions
not of Class Warriors but of Kass Warriors, modern-day equivalents of any race, religion, ethnicity, or national origin like Kass's
family.

Near the end of his first presidential election debate, in October 2012, Obama was on comfortable ground summarizing his
views. But then, lulled into carelessness by rote repetition of slogans, Obama dropped in an amazing admission:

All those things are designed to make sure that the American people, their genius, their grit, their determination, is—*is channeled* [emphasis added] and—and they have an opportunity to succeed. And everybody's getting a fair shot. And everybody's getting a fair share—everybody's doing a fair share, and everybody's playing by the same rules.[19]

Obama was flattering the American people (genius, grit, determination) and promising everyone a fair share (of other's wealth?) and fair shot—terms he never defined. As for everyone playing by the same rules, Obama and his supporters favored different rules for each race, gender, and ethnic group, not to mention crony capitalists.

Yet it is that word *channeled* that gave the game away. Channeled by whom? The government, of course, forcing people to do things for their "own good." Who had ever proposed that some power could override the liberty of the American people to channel them, to tell them what to do in a phrase that sounded like a rancher speaking about cattle? A most elitist revolution indeed.

CHAPTER 9

Liberal, Conservative, Radical

The ex-actor, MSNBC program host, and self-proclaimed socialist Lawrence O'Donnell tried to explain the difference between liberalism and conservatism. Unintentionally, however, he actually explained the differences between liberal, conservatism, and Third Left radicalism.

O'Donnell began by asking:

What did liberals do that was so offensive to the Republican Party? I'll tell you what they did. Liberals got women the right to vote. Liberals got African Americans the right to vote. Liberals created Social Security and lifted millions of elderly people out of poverty. Liberals ended segregation. Liberals passed the Civil Rights Act, the Voting Rights Act. Liberals created Medicare. Liberals passed the Clean Air Act, the Clean Water Act. What did Conservatives do? They opposed them on every one of those things, every one. So when you try to hurl that label at my feet, "Liberal," as if it were something to be ashamed of, something dirty, something to run away from, it won't work, because I will pick up that label and I will wear it as a badge of honor.[1]

Of course, this avoids the actual, real issues of the day entirely. Yet it is likely that O'Donnell sincerely believed what he was saying, his own view of American history being simultaneously significantly distorted and supremely confident.

This shows, though, why rewriting history had to be such a high priority for the Third Left and "Progressive" liberals. They did not then have to prove their programs worked or to deal with the question of whether time and accumulation of change meant self-examination was required. All that was necessary was to demonstrate who was the hero and who the villain of the American drama.

What did O'Donnell claim and what was the truth?

Liberals, he said, got women the right to vote. Of course, the main credit belongs to the nonpartisan, nonideological women's suffrage movement. But which ardent supporter of that movement first introduced the Nineteenth Amendment in Congress? Senator Aaron Sargent was a Republican from California, a conservative, and a leading advocate of women's rights. So was Senator George Sutherland, Republican from Utah, a staunch conservative and anti-Progressive who also supported many regulatory reforms. Most of the state legislatures passing the amendment were also dominated by Republicans.

Liberals, he continued, got African Americans the right to vote. The main opponents of civil rights were not Republicans but southern Democrats. And since the Democratic Party put its own interests above racial justice, the party held back for many decades on this issue.

Abraham Lincoln freed the slaves and Republicans created Reconstruction to empower African Americans in the South, while Democrats were the party of secession, surrender to the Confederacy, the Ku Klux Klan, and the Jim Crow segregationist laws for around eighty years.

President Woodrow Wilson, a Democrat, was a particularly nasty racist. Most politically active African Americans were Republicans. Only President Lyndon Johnson turned around the Democratic Party. Such people as former vice president Al Gore's father, Democratic senator Al Gore Sr., from Tennessee, and the powerful Democratic senator from West Virginia, Robert Byrd, an ex-Klan leader, continued to oppose civil rights. Liberals and Democrats deserve credit for what they did but they did far less than they claim.

Note, too, the patronizing message in O'Donnell's argument so typical of Third Left and "Progressive" behavior, claiming that liberals "got" women and African Americans the right to vote. Supposedly the left celebrates powerful grassroots movements that forced these changes on the Washington power brokers. Yet O'Donnell accurately reflects the profoundly patronizing attitude of today's leftist elite toward the little people. A real liberal or even a historical leftist would stress the role played by average people who had courageously brought change.

This is one more indication of the isolation of the current political-intellectual ruling elite from the liberals of the past. According to O'Donnell—and none of the admirers of his statement saw the incongruity here—the white, male establishment of the 1920s and 1960s gave out these gifts to dependent people the way that government "gives" rights today.

Liberals created Social Security and helped the elderly. That's absolutely true but that was a long time ago. What's relevant today is that contemporary liberals refuse to deal with or even recognize the crisis in Social Security and have done much to make it worse. They may have created it, but who is going to save it?

Liberals ended segregation and passed the civil rights and voting rights laws. See civil rights, above. And certainly since this legislation was passed, Republicans and conservatives immediately accepted it and have not challenged or blocked implementation. And it was the Supreme Court led by a Republican-appointed chief justice, Earl Warren, that made the key decisions ending segregation.

Liberals created Medicare. While this is largely true, Republicans—including George W. Bush—expanded the program considerably. As with Social Security, the key question today is not who created a program but who is going to make sure it doesn't go bankrupt.

Liberals created clean air and clean water laws. True, but the contemporary question is whether it is necessary to expand these continually, make them more expensive and subject to strangling legislation that costs jobs and thus materially injures poorer and working-class Americans.

Of course, one thing O'Donnell doesn't mention was how liberals—but not leftists—joined in a bipartisan policy to fight Communism. There was also a time when liberals supported genuine academic openness and a balanced mass media. Those times are far gone. Moreover, leftists like O'Donnell had historically ridiculed the liberal reforms for which he now wants to claim credit, as insufficient, intended to save capitalism, and subverting the much larger changes that the left wanted to institute.

Finally, O'Donnell concluded that *liberal* should not be a dirty word but a badge of honor. Yet what tarnished it was no conservative attack but a radical redefinition of liberalism that damaged the United States and antagonized many of its people.

Conservatives who sought to prove every liberal president terrible and every liberal act detrimental were perfect counterparts of O'Donnell. But that doesn't make either "my side was always right" school of American history and politics correct. The truth is that neither Democrats nor Republicans, liberals nor conservatives have a monopoly on truth or historical virtue. It all depended on the specific circumstances of the time.

The most reasonable approach might be like this: Conservatives have admitted their mistake in opposing reform and positive legislation many years ago. Now liberals must admit their mistake of not knowing where to stop, piling on more entitlements, regulations, spending, and government. If this rule were to be followed, moderate and traditional liberals would see how their worldview and party have been hijacked and fundamentally transformed by radicals whose ideas and goals were quite different and often the exact opposite.

What people on both sides all too often didn't understand was that it is the historical situation and not an eternal ideology that makes for the right policy. Over the long term of history, neither liberals nor conservatives had a monopoly on correctness, expanding liberty, or making prosperity possible.

What was appropriate for a time when the United States didn't have enough regulation and government was too weak was not appropriate for a time when the United States was overregulated, government too strong, and the country was ridiculously deep in debt. What was appropriate is the concept of "situational politics," which means that no one political standpoint is always right.

Unlike the O'Donnell view, in which history must be distorted to prove that one party—and one only—was always right, was that of Daniel Moynihan, a liberal intellectual disgruntled with the sharp swing to the left in his time. He wrote in 1970 responding to three developments: the New Left's challenge to liberalism; an ever more powerful government's failures (especially on how welfare policies destroyed urban poor families); and the sabotage of institutions, notably universities, that abandoned the values they were supposed to exemplify and protect.

Moynihan wrote, overoptimistically as it would turn out:

In the best universities the best men are increasingly appalled by the authoritarian tendencies of the left. The inadequacies of traditional liberalism are equally unmistakable, while, no less important, the credulity, even the vulgarity of the supposed intellectual and social elite of the country has led increasing numbers of men and women of no especial political persuasion to realize that something is wrong somewhere.[2]

Nowadays, these "best men" are rare in academic institutions swamped with ideologues who are proud to be indoctrinators.

Moynihan also cited increasingly deep divisions that have since then widened into chasms of conflict, and quotes several antiradical liberals.[3]

In fact, the "present generation's" minds went even further in a radical direction and swayed successors to think the same way. SDS and other 1960s revolutionary groups won a posthumous victory as its former activists succeeded in revising liberalism to fit their ideology. Yet liberalism had previously opposed everything the left-dominated version advocated: believing capitalism didn't work; rule by an elite contemptuous of the masses while telling them how to live; an antipragmatic view of reality based on ideology; stifling open debate; and demanding individuals follow the political line of a group into which they were born or be deemed traitors.

But what was liberalism and why is it distinct from the radicalism of the Third Left and their "Progressive" allies? Historically, liberalism had also sought to create a social space in which private property and individual rights would be mutually reinforcing, reducing the state's power, giving society more flexibility, and permitting equal flexibility to conservative-dominated systems. The American Revolution was waged against a British monarchy that stifled individual rights, trussing them by complex regulations and officially dictating which ideas were "politically correct."

America's key to success was to institutionalize a relatively weak state balanced by the society, private groups, the states, and, internally, by the roles of the executive, legislative, and judicial branches. Later, liberalism had fought competing, state-centered fascist and Marxist regimes.

But now historic roles were reversed. A liberalism hijacked by radicalism buried that history. It declared long-rejected ideas and policies to have always been the very soul of liberalism. Yet despite many liberal and Democratic politicians' private reservations, they did not openly battle or systematically critique this coup in their own party and other liberal bastions. Some went along with it; others joined it; and many didn't know it was happening at all.

Ironically, most people who had no difficulty believing that Islam had been hijacked by extremists had no notion that they themselves had been hijacked by the far left. Why could liberals and Democrats claim the Republican Party's far right wing had taken it over while never recognizing how the far left wing had hijacked their own institutions? True, the Democrats had always had their own left wing. But the fact that such candidates were almost always defeated at the polls pushed the party back toward the center.

Now, however, leftism was in fashion and in control of the agenda and ruling the idea-producing sectors. This hegemony was even further intensified in the larger society by Obama's success. Once he was president, Obama could appoint thousands of officials who could run unelected regulatory bodies, nominate judges, and control the party. In effect, the battle was over and there was remarkably little resistance.

The left-wing Congressional Progressive Caucus, established in 1991, is the largest Democratic grouping in the House of Representatives, and its seventy-five members were about 30 percent of the overall party delegation.[4] Thus the "Progressives" ascendancy was not contested. The same point applied for the liberal intelligentsia, academics, journalists, people in the various branches of show business, and other historically liberal constituencies.

This liberal surrender, appeasement, or jumping on the left-wing bandwagon—call it what you will—was revolutionary in its implications. "Liberty," the Italian intellectual Ignazio Silone explained in a 1950 reflection on Communism's failings, "is the possibility of doubting, the possibility of making a mistake, the possibility of searching and experimenting, the possibility of saying 'No' to any authority—literary, artistic, philosophic, religious, social and even political."[5] In the struggle with Communism, Silone had come to understand, like so many liberals then, that the fundamental problem was not conservative authority crushing liberty but of any authority, including that of the left, doing so.

That was why the liberal thinker Arthur Schlesinger Jr. wrote a book in 1949 titled *The Vital Center* to show how liberalism stood between more radical views to the left and right that demand obedience. And it is also why the liberal philosopher Karl Popper explained in his book from 1945, *The Open Society*, that the real enemies of freedom were those who believed they understood the true course of history, human needs, and society's proper organization and thus were entitled to impose their views on everyone else.

For well over a century, liberals had drawn a sharp distinction between their ideas and those of Marxism or radicalism. Indeed, one of their main priorities was to combat leftist revolution. The ideas that the status quo sabotaged the middle class's interests or that protecting America's borders was racism, or that capitalism and market policies had never worked, were totally alien to them.

Antiliberal views were the province of the Communists and later of the New Left. These movements hated real liberals. They merely wanted to fool them, win them over, or destroy them. The moment of greatest clarity regarding this conflict between radicals and liberals was the 1948 presidential election. Real liberals and mainstream Democrats rallied around Truman. The racist right wing of the party went with Strom Thurmond; the far-left, phony liberal wing went with Henry Wallace in a party that was largely a Communist front.

And what could be more appropriate than the name of those covertly led by Communists: the Progressive Party. By choosing that label for themselves, the "Progressive" liberals were openly revealing their historic allegiance and the content of their real views. Suddenly we were supposed to believe class warfare, anticapitalism, disdain for America, Stalinist-style treatment of opponents, mass media devoted to propaganda, and betrayal of professional values among intellectuals were normative liberal ideas.

During the 1930s, the Communist Party tried to take over liberalism but failed miserably. Today, however, the post-Communist left has succeeded in that effort to a remarkable extent, effectively wiping out the memory of what liberalism was actually like.

Remember that Truman led America to recognize and fight the Soviet threat and it was his administration that successfully purged Communists from the U.S. government. Liberal trade union leaders threw out the Communists, too. A perfect symbol of this era was the liberal Americans for Democratic Action, formed in 1947 as an anti-Communist, anti-"Progressive" organization. The ADA wanted to continue the New Deal but warned, "Civil liberties must be protected from concentrated wealth and [from an] overcentralized government."[6]

Within two years of ADA's founding, the left had been defeated and discredited. Facing the Cold War challenge, liberals worked with the mainstream—that is, non-isolationist—conservatives in forging a bipartisan foreign policy. Meanwhile, the conservatives accepted liberal domestic changes, including creation of a social safety net and civil rights. The United States prospered at home and abroad.

And if you want to know how totally the left had triumphed, look at the twenty-first-century ADA lobby and grassroots group: "Americans for Democratic Action has and will continue to be a forthright liberal voice of this nation. We work to advocate pro-gressive stances on civil rights and liberties, social and economic justice, sensible foreign policy, and sustainable environmental pol-icy. The ADA will advance our agenda by maintaining an active and visible presence nationwide, raising the level of debate on the side of the progressive movement and taking action on the national level."[7] While ADA is no longer significant, the positions it holds today sound like Occupy Wall Street, a 180-degree shift from its original purpose of fighting the far left to instead becoming part of it.

The idea that the Third Left and its "Progressive" satellites were merely normative liberals, however, was furthered by many conservatives who insisted that the new movement and the Obama administration were actually heirs of Franklin Roosevelt, Truman, Kennedy, and Johnson. Such an approach—that the problem was liberalism itself—played into the radicals' hands, justifying their claim to the mantle of that historic movement and consolidating its control over its faithful supporters. By the same token, the Third Left and "Progressives" were happy to insist that the only people who opposed them were right-wing.

Yet in fact the Third Left or its new version of liberalism was quite different from historic liberalism. Indeed, the statist radical-ism of the Third Left and "Progressive" liberals was, in histori-cal terms, itself a reactionary worldview. Their effort to centralize intellectual and political power in their own hands, overriding pluralism and individual freedom, because only they knew how to promote the common good, was the same rationale used by feu-dalism, divine-right monarchism, fascism, Communism, and other nondemocratic movements. That is why the Third Left with its late-nineteenth-century solutions must pretend it is dealing with late-nineteenth-century capitalism.

It was easy to show that twenty-first-century "Progressive" lib-eralism was generally quite different from previous mainstream liberalism. The problem was that no one in public life performed that vital task. There were few to provide any "profiles in courage," acts of courage for genuine political moderation.

Yet even if the gap passed largely unnoticed, there were wide differences between the two doctrines. Liberalism wanted to change relatively small aspects of the American system. "Progressive" liberalism considered the entire system objectionable and unworkable. Liberalism had not been antireligious or antipatriotic. Now "Progressive" liberalism demanded religion be systematically scrubbed from every institution and public life while trashing American history and past international behavior. In the new version, America was guilty until proven innocent and the judges instructed the jury that it was guilty as sin.

There were dozens of ways in which the current radical-pretending-to-be-liberal ideology differed from traditional liberalism. "Progressive" economic strategy used class warfare in a demagogic way, claiming that the solution to deficits was not so much to cut spending but to raise taxes on the wealthy who allegedly weren't paying their fair share. Doing so would supposedly generate enough income to pay for Social Security, Obamacare, free condoms, environmentalist perfectionism, an even bigger government bureaucracy, virtually unlimited spending, etc.

It is impossible to conceive of a more antiliberal worldview. The historical liberal demand for more tolerance became a demand for intolerance toward "error," the hallmark of reactionary systems against which liberalism had fought.

Second, liberalism had claimed that there was nothing more dangerous and reactionary than repressing debate. Instead of honestly evaluating what opponents said, such people were intimidated and vilified. Higher education was transformed from a liberating experience in learning how to question through open-minded inquiry into indoctrination that a particular point of view was always correct. The mass media changed from a balanced, fair attempt—no matter how imperfect—to report accurately into becoming a cheerleader for one point of view and advocate of a specific political agenda.

What's the difference between using governmental power and media propaganda to push people into doing what rulers want them to do and the old controls of reactionary social compulsion? By such behavior the traditional advantages of liberalism were thrown away and the American system's corrective mechanisms crippled. In effect, the Third Left implemented what Marx had claimed bourgeois society was doing in only pretending to be democratic: "Each new [ruling] class . . . is compelled in order to [succeed] . . . to represent its interest as the common interest of all the members of society . . . and represent them as the only rational, universally valid ones."[8]

The phrase "politically correct" gave the game away. What should be important is *factual* correctness.

The same was true for the term *multiculturalism*, which abandoned the liberal system of pluralism—individual freedom within an overall unified national identity—for a caste system where each group had varying degrees of privilege. On the other hand, members of so-called oppressed groups were to be denied individual liberty as racial, religious, ethnic, or gender traitors. They must obey the line laid down for them by their leaders, enthroned by Third Left– and "Progressive"–dominated organizations, or be denounced.

In addition, the old racist principle of "separate but equal" was redefined as a glorious example of "Progressive" thought. In a concept straight out of Weatherman ideology, the majority population should rebel against all of its traditions while the "oppressed" should reject loyalty to American society and culture.

These concepts contradicted the liberal idea of a society open to different ideas and giving a monopoly to none. Indeed, such a situation was a genuine liberal's worst nightmare—an intolerant society where everyone was pressured to think the same way and persecuted if they didn't—one brought to life on many college campuses and in mass media, the entertainment industry, and other institutions.

Fourth, the liberal principle of balance was replaced by the radical concept advocating the more the better. The governmental machine could not possibly grow too big nor the national debt too large. The volumes of regulations grew and grew, strangling society, trying to perfect ever-smaller faults at ever-higher prices.

Similarly, policies were now supposed to be judged by stated good intentions, not by any failure to fulfill these alleged goals or even their negative effect on those they supposedly helped. As a result, the infrastructure declined, people's lives worsened, America fell behind other countries, and vast sums of money were thrown away. The quality of public schools declined even as program was piled on program; more people were hired with expensive retirement and benefits' entitlements; costs increased; and educational basics were neglected in favor of social engineering and political indoctrination.

The deep divide separating liberalism from radicalism existed because the two approaches were totally different. Liberalism accepted capitalism as the best of all possible systems. Not everyone receives the same proportion but all do benefit. Some make profits; some, wages; and some, because a wealthier society is better able to pay, receive welfare and other benefits. The system's shortcomings were to be fixed by small adjustments. It was well aware of how capitalism had been the great motive force into providing countries where the majority had lived in poverty to levels of undreamed-of opportunity and prosperity.

In contrast was the radical anticapitalist stance, which viewed that system as inevitably rapacious and unjust. Property, proclaimed the nineteenth-century socialist Pierre-Joseph Proudhon, was theft. And that philosophy dominated the Third Left and the version of "Progressive" liberalism it had created. If you have money it was because you took it from someone else. This was merely Marx's labor theory of value updated. America only had wealth because it was stolen from other countries. That was just Lenin's theory of imperialism updated.

Radicals' viewed capitalism as a zero-sum game, emphasizing redistributing rather than creating wealth. In contrast to the liberal concept of empowering a responsible capitalism to create wealth based on class cooperation was the radical argument that the evil rich were strangling the "middle class."

Fundamentally, radicals argued that all wealth and property rightly belonged to society as a whole. Even if society did not try to take these things directly, it had first claim. The Third Left had modified the Marxist view that this had to be done through revolution into the notion that an existing "bourgeois" government, if properly led, could perform this feat. Liberals understood that a compelling cause could make it necessary for government to override private property, but that this should be kept limited to protect democracy, individual liberty, the balance of institutions, and prosperity.

There were scores of other differences between liberalism and Marxist-influenced "Progressivism."

Radicals believed the United States was an imperialist power and a negative force in the world. They and "Progressive" liberals were sympathetic toward Islamism because it shared their critique of America as colonialist, so foreign anti-Americanism was justified unless the United States demonstrated repentance.

In contrast, liberals knew America had made mistakes but done far more good. They favored American leadership in the world and traditional diplomatic methods like credibility, deterrence through strength, rewarding friends, and punishing enemies. They did not hesitate to identify authoritarian doctrines that ran contrary to American principles.

Liberals believed the pie of prosperity could be made bigger and everyone could live better. While supporting environmental better-ment, they thought this must always be practical-minded so as to be reconciled with material well-being. Like conservatives, liberals had realized that a largely privatized economy allowed millions of minds to operate independently, adapt to the real world, and adjust to changing conditions. Thus it would always do better than an economy that was too centralized and government-directed.

In contrast, radicals were suspicious of other people's high liv-ing standards as based on exploitation. Americans had to give back to the Third World and stop threatening the earth through man-made global warming and other environmental problems.

Liberals historically defended professional ethics and open de-bate in universities. Radicals have tried to force out both real liberal and conservative scholars, to indoctrinate students, and to hire fac-ulty on the basis of ideology so as to have a monopoly on discourse. The quality of academic work in many departments declined as re-search was done mainly to serve a political cause. The radical agenda totally contradicted everything liberals fought for in academia.

The radical policy of fostering division among races, genders, and ethnic groups, plus creating privileged sectors, is in conflict with the liberal doctrine favoring integration and the equal treat-ment of all citizens.

The slippery slope was what Orwell wrote of: "All animals are equal, but some animals are more equal than others." Of class struggle: "four legs good; two legs bad." Dividing citizens into groups with different levels of rights was precisely what liberals had complained about in traditional conservatism. The liberal ideal as expressed by the founders—though imperfectly so, given the existing society—and as expressed by the Reverend Martin Luther King Jr. was equal treatment.

In light of these and many other basic conflicts, radicals hated liberals. This antagonism was in the open during the New Left era of the 1960s and 1970s, only becoming hidden as the Third Left developed and built the "Progressive" liberal interpretation as the conveyor belt for its influence. A good way to understand these real attitudes was through the songs of the radical musician Phil Ochs.

In his song titled "Love Me, I'm a Liberal," Ochs critiqued liberalism from what would become the Third Left position, the theme that liberals were hypocrites because they were not radicals and revolutionaries. Liberals loved civil rights leaders but not Malcolm X; Hubert Humphrey and trade unions, but not Communists or radicals; and they were still (regrettably) patriotic.

Ochs's song reminds us of a deep chasm between liberal and radical that has disappeared today. Liberals liked reform, Ochs sneered, "But don't talk about revolution / That's going a little bit too far." The Third Left, however, overcame that gap by turning liberals into radicals without their knowing it.

From the Weathermen's days to those of Obama and Holder, the Third Left understood that race was a key, perhaps the key, issue they could use to leverage liberals into becoming radicals. They employed liberal guilt but reframed it as white skin privilege. Guilt is a bad feeling that one has that might be groundless. Unearned privilege is a crime that must be atoned. Here is Ochs on this point, mocking liberals:

> I go to civil rights rallies. . . .
> I hope every colored boy becomes a star. . . .
> I love Puerto Ricans and Negros
> As long as they don't move next door
> So love me, love me, love me, I'm a liberal.

Liberals, Ochs said, were hypocrites because they called southern whites racists while they opposed busing their own children. To the New Left, a liberal was a racist who pretended to be enlightened. The Third Left's task was to make liberals feel so bad about this that they would give away rights to make things right.

Of course, all those white (mostly male) professors, journalists, and others could vindicate themselves and justify their own privileges by supporting the Third Left to buy immunity. Thus they could talk of Republicans, conservatives, or any dissenters the way the 1960s liberals spoke of whites in Mississippi who clung to their dislike of people different from themselves. Then, like the 1960s liberals of Ochs's song, they could send their kids to private school with a clear conscience.

Such rich white liberals of the 1960s thus lionized the very lions that would devour them. The Third Left, however, once again did far better. Its own activists now threw the parties and criticized their country's institutions in order to exalt themselves, having become simultaneously "lords" and "fire-breathing Rebels." At such a party, thrown by Ayers and Dohrn, a newly minted politician named Barack Obama made his debut.

In contrast to this way of looking at America, a typical liberal cultural artifact was the 1946 film *It's a Wonderful Life*, whose continuing popularity shows that it expresses something essential about America. The hero, George Bailey, is a banker who cares about his neighbors and helps people. Those he helps in turn support him. It is a pro-capitalist story, albeit one contrasting the good liberal capitalist with his bad conservative rival. And while it took place during the New Deal, the government never appears at all.

No Communist would have approved of this quintessentially liberal film. He would have said it misled the masses by painting a banker as good, making him a virtuous community leader so as to preserve capitalism, and exalting a community rather than class struggle. Rather than demanding banks give loans to people because it was their "right" as reparations for past suffering—as Democrats would do in the Community Development Act, which helped bring about the 2008 economic crash—Bailey loaned money to people who he trusted would work hard and pay him back. The "Progressive" liberals would have driven Bailey into bankruptcy.

This same kind of liberal approach was taken for granted by Hillary Clinton in her 1996 book, *It Takes a Village*. Clinton gave primacy to bottom-up, voluntarily formed communities, not to the federal government. She was still in the traditional liberal approach of praising free citizens making their own decisions. While the seeds of "Progressive" liberalism had already been planted—Clinton was a student of Alinsky and would jump on Obama's bandwagon and declare herself a "Progressive" a dozen years later—they were not yet dominant.

But it was necessary for the Third Left to conceal the real history of America, including the implications of liberalism's achievements. After all, it was precisely these changes that ensured American society didn't need a fundamental transformation to be just. Only if previous efforts had failed or been insufficient would much larger change be needed.

By ignoring the progress of the nation, overstating economic injustice and racism as structural problems, and at the same time exaggerating the degree of social perfection that could be reached and the resources there were to spend, the Third Left and "Progressives" rejected the moderation that arises from realism. Wasn't there a point of diminishing returns in trying to create total equality, the perfect environment, the ideal degree of equality, regulations that covered everything and eliminated any potential risk?

Thus, by its repressive, closed-minded demand that the power of the state be extended ever more into the domain of individual liberty, snobbish contempt for the people, and enthronement of ideology over realism or pragmatism, the "Progressive" liberals ceased to be liberal at all. Ironically, they created a new reactionary equivalent to the old version of conservatism, which they attributed to their political adversaries.

While once conservatives had represented privilege, arrogance of power, the overbearing state, and limiting freedom, today it was liberals—at least in their "Progressive" guise—that played this role. As once conservatism dictated behavior and morality, so now did the we-know-best-for-you nanny state of the left. What kind of car, lightbulbs, toilet, or food one used, how much energy one consumed, had all become a matter of policy. The masses weren't living properly and must be nudged, pressured, or intimidated into doing what their betters dictated.

To see this evolution consider Orwell, in 1943, who asked:

What are the workers struggling for? Simply for the decent life which they are more and more aware is now technically possible. . . . They knew that they were in the right, because they were fighting for something which the world owed them and was able to give them.[9]

In contrast, the reactionaries

are all people with something to lose, or people who long for a hierarchical society and dread the prospect of a world of free and equal human beings. . . . Not one of those who preach against "materialism" would consider life livable without these things. . . . How easily that minimum could be attained if we chose to set our minds to it for only twenty years!

In the left's traditional position, workers were owed a better life not because they existed but because they produced the wealth. And when they were allowed, in liberal capitalist systems, to do so in conjunction with reasonable freedom for their capitalist partners, they were able to better their lives. In America, the result had been achieved in far less than the two decades Orwell envisioned would be needed. The reactionaries were routed; change was so deeply entrenched that conservatives also accepted the reforms.

Historically, conservatives, as guardians of traditional values (religion, patriotism, geographic community, homogeneity, bourgeois lifestyle), wanted to tell people what to do. But today radical-liberals claimed to be guardians of "correct values." These amount to secularism or despiritualized "social justice" religion, antipatriotism, ethno-racial-gender communities governed by a single correct political line, and diversity in the external appearance of the elite combined with their all having a homogeneous worldview. The bottom line was the assertion of a right to tell other people how to live and to pressure them to express a single standpoint or else suffer accordingly.

In contrast, the liberal-conservative consensus in America agreed that success was based on a competition among ideas and viewpoints, on individual choice rather than direction from above. Suddenly, though, liberalism was redefined into the opposite of what it used to be. For instance, there were calls to criminalize wider areas of free speech, a restriction that liberals in the past would have opposed tooth and nail. There were scores of other such situations.

The "Progressive" brand of liberalism rewrote the history of that political standpoint. After all, America had changed. But it was in a very different way than it claimed.

Were American society and the middle class in the early twenty-first century jeopardized by a surfeit of unbridled capitalism? Did the government tremble because of Ford, General Motors, US Steel, Standard Oil of New Jersey, the Pennsylvania Railroad, and other mighty enterprises, many of which have collapsed completely?

No. It was the opposite. Corporations trembled before government regulators who had the power to tie them into knots, and competed for their favor. Indeed, many of their executives sympathized with Third Left positions or at least saw the advantages of pretending to do so.

Did workers living in hovels fear the boss telling them at a whim that they were now out of work, without unemployment compensation or pension; that their hours were arbitrarily increased; that they were going to be thrown out of their company homes because they were ten minutes late at work? No, it was the unions in a number of sectors that had the whip hand, with the government 100 percent on their side.

Did big-bellied capitalists blow cigar smoke into newspaper editors' faces and threaten to cut off advertising unless their corporate scandals were covered up? No, it was the scandals of the left and its favored political figures that the mass media generally excused while their opponents were excoriated. Meanwhile, most corporate executives were desperate to have the media proclaim them to be good citizens. Instead of battling the political forces opposing them, they tried to cut the best possible deal, including spending money running image ads about their good works for environment and social justice; giving money to left-wing-backed causes; and hiring in left-wing consultants to put their employees through sensitivity training.

Thus it is quite responsible to believe that in the past the main threat to liberty came from big corporations and underrestrained capitalism. But today, the main threat comes from an out-of-control bloated government every bit as corrupt, greedy for power, incompetent, and inefficient as laissez-faire capitalism's worse abuses. Liberals should be arguing—and compromising—with conservatives over the details of massive cuts in government spending, regulation, and size, not over whether such things are needed at all.

There has also been growing evidence that the endless expansion of spending, debt, government, and regulation has reached its limit—and exceeded it—in Western democratic societies. The fiscal problems of Europe, where such excessively ambitious welfare state policies failed badly, have clearly shown that to be true.

To see government as deity or inevitable friend of the poor and downtrodden is an illusion. What could be more ironic than that American capitalism's ultimate crisis was caused not by stealing the workers' productive labor but by the exact opposite: payment of more than society could afford, as politicians competed to pour out money to useless or counterproductive projects and entitlements. Thus the workers and their descendants found themselves paying for the poor, lumpenproletariat, illegal immigrants, and most of all for the privileges of a parasitic, pampered bourgeoisie of bureaucrats, academics, shady businessmen, and legions of others.

There have been times when government has been a positive force. But "government" is composed of people. These human beings are often no better, and often worse than average people. Government and its specific agencies have their own goals, and their ways of functioning have built-in shortcomings (bureaucratic rigidity, indifference to the money and distant lives of others, lust for the accumulation of power, etc.).

So to say that government as a whole and its parts have no interests of their own is not true. The government is not a solution to all things—a kind of secular god—but a party with its own selfishness, goals, and negative aspects. Consequently, citizens must guard against its usurpation of their liberty, wealth, and objectives. Government is not a disinterested shepherd, but in reality just another wolf.

Such was also the view of the Marxist left, at least concerning the "bourgeois" governments that existed prior to the projected revolution. Only when the Third Left conceived that it might direct policies toward its goals did government suddenly become the solution; more money to government was an absolute good; and more regulation from government was a font of virtue because the government was a knight in shining armor and protector of the downtrodden.

Liberals used to understand these dangers yet they now refuse to ask the most urgent and basic questions: Could it possibly be that a government that has grown steadily for so many decades might have become too big? Is it conceivable that regulations imposed by the thousands have become too onerous? Is it within the realm of the real world that the burdens of salaries and retirements for those who draw government paychecks have become too onerous? Might it be true that if you keep dividing society into warring groups they will eventually go to war against each other?

Or is this all a fantasy of a reactionary, evil, woman-hating, racist mind-set that should be dismissed by any civilized being? Yet by portraying the critique of solution by government in roughly those terms, the debate became unglued. Bipartisan compromise would have been based on mutual agreement that massive spending cuts and priority changes were needed. But with liberals insisting for all practical purposes that continuing the ever-accelerating pace and the never-changing course they had been on for a century required no further thought, no cooperation was possible.

Once the deliberate division and limitation of power is abandoned, spiraling abuse of power is inevitable. In Franklin Roosevelt's phrase, the government is no longer ruled by the voters but is in practice an "alien power" ruling over them, telling them how to live, what to do, messing up the functioning of the society and draining more and more of its wealth.

Like any institution that becomes too powerful, government has turned from a helping hand to a strangling hand. There are elements in its nature that make it especially dangerous in that regard. It is precisely the same problem as having overly powerful banks, corporations, military officers, or anything else. And the government's victories are at the expense of the liberty of individuals.

Human beings are imperfect. They are subject to a range of behavior that include ambition, arrogance, bullying, corruption, cravenness, dictatorial tendencies, greed, inability to understand others' needs or viewpoints, lack of imagination, and being controlled by a specific caste for that group's own selfish interests.

Government, then, is not a referee but just another special-interest group.

Yes, the same is true of any human institution. That's why institutions should be in balance. But, of course, government controls the laws and so can compel the action of others to an extent that no one else can. It has a monopoly on force and power far beyond any other institution. The mafia can try to compel obedience but citizens can seek the protection of the law. In contrast, government makes the laws and sets the rules. To whom can a citizen flee for help against a government that is too powerful?

There's more. The kinds of people who become politicians and government bureaucrats have specific and especially developed character traits. They are people who crave power—I know this firsthand from growing up and living in in these circles in Washington, D.C.—and who are prone to arrogance once they achieve that status. They do not like to be criticized and they are even more prone than most mortals to believe that they cannot be wrong.

Isolated largely in a single city, Washington, D.C., and even isolated within that city, they lose contact with ordinary people. When they do encounter non-elite people they see them in a way that reinforces their own sense of superiority. The more they talk of standing up for the little guy and promulgating social justice, the more likely are these things cynically manipulated for their own empowerment.

Even when virtuous—and many originally take up political or bureaucratic careers intending to help others—they are limited by their own lack of knowledge and experience. Having followed a narrow course in life—years of formal education and then public office—they honestly don't know much about the real lives of those they rule. Their desire to help often becomes harmful. And even beyond this, they are focused on a narrow piece of reality. If your job is to save endangered species, you don't think of that mission's effect on other people's livelihoods.

In addition, of course, you are using other people's money; a factor that also makes people careless and spendthrift. You are not subject to the demand for rigorous cost-effectiveness that business faces. It is easy to conclude that you know best and that it is necessary to make others do things for their "own good."

Self-interest dictates the maximum accumulation of power and money for yourself and your department. To fill up the day you must produce regulations and reports on others' compliance with existing regulations. As a result, there is a strong tendency to tighten the noose around the freedom of your subjects. And for many this is reinforced by a specific agenda to be put into place whatever the cost or effect on the citizenry.

Communism should have provided the critical lesson in understanding all these things. It had no exploitive capitalists but only an exploitive state ruled by a ruling class that, in effect, controlled everything by "owning" the government. That system produced far more waste and unhappiness, and far less wealth, than the American system, not to mention totalitarian repression. The lesson should have been clear—as it had been in the nineteenth century—that both unchecked private capital and government can strangle a society and usurp freedom.

A reasonable balance must be reestablished. One shouldn't have to be a conservative to understand that reality. Indeed, it was liberals who had opposed big government when it was very strong and conservative in Europe. They complained of restrictions on rights; on the enforcement of morality; on the protection of the power of state-backed groups like the aristocrats and the church, and others.

Many of the liberal positions of today are based not on philosophical principle but simply on the use of a controlled institution to give one's own faction more power, money, and ability to implement its own agenda. Only now that liberals think they can have government do whatever they want has the position turned around 180 degrees.

If the liberal stance has become one of radical-dominated opportunism rejecting past principle, what of the liberal definition of conservatives as evil, incomprehensible, and without any merit, so that the opposite of what they say must always be embraced? Are Christian believers scarier than revolutionary Islamists? Is the worldview of America's hinterland, of the non-elite, more distasteful than foreign cultures whose values are alien to democracy and freedom?

The demonization of Christians, Republicans, and large areas of America by an intolerant elite is one of the most absurd features in the terrible distortion of reality so powerful in the contemporary United States. While it is rooted in historic snobbery and the battles of the past, much of this conflict stems from the infusion of radical ideas.

Yet just as the image of the liberal is out of date, so is that of the conservative. When Republicans and conservatives boast as many or more female and non-white candidates than do their counterparts, while liberals and Democrats preach censorship and deify government power over freedom, something is very different from the past.

The liberal has contempt for the conservative as an authoritarian who wants to tell him what to do, say discriminating against gays and nonwhites, and make abortion illegal. Yet the shoe in practice is on the other foot. Traditionally a conservative was someone who wanted more social constraints and a more powerful state, church, and conformity. Today, generally speaking, conservatives want more liberty for the individual, while Third Left–influenced liberals want more social constraints, enforced by a strong government.

As one conservative writer put it:

Conservatism now stands for freedom *from* authority, while it is *progressivism* that seeks to implement the . . . "nanny state." It's *liberals* who want to tell you what to do and what is allowed, not conservatives. . . . It is mostly liberal politicians, not conservative politicians, who pass laws and regulations telling citizens what they can and cannot do, what they must and must not buy, what they are and are not allowed to say.[10]

Modern Western conservatism, dethroned from its position as social arbiter and chastened by the experience of fascism, accepted liberal reforms and took on a libertarian edge, reaching similar conclusions. Historically, one might say that roughly before World War I in the West, conservatives had dominated states and directed the course of powerful religious forces. They had used their position to impose their will, to narrow the scope of liberty. Liberals had rebelled against their power.

The truth is that while there are indeed reactionary, even lunatic forces on the right, conservatives have learned a lot more in recent years than their counterparts. They have accepted large elements of progress—including racial and gender equality, reasonable regulation and environmental programs—but without abandoning vital basic principles of an economy that worked to produce wealth and a government that did not strangle commerce or freedom.

A key element in the conservative transformation was the experience of Communism. Many conservatives began to fear the power of a state that was in the hands of the other side. Seeing top-down, state-embodied power used to impose things they didn't like forced reconsideration, with the rise of a strong libertarian element in their thinking.

There were also widespread social changes that became irreversible. Few conservatives sought to roll back the basic innovations. And the same applied to such later initiatives as civil rights along racial and gender lines or the main and much-needed environmental legislation following the discovery of just how much

America's water and air had deteriorated. In other cases, while many conservatives would have liked to restrict abortions, that simply was not within their conceivable power. The issue had now moved on to the much narrower one of ensuring that taxpayers and dissenting religious institutions didn't have to pay for them.

What's "conservative" about believing that the United States should not go further and further into debt; massive regulation; the restriction of individual freedom; higher taxes; and past a certain point bigger government? What's liberal about supporting revolutionary Islamism's empowerment, failing to help allies, etc.? The effort is to define liberalism as radicalism, and anything in liberalism that is not radically left—even if it has been a major theme of that view for a century or more—is redefined as conservative. But you don't need to be a conservative to tell which way the wind blows.

All of the demonizing myths, however, were not on the liberal side. The basic problem of the debate had become that the two contending groups produced histories in which their rival was always wrong throughout all of American history. While the conservative version of U.S. history was often more accurate than the currently fashionable radical, Marxist-style, anti-American view—indeed, it was usually identical to the traditional liberal view—it faced a temptation to turn the recent struggle with radicalism into a much older, broader conflict.

While America itself was the villain for the Third Left and "Progressive" liberals, liberalism became the eternal villain for some on the right. In this approach the great work of the founders was going well until the real Progressives decided to trash the Constitution and turn power over to an elite operating through a powerful central government.

What did this leave out? When governments were monarchies and the wealthy were landowning aristocrats, conservatives backed the authoritarian status quo. Liberals rebelled against state power and demanded representative government. They fought the conservative-backed excessive regulations left over from the Middle Ages, battled monarchies that choked trade and industry, and opposed the special treatment given to different classes, ethnic groups, and religions.

That's what the American Revolution was about. The Constitution was designed to strike a balance between the dangers of a government so weak as to ensure anarchy and a government so strong as to ensure tyranny. Its authors didn't look at government as the solution but as a necessary evil and a tremendous danger to liberty.

It also omitted the fact that the balance was upset not by the Progressive reformists but by post–Civil War industrialization. New giant corporations—Standard Oil of New Jersey, Carnegie Steel, J. P. Morgan, big railroads, and so on—were too powerful to be contained by the old system. Robber barons flouted the law, bought and sold state and national governments, and imposed monopolies that crushed workers, farmers, and small businesses.

With the rise of corporate capitalism, the pendulum swung in favor of the wealthy. Riches bought power, even the virtual ownership of government. Against robber barons and monopolies, liberals fought to strengthen an independent government as a counterweight. They won.

This didn't mean America or its history is evil but they were necessary transitional processes to a modern industrial society and the creation of the massive wealth that made possible progress, opportunities, and high living standards today. The modernization process in America was better than no modernization process at all and certainly better than its equivalent in the Soviet Union, Germany, or even Great Britain. The effects were cushioned by the founders' system and the American character built up by the frontier, individualism, and democratic society, letting the United States industrialize quickly and at relatively low costs compared to elsewhere. By the same token, those who exposed these ills and brought reforms to fix them were equally essential.

The conservatives forgot that there was a day when Standard Oil of New Jersey and J. P. Morgan and the Pennsylvania Railroad and the Carnegie Steel Company and other such banks or companies ruled America and did as they liked. The liberals forget that those days are long gone. The conservatives forgot that there was a day when workers were trampled on and had no rights. The liberals forgot that those days are long gone and that trade unions are more likely to get their way by bullying than are corporations.

In addition, that was the era of the powerful, corrupt urban political machines based on immigrant votes and populist payoffs. The last of these, in Chicago, produced Obama's political career, and ironically the corralling of immigrants and government financial payoffs are two central strategies of today's Third Left and "Progressive" liberals.

Finally, there was the threat of the revolutionary left. Liberals, then, had a difficult task: to defeat the powerful corporations and revolutionaries without creating a dictating state and to rein in the corrupt politicians. They showed how socialism wasn't needed because capitalism could be reformed; laissez-faire capitalism had to be balanced by government, unions, a free press, and other institutions. Conservatives were able to keep things from going too far.

The crisis of adjusting to modern industrial capitalism by strengthening the state and other institutions, however, was not the end of history for America. The power of government kept growing. The pendulum kept moving ever onward in the same direction.

A new class of professional managers, bureaucrats, and those who controlled the commanding heights of idea and attitude production was empowered. And the giant federal government turned to crony capitalism, a different form of the late-nineteenth-century corruption of favoritism; massive handouts to buy votes; and ever-tighter regulation.

There were diminishing returns, too. It's the difference between hand-feeding a cute little cat and a ravenous, snarling lion. Surely these differences should figure into political programs. Massive spending and programs did not eliminate poverty. By pushing further and further, liberals could claim to be doing good and helping the downtrodden, but after a certain point this was no longer true. The environment needed cleaning up, but after a certain point the costs outweighed the benefits. Once poisoned rivers and air were purified the movement went into ever-smaller details that cost ever-larger amounts of money. Backing a bigger government in 1935 or 1965 was a much smaller risk than doing so at a time when government had already grown to such enormous size.

It is amazing that almost a century after the institution of Communism in Russia and almost a quarter century after its fall, the Marxist-Leninist system's most basic mistake was still being ignored by those called the "smartest" people in society. Here is the simple, catastrophic mistake: the idea that the capitalist is greedy and shortsighted. And that the commissar, in other words, the government official, looks after the interests of everyone, having no character or interest of his own. He is purely the people's servant, even though centuries of history showed that idea to be ridiculous.

Why should the commissar be so trusted? Can't he use government to enrich himself and his friends? Doesn't he use the power of government to force his individual preferences on others? Won't his thirst for power be equally desperate? Moreover, he is likely to be more careless with funds, since the money he spends is not his. He is far more shielded from personal responsibility for mistakes or misdeeds.

This of course is precisely what the radicals pretending to be liberals wanted people to believe and what the Third Left cadre often believed themselves, just as they had as New Leftists in the 1960s. America was imperialist abroad and oppressive at home; conservatives were racist, greedy people in the pockets of big corporations who wanted to destroy unions, oppress African Americans and women, and make people drink bad water and breathe polluted air. All virtue came from the left; the left was the heir of the liberals.

But then, even if it is true that the new "Progressives" are far to the left of liberals, will they succeed in fundamentally and permanently transforming America? There are factors that can be argued on either side about such an outcome.

The left's success has been to capture most of liberal and even a great deal of moderate opinion, thus expanding its base from about 10 percent of the population to about 40 or even potentially 50 percent. What the Third Left had achieved was not just some narrow electoral victory but indeed a fundamental paradigm shift. It also involved the conquest of institutions from which the Third Left cannot easily be expelled or diminished, and the redefinition of issues—like gay marriage—that no one would have believed possible a few years earlier.

The movement has created what might be called, in terms of its self-image, a coalition of those simultaneously believing themselves to be virtuous and victimized. All of these groups—African Americans, Hispanics, gays, Jews, young people generally (especially as students and young, unmarried women)—generally supported Third Left candidates and causes by a large margin.

They have all suffered in the past from unequal status, and a majority in each case was convinced, no matter how far-fetched that was, that those who opposed Obama and Third Left stances generally might return them to that suffering status. What is important here was not the stridency or improbability of some of these fears but the strength with which such beliefs were held, strength that made them impervious to argument or facts to the contrary.

On one hand, opposition forces have been demoralized, divided, and discredited. On the other hand, the indoctrination from education is long-term and reinforced by ongoing, daily doses from other areas of culture.

Then there is the element of material self-interest, especially in the areas of entitlements for those poorer, in specific benefits for elements in the middle class, and in the creation of a large crony capitalist sector where the advantage of going along with a powerful government is the road to prosperity. And finally there are powerful single-issue passions.

This combination of past suffering—identification of conservatism with evil (neo-fascism, paternalistic, reactionary religious), and the fear that the opposition wanted to return them to the bad old days of slavery, barefoot in the kitchen and having to bear unwanted babies, cowering in the closet, or deported—overwhelms rational considerations. And it has all been stoked brilliantly by the Third Left. While the level of support can be reduced, it was not going to change much. It is impervious to facts and developments.

The Third Left, however, had put mechanisms into place to avoid such an outcome. One line of defense was to deny that the problem existed in the first place. The recession was ending and the economy was recovering, as shown by those lower unemployment statistics, for example. Or it could be argued that the quality of life was improving, that what was important was the increase in equality and social justice, of environmental well-being and an earth saved from man-made global warming. Meanwhile, the proportion of those successfully indoctrinated would steadily increase as new generations came of age that didn't remember pre–Third Left Communism or liberalism, a time when the media aspired to balance, and education to open inquiry. Their reflexes would be prepared to reject counterarguments even before hearing them.

To the extent that growing problems were recognized, that could be managed, too. If the masses were persuaded to blame the greed of the rich and the incompetence of capitalism, they would only support the further tightening of the system.

And that brings us to the key counterargument, that a dose of reality, especially the inability to sustain this pyramid scheme of spending, debt, and entitlement, will collapse in front of everyone. That reality will impose itself decisively on the managed state. Or, in other words, it wasn't working and people don't like the results that they see.

There are indeed many reasons to expect that this will happen. The statist structure of the Third Left and "Progressive" liberals simply doesn't fit the American economic system, ensuring continued high unemployment and recession. By punishing the productive and rewarding failed or inefficient enterprises, the ruling ideas threatened to wreck the economy on a long-term basis.

American culture is based on a high level of individualism and a large margin of freedom that will not accept a continually stronger, more restrictive level control by intellectuals or government over society and restrictions on individual freedom.

Failures in policy and at the ballot box, along with a growing understanding of the situation, have triggered a stronger anti-"Progressive" reaction led by conservatives.

A demand for abstract equality "fairness" is not going to motivate the overturn of existing social arrangements. And the objectively improving status of minority groups will also give them incentives for rejecting ideas and policies that damage most of their material interests, which increasingly parallel those of the rest of the population.

The Third Left–"Progressive" foreign policy empowers authoritarian enemies of America, leading to crises and conflicts abroad that the radical approach cannot handle.

Ironically, the Third Left succeeded too fast before the indoctrination of several generations and their placement in control of institutions gave its ideas overwhelming, irreversible hegemony. In that sense, the Obama phenomenon, which appeared to advance so much the radical agenda, may appear in the long run to have subverted it.

One weakness of the radical movement, however, was clear. The earlier revolutionaries intended to destroy the existing government to create a completely new regime structured to ensure their hold on power. Failures, such as economic decline, didn't worry them because they could repress any dissent and didn't need to win fair elections.

What might bring the Third Left–dominated era to an end? In broad historical terms, there are five factors to be considered:

Will the ideas and projects of the Third Left at home and abroad fail badly enough that this will be recognized by the majority of Americans, who would then reject it?

Will the outcome of the Third Left's philosophy become objectionable to the majority of Americans due to its effect on their own lives and psyches?

Is the high tide of Third Left hegemony linked to the personality of Obama to the extent that after his departure from the political scene a fad-oriented society that yearns for new trends will seize on someone or something else? In short, will Barack Obama prove to be a unique phenomenon and the Third Left's leadership a unique generation?

Has the Third Left era been largely the result of experience by a single generation, that is, the 1960s baby boomers, and so will not match the demands and needs of successors?

And will structural changes in the United States, say, for example, the entrance of more African Americans and Hispanics into greater affluence, or even the mere aging of a young cohort that finds its indoctrination to have been misleading, shift political and social attitudes?

So the economy and society would stagnate, development slow, innovation stall, and the proportion of producers to receivers decline. There is, however, a planned escape route. This critical situation, which would, under normal conditions, unseat the Third Left, now became another asset in its favor. Instead of furnishing proof that the

Third Left had failed, it was merely to be counted as proof that the situation required even more fundamental transformation, and that the opposition was stronger and more evil than previously thought.

What are the main principles required to challenge the immense cultural and political power of the Third Left and "Progressive" liberals?

While capitalism must be regulated, it cannot work if it is being strangled. Capitalists are no more prone to illegal and immoral activity than are college professors, government bureaucrats, and politicians. Excessive spending is dangerous for American society and the economy. Liberals accepted the concept of deficit spending but not insanely high deficits.

One must value success honestly achieved and wealth honestly gained. If success is no longer respected it will become increasingly rare. Class warfare is alien to Western liberalism. While, of course, people who are wealthier should pay more in taxes, the idea that they should pay virtually everything is financially unworkable and bad for the society.

Improving the environment was good; destroying American industry and refusing to drill for oil or mine for coal is bad. Such common sense is needed on all issues.

Social snobbery is reactionary and antiliberal. Millions of minds able to operate flexibly and willing to adapt to the real world and changing conditions will do better than a handful of self-proclaimed geniuses who only talk to each other, have a rigid worldview, and possess only narrow experience.

American society does not guarantee equality of result. Granting special privileges to certain groups on the basis of wrongs suffered generations ago is neither liberal nor democratic. Civil rights and racial equality were good; quotas and obsessive division of America's people into groupings with unequal rights is bad. To encourage groups to view others as their eternal oppressor only breeds bitterness and conflict.

Traditional standards of intellectual debate and academic honesty should be upheld. Liberals should not engage in politically correct exercises in intimidation. Schools should not be places for partisan and ideological indoctrination; universities should present a real diversity of opinion.

The mass media should strive to be balanced and fair to the utmost extent. Any editor or journalist who consistently slants or hides stories should be fired.

Conservatives are not monsters. Those who demonize them are simply incapable of answering their arguments rationally.

Many of these points would have been regarded as obvious a generation ago, and they are probably capable of winning a majority today—if the issues at stake are clearly comprehended, which is a very difficult proposition indeed.

One thing is certain: The Third Left–"Progressive" program in America will fail. It will fail out of political defeat or it will fail to make the United States a better place due to the disasters brought about by its victory.

The Third Left, however, was trying to run an existing capitalist society in which its misfit policies inevitably produced failure and even disaster. What they were doing was somewhat akin to trying to get your computer to boot up by hitting it with a club. There were also still big holes in its control over information and education, allowing reality to shine through. The accidental and too-fast ascent of the Obama administration was very dangerous for the movement, since that government's failures repelled the public, while its high profile mobilized opposition and the discovery of the silent revolution.

Thus the mountain of failure can rise so high and become so obvious that it undermines the movement that is responsible for the problems. To put it in Abraham Lincoln's words, "you may fool all the people some of the time; you can even fool some of the people all the time; but you can't fool all of the people all the time"—at least after enough time has elapsed.

Already the evidence shows this failure of accomplishment, but does that inevitably mean its political defeat? In short, might the Third Left strategy of controlling mental superstructure, of controlling beliefs, be triumphant even though reality contradicted its every claim?

Yes. The Third Left's political triumph should teach two lessons.

First, pragmatism—the test of success in reality—does not necessarily work. To make this claim to Westerners, it is as if gravity has suddenly ceased functioning, as if results don't matter anymore. Yet at least for a period of many years that can in effect be true, as was shown in the history of Marxism as so intellectually powerful, and of Communism, able to keep power for many years despite its manifest, abject failure.

Second, there is something strange in Western civilization, which has achieved such heights of greatness and prosperity and yet, in Europe even more than in America, seems to be facing decay with no easy or clear way out. The reasons for this situation are unknown but might be found in the very benefits of prosperity, which have brought the irreversible decline in religion and patriotism; a huge shift in gender roles and the family; a desire for an easy and rich life based on entitlement rather than hard work, now possible for the first time in the history of humanity; new technologies; and demographic shifts.

Otherwise, one would have expected that the twenty-first century should have been spent in celebration of this progress instead of giving rise to a powerful movement that ignored the successes and cursed America. Yet American values—some liberal, some conservative—must meld in order to work. If successfully hijacked by the left, America will fail at home and abroad, while *liberalism* itself will become a dirty word, fundamentally transformed into the opposite of itself.

The outlook is, however, a pessimistic one. Of course, there will be some partial recovery. But is there a unity of opposition, clarity of vision, charismatic leadership, and coherent doctrine that can inspire a reversal? This seems doubtful. America may decline more slowly but it is hard to see where the courage, determination, unity, and money would come from to revive the traditional American virtues.

It is not only that things have gone too far. It is also that the indoctrination may have gone too deep, into the basic structures of attitudes toward people, society, and philosophy, and so may be too hard to root out. This is especially true because a large crisis involving violence and instability that shakes people's lives or puts their financial survival in visible doubt is unlikely.

Moreover, any attempt to change course would be subject to strong resistance and weak implementation in presenting different values by the schools, media, nonprofit organizations, and entertainment industry. The Third Left–managerial caste would protest that this was the real face of capitalism's failure and cutbacks: its lack of sympathy to the people's suffering.

Finally, there are those mysterious structural changes in Western society that are seen in both Europe and America, from crashing birth rates, declining cultures, a loss of self-confidence, and worsening economies. A comeback cannot be achieved easily.

Here is the problem in brief. Bad things are happening in the direction of American society, including mounting debt, regulation, declining educational quality, international credibility, and standards of behavior. It is true that the Third Left has received far less than it desired but it is continually indoctrinating through schools, the media, and entertainment or cultural sources, and winning through regulatory agencies and court decisions, too. Moreover, the very fact of deadlock—especially on legislative decisions—means that the rolling back of negative changes would also be harder.

If someone is persuaded of something, they can change their mind relatively easily based on facts or developments. But if they are indoctrinated by an ideological framework, a worldview, that is a very different situation, because evidence and experience that contradict it will be ignored or misinterpreted.

While there will be inevitably electoral reverses, they will be by relatively small margins, and often by people who lack the courage or resources to battle against the winds of popularity, needing the services of ideologically opposed cadre. Thus, while the slide may be slowed down, there is no mandate for a social and ideological counterrevolution.

Or to put it another way, the brakes can be applied, but will there be a U-turn?

The result may be a very long term and even permanent— inasmuch as it is possible to use such a word in discussing history— change of the United States into something else, a nation far less affluent and far less free. Whatever the course of this struggle, its outcome will determine whether America will again prosper at home, maintain social peace, and remain a great power internationally, or sink gradually but ever downward, as so many societies have in the past.

NOTES

CHAPTER 1: AMERICA'S FUNDAMENTAL TRANSFORMATION HAS ALREADY HAPPENED

1. "Obama: We Are 5 Days from Fundamentally Transforming America," YouTube video, posted by "PatriotPost," February 2, 2012, www.youtube.com/watch?v=oKxDdxzX0kI.
2. Inaugural Address by President Barack Obama, January 21, 2013, www.whitehouse.gov/the-press-office/2013/01/21/inaugural-address-president-barack-obama.
3. Ibid.
4. Ibid.
5. Victor Davis Hanson, "Good News, What Good News?" *PJMedia*, http://pjmedia.com/victordavishanson/good-news-what-good-news/2.
6. Dieter Farwick, "Walter Laqueur: Europe—Recovery or Collapse?," *World Security Network*, April 23, 2012, www.worldsecuritynetwork.com/Europe/dieter-farwick-1/Walter-Laqueur-Europe-Recovery-or-Collapse.

CHAPTER 2: THE MARXIST CHALLENGE TO WESTERN SOCIETY

1. David Thomson, *England in the Nineteenth Century* (London: Penguin, 1961), pp. 18–19.
2. For Marx's use of Cobbett's report see his "Inaugural Address of the International Working Men's Association," October 21, 1864, http://marxists.org/archive/marx/works/1864/10/27.htm; Thomson, *England in the Nineteenth Century*, p. 12.

3. Robert Roswell Palmer, Joel Colton, Lloyd Kramer, *A History of the Modern World Since 1815*, 10th ed. (Boston: McGraw-Hill, 2007).
4. Vladimir I. Lenin, *The State and Revolution* (London: Penguin Books, 1993) (original published in 1917).
5. Karl Marx, *The German Ideology*, 1845.
6. Ibid.
7. Ibid.
8. Karl Marx and Friedrich Engels, *Manifesto of the Communist Party*, 1848.
9. Ibid.
10. Ibid.
11. Leon Trotsky, *Our Political Tasks* (Geneva, 1904), p. 54.
12. Karl Marx, *The German Ideology* (1845).
13. Vladimir I. Lenin, *The State and Revolution*.
14. Ibid.
15. Ibid.
16. Ibid.
17. Karl Marx and Friedrich Engels, *Manifesto of the Communist Party*, 1848.
18. Ibid.
19. Ibid.
20. Ibid.
21. Karl Marx, "Theses on Feuerbach," in Karl Marx and Friedrich Engels, *The German Ideology* (New York: Prometheus Books, 1998).
22. Karl Marx and Friedrich Engels, *Manifesto of the Communist Party*, 1848.
23. Karl Marx, "Address of the International Working Men's Association to Abraham Lincoln, President of the United States of America," January 28, 1865, http://marxists.org/history/international/iwma/documents/1864/lincoln-letter.htm#a.

CHAPTER 3: WHY MARXISM FAILED AND THE WEST SUCCEEDED

1. Cliff Stratton, "Browder Shies from Friendly Reception Here . . . ," *Wichita Eagle*, June 30, 1936, www.kshs.org/kansapedia/earl-browder-newspaper-articles/11697
2. George Orwell, "Mark Twain, the Licensed Jester," *Tribune*, November 26, 1943, www.online-literature.com/orwell/894/.
3. Karl Marx, *The German Ideology*, 1845.
4. Karl Marx and Friedrich Engels, *Manifesto of the Communist Party*, 1848.
5. Ibid.
6. Ibid.
7. Ibid.
8. Michael Kazin, "The Port Huron Statement at Fifty," *Dissent*, Spring 2012, www.dissentmagazine.org/article/the-port-huron-statement-at-fifty.
9. Karl Marx and Friedrich Engels, *Manifesto of the Communist Party*, 1848.
10. "You Don't Need a Weatherman to Know Which Way the Wind Blows,"

New Left Notes, June 18, 1969, www.sds-1960s.org/NewLeftNotes-vol4-no22
.pdf; also available at www.archive.org/stream/YouDontNeedAWeatherman
ToKnowWhichWayTheWindBlows_925/weather_djvu.txt.

CHAPTER 4: THE MAKING OF THE THIRD LEFT

1. Karl Marx and Friedrich Engels, *Manifesto of the Communist Party*, 1848.
2. Mark Oppenheimer, "Free Bob Avakian!," *Boston Globe*, January 27, 2008, www.boston.com/bostonglobe/ideas/articles/2008/01/27/free_bob_avakian.
3. David Horowitz, *Radicals: Portraits of a Destructive Passion* (Washington, DC: Regnery Publishing, 2012), p. 185.
4. "From Pineapples to Small Schools, Alum Mike Klonsky's Work Is No Small Talk," University of Illinois at Chicago College of Education, http://education .uic.edu/alumni/620-from-pineapples-to-small-schools-alum-mike-klonskys-work-is-no-small-talk; "Bill Ayers," The Biography Channel, www.biography .com/people/bill-ayers-380916.
5. Klonsky even ran a blog on the official Obama campaign website until the blogger Stephen F. Diamond—not the mass media—exposed this connection. Stephen F. Diamond, "Berkeley Law's Edley Joins Ayers Renaissance–Maoist Klonsky Applauds," October 22, 2009, http://stephen-diamond .com/?p=1689.
6. Ylan Q. Mui, "Michelle Obama, Grocers Join Forces on Food Deserts," *Washington Post*, July 20, 2011, www.washingtonpost.com/blogs/federal-eye/post/obama -grocers-join-forces-on-food-deserts/2011/07/20/gIQAgf5FQI_blog.html.
7. The Middle East Media Research Institute TV Monitor Project, clip 1250, August 22, 2006, www.memritv.org/clip/en/1250.htm.
8. Barack Obama, *Dreams from My Father: A Story of Race and Inheritance* (New York: Broadway Books, 1995, 2004), p. 101.
9. "You Don't Need a Weatherman to Know Which Way the Wind Blows," *New Left Notes*, June 18, 1969, www.sds-1960s.org/NewLeftNotes-vol4-no22 .pdf; also available at www.archive.org/stream/YouDontNeedAWeatherman ToKnowWhichWayTheWindBlows_925/weather_djvu.txt. All quotes are taken from this text.
10. Klonsky, for example, was codirector of the Small Schools Workshop at the University of Illinois at Chicago, which ran the Teacher Leadership Academy. The program received funding from the Chicago Annenberg Challenge public school reform project, of which Obama was on the board. See *Memo, Chicago Annenberg Challenge Report*, May 8, 1996, http://sonatabio.com/CAC/CAC-1996-first.pdf, pp. ii, 10. See also Stanley Kurtz, "Obama and Ayers Pushed Radicalism on Schools," *Wall Street Journal*, September 23, 2008, http://on line.wsj.com/news/articles/SB122212856075765367.
11. Note that the manifesto did not mention the many Catholic or conservative Protestant churches that do the bulk of such charity work but picked the most left-wing religious group they could think of.
12. Karl Marx, *The German Ideology*, 1845.

13. Karl Marx, "Theses on Feuerbach," in Karl Marx and Friedrich Engels, *The German Ideology* (New York: Prometheus Books, 1998).
14. Francis Bacon, *The Great Instauration*, (1620).
15. Francis Bacon, *The Advancement of Learning* (1605), http://ebooks.adelaide .edu.au/b/bacon/francis/b12a/complete.html.
16. Mao Zedong, "Draft Decision of the Central Committee of the Chinese Communist Party on Certain Problems in Our Present Rural Work," May 1963, http://www.marxists.org/reference/archive/mao/selected-works/volume-9/ mswv9_01.htm.
17. Andrei S. Markovits, "The European and American Left since 1945," *Dissent*, Winter 2005.
18. Ibid.
19. Ibid.
20. Karl Marx and Friedrich Engels, *Manifesto of the Communist Party*, 1848
21. Obama said a greedy surgeon would make $30,000 to $50,000 to amputate the foot of a diabetic and thus a doctor would do that rather than prevent diabetes. The actual amount is between $740 and $1,140. Cheryl Clark, "Obama Missteps on Foot Amputation Pay to Surgeons," Health Leaders Media, August 14, 2009, www.healthleadersmedia.com/content/237492/topic/WS_HLM2_ PHY/Obama-Missteps-on-Foot-Amputation-Pay-to-Surgeons.html.
22. "If you don't have your papers and you took your kid out to get ice cream, you're going to be harassed, that's something that could potentially happen." Obama misstated the law, which said that people's citizenship or legal immigration status could be checked only if they were being stopped by police for suspected criminal action. Kristina Wong, "President Obama Says Arizona's 'Poorly Conceived' Immigration Law Could Mean Hispanic-Americans Are Harassed," ABC News, April 27, 2010, http://abcnews.go.com/blogs/poli tics/2010/04/president-obama-says-arizonas-poorlyconceived-immigration- law-could-mean-hispanicamericans-are-haras/.
23. Michael Moore, *Sicko*, The Weinstein Company, 2007.
24. Joseph Schumpeter, *Capitalism, Socialism, and Democracy* (New York: Harper & Row, 1942), p. 153.
25. James Burnham, "Letter of Resignation from the Workers Party," May 1940, www.marxists.org/history/etol/writers/burnham/1940/05/resignation.htm. One of Burnham's most careful readers was the writer George Orwell, who based his novel *1984* on what might eventually result if Burnham's prediction was fulfilled.

CHAPTER 5: A NEW POLITICAL PHILOSOPHY IN POWER

1. Barry Rubin, "Barack Obama and the Cruise Ship Theory of Underdevelopment: A Formula for . . . Permanent Underdevelopment," *Rubin Report*, July 3, 2010, http://rubinreports.blogspot.co.il/2010/07/by-barry-rubin-in-his-autobio graphy.html.
2. "Mayhill Fowler, "Obama: No Surprise That Hard-Pressed Pennsylvanians

Turn Bitter," *Huffington Post*, April 11, 2008, www.huffingtonpost.com/ mayhill-fowler/obama-no-surprise-that-ha_b_96188.html.
3. Karl Marx and Friedrich Engels, *Manifesto of the Communist Party*, 1848.
4. David Nakamura, "Obama at New York Celebrity Fundraiser: 'Manhattan Isn't a Battleground,'" *Washington Post*, June 15, 2012, www.washington post.com/blogs/election-2012/post/obama-at-new-york-celebrity-fundraiser-manhattan-isnt-a-battleground/2012/06/15/gJQARiuydV_blog.html; Ben Feller, "Obama to Celebrities: 'You're the Ultimate Arbiter of Which Direction This Country Goes,'" CSNNews (Associated Press), June 14, 2012, http://cnsnews.com/news/article/obama-celebrities-youre-ultimate-arbiter-which-direction-country-goes.
5. Popsugar Sex & Culture, "Anna Wintour in Minnesota: People Are Little Houses Here," *Popsugar*, www.tressugar.com/Anna-Wintour-Minnesota-People-Little-Houses-Here-3165175; "Anna Wintour Obama Video Invites You to Dine with Her, Sarah Jessica Parker & FLOTUS," *Huffington Post*, June 1, 2012, www.huffingtonpost.com/2012/06/01/anna-wintour-obama-video-sarah-jessica-parker_n_1562166.html.
6. After all, if Chief Justice John Roberts of the Supreme Court made his decision on Obamacare because, as some reliable reporters wrote, he was concerned to retain his reputation among the media, law schools, and the socially dominant left, that too constitutes accepting a bribe.
7. Lindsey Ellerson, "Obama to Bankers: I'm Standing 'Between You and the Pitchforks,'" ABC News, http://abcnews.go.com/blogs/politics/2009/04/obama-to-banker/.
8. See chapter 2.
9. "YouTube Debate: Hillary—Are You a Liberal?" YouTube video, posted by "Politicstv," July 23, 2007, www.youtube.com/watch?v=C2oOoCdFblc; http://articles.cnn.com/2007-07-23/politics/debate.transcript_1_new-ideas-issues-don-t-matter-child-care-legislation/4?_s=PM:POLITICS.
10. These issues are discussed in more detail in chapter 7.
11. How ironic that George Soros was a student of Popper, who claimed to admire him and even named his own main project "Open Society"! To put it humorously, Soros must not have been paying attention in class. Or, perhaps more seriously, what Soros did in this regard was an act of such supreme cynicism as to have been a deliberate act of flaunting evil, an inside joke the likes of which can only be found in John Milton's description of another traitor disciple in *Paradise Lost*.

CHAPTER 6: THE CONQUEST OF INSTITUTIONS

1. Tom Wolfe, "Radical Chic: That Party at Lenny's," *New York*, June 8, 1970, http://nymag.com/news/features/46170/.
2. Bruce Bawer, "Today's Radical Chic," *Front Page Mag*, March 19, 2012, http://frontpagemag.com/2012/bruce-bawer/todays-radical-chic/.
3. Ibid.

4. The mass media reaction was enthusiastic about Obama making jokes about these and similar incidents. See "President Obama at White House Correspondents Dinner," whitehouse.gov, April 27, 2013, www.whitehouse.gov/photos-and-video/video/2013/04/28/president-obama-white-house-correspondents-dinner; Hannah Lyons Powell, "Barack Obama Jokes about Taylor Swift and Jay-Z at White House Dinner," *Glamour*, April 29, 2013, www.glamourmaga zine.co.uk/celebrity/celebrity-news/2013/04/29/barack-obama-jokes-taylor-swift-jay-z-white-house-dinner.

5. Joel Gehrke, "Pastor Who Prayed at Obama's Inauguration Says All White People Will Go to Hell," *Washington Examiner*, October 31, 2012, http://washingtonexaminer.com/pastor-who-prayed-at-obamas-inauguration-says-all-white-people-will-go-to-hell/article/2512272#.UKGQGuSTyvM.

6. Although the passage was restored by the convention leadership, it clearly failed a majority vote.

7. See, for example, Hans A. Von Spakovsky, "Federal Court: DOJ Official May Have Lied about the New Black Panther Case," *PJMedia*, July 30, 2012, http://pjmedia.com/tatler/2012/07/30/federal-court-doj-official-may-have-lied-about-the-new-black-panther-case/; J. Christian Adams, "How Many Crimes Did the New Black Panthers Commit in Florida?" *PJMedia*, March 26, 2012, http://pjmedia.com/jchristianadams/2012/03/26/how-many-crimes-did-the-new-black-panthers-commit-in-florida/.

8. Cathy Wilkerson, *Flying Close to the Sun: My Life and Times as a Weatherman* (New York: Seven Stories Press, 2007), p. 371.

9. One of them was the Chicago New Party, which Barack Obama would join.

10. The term has roots in the writings of the Italian Communist Party leader Antonio Gramsci but was coined in modern times by the West German radical leader Rudy Dutschke in 1968. "The permanent revolutionaries can be thrown out time and time again, [but] they will always penetrate new institutions: That is the long march through the institutions." Ulrike Marie Meinhof, *The Dignity of Man Is Tangible: Essays and Polemics.* (Berlin: Klaus Wagenbach, 1980). Meinhof was the co-leader of Germany's worst terrorist group.

11. Ronald Radosh, "A Story Told Before," *Weekly Standard*, November 12, 2012, www.weeklystandard.com/articles/story-told_660176.html; Michael Moynihan, "Oliver Stone's Junk History of the United States Debunked," *Daily Beast*, November 19, 2012, www.thedailybeast.com/articles/2012/11/19/oliver-stone-s-junk-history-of-the-united-states-debunked.html.

12. Barack Obama was a member of the foundation's board between 1994 and 2002. See, for example, the Joyce Foundation's 1999 Annual Report, http://www.joycefdn.org/assets/1/7/99_AnnualReport.pdf , where Obama is listed under the board of directors. See also Ellen Alberding's biography on the Joyce Foundation's website, http://www.joycefdn.org/newsroom/our-experts/ellen-alberding/.

13. "You Don't Need a Weatherman to Know Which Way the Wind Blows," *New Left Notes*, June 18, 1969, www.sds-1960s.org/NewLeftNotes-vol4-no22.pdf; also available at www.archive.org/stream/YouDontNeedAWeatherman ToKnowWhichWayTheWindBlows_925/weather_djvu.txt.

14. John Fonte, "Why There Is a Culture War," *Policy Review*, no. 104, December 1, 2000, www.hoover.org/publications/policy-review/5100.
15. Ibid.
16. Ibid.
17. A reference to Allan Bloom, *The Closing of the American Mind* (New York: Simon & Schuster, 1987).
18. John Roche, *The History and Impact of Marxist-Leninist Organizational Theory* (Cambridge, MA: Institute for Foreign Policy Analysis, 1984) p. 64.
19. Ibid.
20. Robert Hughes, "Pulling the Fuse on Culture," *Time*, June 24, 2001, www .time.com/time/magazine/article/0,9171,134526,00.html; "Ten Questions for Arianna Huffington," *Time*, September 18, 2006, www.time.com/time/na tion/article/0,8599,1536338,00.html.
21. Jonathan Strong, "Liberal Journalists Suggest Government Shut Down Fox News," *Daily Caller*, July 21, 2010, http://dailycaller.com/2010/07/21/liberal-journalists-suggest-government-shut-down-fox-news/; Jonathan Strong, "Documents Show Media Plotting to Kill Stories about Rev. Jeremiah Wright," Daily Caller, July 20.2010, http://dailycaller.com/2010/07/20/documents-show-media-plotting-to-kill-stories-about-rev-jeremiah-wright.
22. Jonathan Strong, "When McCain Picked Palin, Liberal Journalists Coordinated the Best Line of Attack," *Daily Caller*, July 22, 2010, http://dailycaller .com/2010/07/22/when-mccain-picked-palin-liberal-journalists-coordinated-the-best-line-of-attack/.
23. Howard Kurtz, "Getting the Message on Journolist's Controversial Postings," Media Notes, *Washington Post*, July 23, 2010, www.washingtonpost.com/wp-dyn/content/article/2010/07/22/AR2010072206024.html?sub=AR.
24. Rasmussen Reports, "Just 53 Percent Say Capitalism Better than Socialism," April 9, 2009, www.rasmussenreports.com/public_content/politics/general_ politics/april_2009/just_53_say_capitalism_better_than_socialism.
25. Galileo Galilei, *Dialogue Concerning the Two Chief World Systems*, 1632, http://law2.umkc.edu/faculty/projects/ftrials/galileo/dialogue2.html.
26. Personal observations.
27. Bruce Bawer, *The Victims' Revolution: The Rise of Identity Studies and the Closing of the Liberal Mind* (New York: Broadside Books, 2012). See also Chris Haire, "Defending Western Culture, Decrying Multiculturalism . . . Restoring Education?," *Downtown*, September 4, 2012, http://downtownmagazine nyc.com/the-victims-revolution-review-defending-western-culture-decrying-multiculturalism-restoring-education/.
28. Oliver Stone, *Oliver Stone's Untold History of the United States*, Showtime, www.sho.com/sho/oliver-stones-untold-history-of-the-united-states/home.
29. Ronald Radosh, "How the Academic Establishment Has Silenced a Major Critic of the Field of 'Black Studies,'" *PJMedia*, May 8, 2012, http://pjmedia .com/ronradosh/2012/05/08/how-the-academic-establishment-has-silenced-a-major-critic-of-the-field-of-black-studies/.
30. Bruce Kesler, "Working Hard to Convince Freshmen They Are Victims," *Minding the Campus*, June 5, 2012, www.mindingthecampus.com/fo rum/2012/06/working_hard_to_convince_freshmen_they_are_victims.html;

Bruce Kesler, "Fact and Fiction at Brooklyn College," *Maggie's Farm*, October 14, 2010, http://maggiesfarm.anotherdotcom.com/archives/15628-Fact-and-Fiction-at-Brooklyn-College.html; Bruce Kesler, "More of the Same: Brooklyn College Common Reading a Year Later," *Maggie's Farm*, August 5, 2011, http://maggiesfarm.anotherdotcom.com/archives/17706-More-Of-The-Same-Brooklyn-College-Common-Reading-A-Year-Later.html.

31. Bruce Kesler, "Working Hard to Convince Freshmen They Are Victims."

32. Karl Marx, *The German Ideology*, http://www.marxists.org/archive/marx/works/1845/german-ideology/ch01b.htm.

33. "Van Jones 'Top Down, Bottom Up Movement,'" YouTube video, posted by "Brent Hellendoorn," March 20, 2011, www.youtube.com/watch?v=TWrdgkt9z_c; University of California Television (UCTV), "Van Jones: The Green Collar Economy," YouTube, June 17, 2010, www.youtube.com/watch?v=RBM1qgnTz4s.

34. Bureau of Labor Statistics, United States Department of Labor, "Union Members Summary," news release, January 23, 2013, www.bls.gov/news.release/union2.nr0.htm.

35. Service Employees International Union, "About SEIU," [n.d.], www.seiu.org/our-union/; http://www.unionfacts.com/union/National_Education_Association; http://www.unionfacts.com/union/American_Federation_of_State_County_%26_Municipal_Employe; http://www.iaff.org/about/history/whoweare.htm; http://www.unionfacts.com/union/Fire_%26_Security_Officers; http://www.aft.org/about/.

36. Tom McGinty and Brody Mullins, "Political Spending by Unions Far Exceeds Direct Donations," *Wall Street Journal*, July 10, 2012, http://online.wsj.com/article/SB10001424052702304782404577488584031850026.html.

37. Ibid.

38. Andrew J. Coulson, "America Has Too Many Teachers," *Wall Street Journal*, July 10, 2012, http://online.wsj.com/article/SB10001424052702303734204577465413553320588.html.

39. Ibid.

40. See chapter 8.

41. Fonte, "Why There Is a Culture War."

42. Catherine MacKinnon, *Toward a Feminist Theory of the State* (Cambridge, MA: Harvard University Press, 1989), p. 170.

43. Walter Russell Mead, " 'Liberal' Think Tank Caught with Hand in the Cookie Jar," *American Interest*, May 23, 2913, http://blogs.the-american-interest.com/wrm/2013/05/23/liberal-think-tank-caught-with-hand-in-the-cookie-jar/.

44. "Warren Buffett, Hypocrite," editorial, *New York Post*, August 29, 2011, www.nypost.com/p/news/opinion/editorials/warren_buffett_hypocrite_E3BsmJmeQVE38q2Woq9yjJ#ixzz1WRoIlYSf ; Newsmax Wires, "Report: Buffett's Berkshire Owes $1 Billion in Back Taxes," *Newsmax*, September 1, 2011, www.newsmax.com/Headline/buffett-irs-back-taxes/2011/09/01/id/409520; Barbara Hollingsworth, "Warren Buffett's Latest Tax Dodge," *Washington Examiner*, April 15, 2012, http://washingtonexaminer.com/article/1231806; "Warren Buffett's Tax Dodge," editorial, *Wall Street Journal*, August 17, 2011, http://online.wsj.com/article/SB10001424053111903918104576504650932556900.html.

45. Margaret Carlson, "Should the Huffingtons Be Stopped?" *Time*, October 3, 1994, www.time.com/time/magazine/article/0,9171,981544,00.html; Belinda Luscombe, "*Time*'s Top 100 Influential People of 2011: Arianna Huffington," *Time*, April 21, 2011, www.time.com/time/specials/packages/arti cle/0,28804,2066367_2066369_2066496,00.html.

46. This and following quotes are taken from Zombie [pseud.], " 'Teaching as a Subversive Activity': The Theory of Political Indoctrination," *PJMedia*, April 12, 2012, http://pjmedia.com/zombie/2012/04/12/teaching-as-a-subversive-activity-the-theory-of-political-indoctrination/. The author is a well-known writer who documents his work thoroughly but must use a pseudonym, "Zombie," to avoid jeopardizing his job.

47. H. Douglas Brown, *Teaching as a Subversive Activity—Revisited*. April 6, 2012, http://blc.berkeley.edu/index.php/blc/post/lecture_april_6_2012_h._doug las_brown/.

48. Zombie [pseud.], " 'Teaching as a Subversive Activity': The Theory of Political Indoctrination."

49. Congressional Progressive Caucus, "The Progressive Promise: Fairness for All," [n.d.] http://cpc.grijalva.house.gov/index.cfm?sectionid=63&sectiontree=2,63.

50. Zombie [pseud.], "Another Hollywood Millionaire Outs Self as Faux-Socialist Hypocrite," *PJMedia*, July 15, 2012, http://pjmedia.com/tatler/2012/07/15/ another-hollywood-millionaire-outs-self-as-faux-socialist-hypocrite-joss-whedon-rants-against-capitalism/.

51. Herman Wouk, *The Caine Mutiny*. (New York: Doubleday, 1951).

52. The late Michael O'Hare, who originated the role of Jessep on Broadway.

53. Aaron Sorkin, *A Few Good Men*, Broadway, 1989.

CHAPTER 7: BARACK OBAMA AS CASE STUDY OF A THIRD LEFT CADRE

1. Charles C. Johnson, "Who Were Barack Obama's Marxist Professors?" *PJMedia*, September 17, 2012, http://pjmedia.com/blog/who-were-barack-obamas-marxist-professors/.

2. Anne Ball, "Caldwell Charts Decline of American-Soviet Relations," *Occidental*, May 1, 1981.

3. Gretchen Lux, "Caldwell Shares His 'Last' Views," *Occidental*, May 8, 1981.

4. Kerry Eleveld, "Obama Talks All Things LGBT with the Advocate," *Advocate*, December 23, 2008, www.advocate.com/news/2008/12/23/obama-talks-all-things-lgbt-the%C2%A0advocate.

5. Lisa Messinger and Debra Lewinter, "Egan Links Economics and Latin Repression," *Occidental*, [n.d.].

6. Susan Keselenko, "Boesche Synthesizes Political Convictions," *Occidental*, May 1, 1981.

7. Johnson, "Who Were Barack Obama's Marxist Professors?"

8. Steven R. Weisman, ed., *Daniel Patrick Moynihan: A Portrait in Letters of an American Visionary* (New York: PublicAffairs, 2010), pp. 232–33.

9. Ibid.

10. George Orwell, *Horizon*, September 1943.

11. Ibid.

12. Ben Smith, "The Real Story of Barack Obama", *BuzzFeed Politics*, June 17, 2012, www.buzzfeed.com/bensmith/the-real-story-of-barack-obama.

13. Ibid.

14. Barack H. Obama [Sr.], "Problems Facing Our Socialism," *East Africa Journal*, July 1965, available at www.politico.com/static/PPM41_eastafrica.html. He notes that "in most African societies the individual had sole right as to the use of land and proceeds from it. He did, however, own it only as a trustee to the clan, tribe, and society."

15. Ibid. In land ownership, he favors clan cooperatives, an example of how he was an African socialist rather than a Communist.

16. Ibid.

17. Since the FBI knew that Davis was a Communist, however, it might have been using his assessment in the opposite way, knowing that anyone he recommended would be suspect.

18. John Edgar Tidwell, "An Interview with Frank Marshall Davis," *Black American Literature Forum*, Autumn 1985; "Frank Marshall Davis' Blog 1949," http://www.hawaii.edu/uhwo/clear/HonoluluRecord1/frankblog1949.html.

19. "God Damn America Rev Jeremiah Wright, Farrakhan & Obama," YouTube video, posted by "Obamamania," March 14, 2008, www.youtube.com/watch?v=9hPR5jnjtLo.

20. Taylor Marsh, "Obama: Grandmother 'Typical White Person,'" *Huffington Post*, March 20, 2008, www.huffingtonpost.com/taylor-marsh/obama-grandmother-typical_b_92601.html.

21. Ed O'Keefe, "Obama Condemns Wright's Defense," ABC News, April 29, 2008, http://abcnews.go.com/blogs/politics/2008/04/obama-condemns-3/.

22. Ibid.

23. "Obama Speaks of Rev. Wright in This 1995 Interview," YouTube video posted by "Doyouhearwhatihear08," October 27, 2008, www.youtube.com/watch?v=Fh7xMhsLnac.

24. Brian Ross and Rehab El-Buri, "Obama's Pastor: God Damn America, U.S. to Blame for 9/11," ABC News, March 13, 2008, http://abcnews.go.com/Blotter/DemocraticDebate/story?id=4443788&page=1#.UaUbJqKnqLg.

25. "Moment of Truth," editorial, *Washington Post*, March 19, 2008, www.washingtonpost.com/wp-dyn/content/article/2008/03/18/AR2008031802704.html.

26. Ibid.

27. Ibid.

28. Ben Wallace-Wells, "Destiny's Child," *Rolling Stone*, February 22, 2007.

29. Richard Wolf, Jessica Ramirez, and Jeffrey Bartholet, "When Barry Became Barrack," *Daily Beast*, March 22, 2008, www.thedailybeast.com/newsweek/2008/03/22/when-barry-became-barack.html.

30. Ben Smith, "Obama's Wright: White Folks' Greed," *Politico*, March 14, 2008, www.politico.com/blogs/bensmith/0308/Obamas_Wright_White_folks_

greed.html; Barack Obama, *Dreams from My Father* (New York: Three Rivers Press, 2004), p. 293.

31. Obamamania, "God Damn America Rev Jeremiah Wright, Farrakhan & Obama."

32. Elliot C. McLaughlin, "Rev. Wright More than Sound Bite, Obama's Ex-Pastor," CNN, April 29, 2008, http://articles.cnn.com/2008-04-29/politics/wright.bio_1_obama-campaign-chicago-s-trinity-united-church-barack?_s=PM:POLITICS.

33. "Rev. Wright; 9/11, Blame America. Long Version," YouTube video, posted by "jbranstetter04," April 26, 2008, www.youtube.com/watch?v=fXDWLDvxth8.

34. Ibid.

35. Stanley Kurtz, *Radical-in-Chief: Barack Obama and the Untold Story of American Socialism* (New York: Threshold Editions, 2010); Stanley Kurtz, "Obama's Third-Party History," *National Review*, June 7, 2012, www.nationalreview.com/articles/302031/obamas-third-party-history-stanley-kurtz.

36. This issue is discussed at greater length in chapters 6 and 7.

37. Glenn Beck, "Rewriting Our History, Changing Our Traditions," Fox News, December 16, 2009, www.foxnews.com/story/0,2933,580414,00.html.

38. Jack Tapper, "McCain to Attack Obama for Public Radio Comments from 2001," ABC News, October 27, 2008, http://abcnews.go.com/blogs/politics/2008/10/mccain-to-attac/.

39. "Obama: We Are 5 Days from Fundamentally Transforming America," YouTube video, posted by "PatriotPost," February 2, 2012, www.youtube.com/watch?v=oKxDdxzX0kI.

40. Thomas S. Kidd, "Watch Your Religious Language, Mr. President," *USA Today*, December 10, 2010, www.usatoday.com/news/opinion/forum/2010-12-09-kidd10_ST_N.htm; Fred Lucas, "Obama Restores the 'Creator' to His Recitation of the Declaration of Independence," CNSNews, October 25, 2010, http://cnsnews.com/news/article/obama-restores-creator-his-recitation-declaration-independence; Aliyah Shahid, "President Obama Slams GOP Decision to Vote on "In God We Trust" Motto Instead of His Job Creation Bill," November 3, 2011, www.nydailynews.com/news/politics/president-obama-slams-gop-decision-vote-god-trust-motto-job-creation-bill-article-1.971640.

41. Obama's ability to explain away—or more accurately his immunity from serious questions about—his radical associations is enhanced by media behavior. Obama could say he barely knew Ayers when they had numerous associations on foundations and other places. Indeed, the only book review Obama ever wrote was to heap lavish praise on Bill Ayers's *A Kind and Just Parent* in the *Chicago Tribune* in December 1997. Martin Chilton, "President Obama's Reading Habits," *Daily Telegraph*, January 23, 2012, www.telegraph.co.uk/culture/books/booknews/9028331/President-Obamas-reading-habits.html.

42. Brian Friel, Richard E. Cohen, and Kirk Victor, "*National Journal*'s 2007 Vote Ratings," *National Journal*, January 31, 2008, http://news.nationaljournal.com/articles/voteratings/.

43. Johnson, "Who Were Barack Obama's Marxist Professors?"

44. Obama, *Dreams from My Father*, p. 101.

45. Kurtz, *Radical-in-Chief*.

46. The one "defector" from Obama's circle at Occidental who has written in detail about Obama's Marxist views is John Drew. See Drew, "Meeting Young Obama," *American Thinker*, February 24, 2011, www.americanthinker .com/2011/02/meeting_young_obama.html; "My White Girlfriend Inspired Obama's Big, Dark Regina in *Dreams from My Father*," *American Thinker*, July 17, 2012, www.americanthinker.com/2012/07/my_white_girlfriend_in spired_obamas_big_dark_regina_in_dreams_from_my_father.html; and "Face-to-Face with Young Marxist Obama: Remembering My Days as an Anti-Apartheid Student Activist," *NewsRealBlog*, February 17, 2010, www .newsrealblog.com/2010/02/17/face-to-face-with-young-marxist-obama-remembering-my-days-as-an-anti-apartheid-student-activist/.

47. Obama, *Dreams from My Father*, pp. 17, 214.

48. FoxNews.com, "Obama Mistakenly Refers to Hawaii as 'Asia' During Summit," Fox News, November 15, 2011, www.foxnews.com/politics/2011/11/15/ obama-mistakenly-refers-to-hawaii-as-asia-during-summit/; "Obama: Hawaii in Asia," YouTube video, posted by "Ed Morrissey," November 15, 2011, www .youtube.com/watch?v=h9hPXHD4WH0.

49. Obama, *Dreams from My Father*, pp. 17, 214.

50. Jaketapper, "Michelle Obama: 'For the First Time in My Adult Lifetime, I'm Really Proud of My Country,'" Political Punch, ABC News, February 18, 2008, http://abcnews.go.com/blogs/politics/2008/02/michelle-obam-1-2/.

51. Lauren Collins, "The Other Obama: Michelle Obama and the Politics of Candor," *New Yorker*, March 10, 2008, www.newyorker.com/ reporting/2008/03/10/080310fa_fact_collins#ixzz20odlKENI.

52. Karen Russell, "Obama: People Are Hungry for Change," *Huffington Post*, June 2, 2007, www.huffingtonpost.com/karen-russell/obama-people-are-hungry-f_1_b_50423.html.

53. Michelle LaVaughn Robinson, "Princeton Educated Blacks and the Black Community," master's thesis, Princeton University, 1985. See also, Jeffrey Ressner, "Michelle Obama Thesis Was on Racial Divide," *Politico*, February 22, 2008, www.politico.com/news/stories/0208/8642.html. The full text of the thesis is available at www.politico.com/pdf/080222_MOPrincetonThesis_26-501 .pdf, www.politico.com/pdf/080222_MOPrincetonThesis_51-751.pdf, www .politico.com/pdf/080222_MOPrincetonThesis_1-251.pdf.

54. Obama, *Dreams from My Father*, 2004 ebook.

55. Terence P. Jeffrey, "Obama on Why Michelle Was a Working Mom (at $316K per Year): 'We Didn't Have the Luxury for Her Not to Work,'" CSNNews, April 9, 2012, http://cnsnews.com/news/article/obama-why-michelle-was-working-mom-316k-year-we-didnt-have-luxury-her-not-work; Mike Dorning, Bruce Japsen, and David Mendell, "Employer: Michelle Obama's Raise Well-Earned," *Chicago Tribune*, September 27, 2006, http://articles.chicagotribune .com/2006-09-27/news/0609270216_1_greenville-hospital-system-university -of-chicago-hospitals-michelle-obama; Cassandra West, "Her Plan Went Awry, but Michelle Obama Doesn't Mind," *Chicago Tribune*, September 1, 2004, http://articles.chicagotribune.com/2004-09-01/features/0408310383_1_ michelle-obama-sidley-austin-brown-best-laid-plans.

56. Anne Zieger, "U of Chicago Plans Major Restructuring," *FierceHealthcare*, February 9, 2009, www.fiercehealthcare.com/story/u-chicago-plans-major-restructuring/2009-02-09.

57. Christopher Drew and Jo Becker, "Obama Lists His Earmarks, Asking Clinton for Hers," *New York Times*, March 14, 2008, www.nytimes.com/2008/03/14/us/politics/14campaign.html?_r=2; mybudget360, "How much does the Average American Make? Breaking Down the U.S. Household Income Numbers," MyBudget360 [n.d.], www.mybudget360.com/how-much-does-the-average-american-make-breaking-down-the-us-household-income-numbers/.

58. Robinson, "Princeton Educated Blacks and the Black Community."

59. Obama, *Dreams from My Father.*

60. Hans A. Von Spakovsky, "Every Single One: The Politicized Hiring of Eric Holder's Voting Section," *PJMedia*, August 8, 2011, http://pjmedia.com/blog/every-single-one-the-politicized-hiring-of-eric-holder%E2%80%99s-voting-section/ (and http://pjmedia.com/blog/every-single-one-the-politicized-hiring-of-eric-holders-appellate-section/, with links to parts one to ten of the series).

CHAPTER 8: OBAMA AT OSAWATOMIE

1. "Obama's State of the Union Address: Everybody Must Play by the Same Rules," *Huffington Post*, January 24, 2012 www.huffingtonpost.com/2012/01/24/obama-state-of-the-union_n_1229720.html; "2012 State of the Union Address: Enhanced Version," YouTube video, posted by "The White House," January 24, 2012, www.youtube.com/watch?v=Zgfi7wnGZlE.

2. Jeffry Bartash, "Romney and Detroit: Did He Really Say Let US Automakers Fail?," Marketwatch, *Wall Street Journal*, September 5, 2012, http://blogs.marketwatch.com/election/2012/09/05/romney-and-detroit-did-he-really-say-let-u-s-automakers-fail/.

3. "Remarks by the President on the Economy in Osawatomie, Kansas," December 6, 2011, www.whitehouse.gov/the-press-office/2011/12/06/remarks-president-economy-osawatomie-kansas. All of Obama's quotations from Osawatomie in this chapter come from here.

4. Andrea Coombes, "Taxes—Who Really Is Paying Up," *Wall Street Journal*, April 15, 2012, http://online.wsj.com/article/SB10001424052702304356604577338122267919032.html.

5. "Taxes Are for the Little People," editorial, *New York Post*, December 6, 2012, www.nypost.com/p/news/opinion/editorials/taxes_are_for_the_little_people_cLuVKa0gfnxIVaKJvHRFmI.

6. Wayne Crews, "The Cost of Government Regulation," *Forbes*, June 6, 2011, www.forbes.com/sites/waynecrews/2011/07/06/the-cost-of-government-regulation-the-barack-obama-cass-sunstein-urban-legend/.

7. "Chick-Fil-A Controversy Heats Up," *Washington Post*, July 27, 2012, www.washingtonpost.com/chick-fil-a-controversy-heats-up/2012/07/27/gJQAGJXJEX_video.html; Carrie Dann, "Pawlenty Calls Officials' Thumbs Down on Chick-Fil-A 'Chilling, Jaw-Dropping,'" July 28, 2012,

First Read, NBC News, July 28, 2012, http://firstread.msnbc.msn.com/_news/2012/07/28/13010224-pawlenty-calls-officials-thumbs-down-on-chick-fil-a-chilling-jaw-dropping?lite.

8. Bob Egelko, "Top Court Turns Down Wal-Mart—Cities Can Ban Big-Box Stores/Justices Decline to Take Up Appeal of Turlock Ordinance," *San Francisco Chronicle,* July 13, 2006, www.sfgate.com/bayarea/article/CALIFORNIA-Top-court-turns-down-Wal-Mart-2531747.php; Shirley Svorny, "Banning Wal-Mart May Prove Costly," *Los Angeles Times,* January 30, 2004, http://articles.latimes.com/2004/jan/30/opinion/oe-svorny30.

9. "Remarks by the President on the Economy in Osawatomie, Kansas," December 6, 2011, www.whitehouse.gov/the-press-office/2011/12/06/remarks-president-economy-osawatomie-kansas.

10. "Rahm Emanuel: You Never Want a Serious Crisis to Go to Waste," YouTube video, posted by "Jim Swift," February 9, 2009, www.youtube.com/watch?v=1yeA_kHHLow.

11. "Remarks by the President on the Economy in Osawatomie, Kansas."

12. John M. Broder, "E.P.A. Official in Texas Quits over 'Crucify' Video," *New York Times,* May 1, 2012, www.nytimes.com/2012/05/01/us/politics/epa-official-in-texas-resigns-over-crucify-comments.html?_r=1.

13. On his background, see Bryan Preston, "Who Is EPA Crucifixion Chief Al Armendariz?," *PJMedia,* April 27, 2012, http://pjmedia.com/tatler/2012/04/27/who-is-epa-crucifixion-chief-al-armendariz/.

14. "Remarks by the President at a Campaign Event, Pueblo, Colorado," August 9, 2012, www.whitehouse.gov/the-press-office/2012/08/09/remarks-president-campaign-event-pueblo-colorado.

15. Angie Aker, "The Elizabeth Warren Quote Every American Needs to See," MoveOn.org, September 21, 2011, http://front.moveon.org/the-elizabeth-warren-quote-every-american-needs-to-see/.

16. L. Gordon Crovitz, "Who Really Invented the Internet?" *Wall Street Journal,* May 6, 2010, http://online.wsj.com/article/SB10000872396390444464304577539063008406518.html.

17. There are, of course, some exceptions regarding toll roads and user fees, but this does not change the overall picture; indeed these were usually instituted when the deficit became so unmanageable.

18. John Kass, "Who Else Mr. President?," *Chicago Tribune,* July 18, 2012, www.chicagotribune.com/news/columnists/ct-met-kass-0718-20120718,0,2313230.column.

19. Transcript of debate, www.npr.org/2012/10/03/162258551/transcript-first-obama-romney-presidential-debate.

CHAPTER 9: LIBERAL, CONSERVATIVE, RADICAL

1. "Lawrence O'Donnell Likes Liberals," MSNBC, February 2, 2012, www.msnbc.com/the-last-word/lawrence-odonnell-likes-liberals.

2. Weisman, ed., *Daniel Patrick Moynihan.*

3. Ibid.
4. Congressional Progressive Caucus, "What is CPC?" [n.d.] http://cpc.grijalva .house.gov/index.cfm?sectionid=74&sectiontree=2,74.
5. In *The God that Failed* (London: Hamilton, 1950).
6. Associated Press, "Americans for Democratic Action Yields Big Influence from Unpretentious Headquarters," *Daytona Beach Morning Journal*, March 24, 1962, http://news.google.com/newspapers?nid=1873&dat=19620324&id =iKEtAAAAIBAJ&sjid=hNEEAAAAIBAJ&pg=685,4351765.
7. Americans for Democratic Action Website, http://www.adaction.org/pages/ about.php.
8. Karl Marx, *The German Ideology*, http://www.marxists.org/archive/marx/ works/1845/german-ideology/ch01b.htm.
9. George Orwell, *Looking Back on the Spanish Civil War* (London: New Road, 1943).
10. Zombie [pseud.], "*The Little Blue Book*: Quotations from Chairman Lakoff," *PJMedia*, July 9, 2012, http://pjmedia.com/zombie/2012/07/09/the-little-blue-book-quotations-from-chairman-lakoff/1/.

INDEX

Page numbers followed by *n* indicate notes.

ABOUT THE AUTHOR

Barry Rubin was the director of the Global Research for International Affairs (GLORIA) Center and a professor at the Interdisciplinary Center Herzliya as well as editor of the journals *Middle East Review of International Affairs* and *Turkish Studies*. The author or editor of more than thirty books, he was also a columnist for the *Jerusalem Post*. Professor Rubin passed away in February 2014.